DEPARTMENT OF HEALTH

COMMITTEE OF INQUIRY

INDEPENDENT INVESTIGATION INTO HOW THE NHS HANDLED ALLEGATIONS ABOUT THE CONDUCT OF CLIFFORD AYLING

Submitted to
The Secretary of State for Health
on 15th July 2004
by The Honourable Mrs Justice Pauffley, DBE

Presented to Parliament by the Secretary of State for Health
by Command of Her Majesty
September 2004

Cm 6298

**COMMITTEE OF INQUIRY
TO INVESTIGATE HOW THE NHS HANDLED
ALLEGATIONS ABOUT THE CONDUCT
OF CLIFFORD AYLING**

Inquiry Chairman: Dame Anna Pauffley

Inquiries team, 7th floor, Hannibal House, Elephant and Castle, London, SE1 6TE

The Rt. Hon. John Reid MP
Secretary of State for Health
Richmond House
79 Whitehall
London
SW1A 2NS

15 July 2004

Report of the Clifford Ayling Inquiry

As you will know, I was appointed in September 2002, by your predecessor, to
Chair an Independent Investigation into how the NHS handled allegations about
the conduct of Clifford Ayling. I am grateful to have had the advice and support
of Mary Whitty and Peter Berman, who were my panel members.

Under the terms of reference of the Inquiry, I now submit my report to you for
publication.

Dame Anna Pauffley

REPORT STRUCTURE

CHAPTER 1
1. THE INQUIRY

Establishing The Inquiry

1.1   On 11 November 1998 officers of the Kent County Constabulary arrested Clifford Ayling and the following day he was charged with indecently assaulting former patients. Following the initial charge, Ayling was given conditional bail by the Police to appear at Folkestone Magistrates' Court on 13 November 1998. He was placed on conditional bail on terms that he should not practice as a medical practitioner, attend his surgery at 19 Cheriton High Street, Folkestone or touch any patient records. He was also made subject to a condition not to contact or interfere with prosecution witnesses, in particular those involved with the charges.

1.2   Ayling applied to the High Court for a variation of the condition not to practise as a medical practitioner. The application was heard on 23rd November 1998 when new bail conditions were substituted for those imposed in the Magistrates' Court. These included the following:

- At all times not to examine any female patient without a qualified nurse being present;
- Not to access any patient records save as is necessary for the defendant to see the medical records of patients who require medical services and where the patient record is handed to him by a practice receptionist;
- Not when acting for SEADOC (a deputising service) to conduct any home visits or clinical examinations.

1.3   On 15 March 2000 Ayling was committed for trial at the Crown Court by Folkestone Magistrates' Court. The trial commenced at Maidstone Crown Court on 16 October 2000. On 20 December 2000 Ayling was convicted on 12 counts of indecent assault, relating to 10 female patients, and sentenced to four years' imprisonment. His name was placed indefinitely on the sex offender's register under the Sex Offenders Act 1997. He was acquitted of a further 9 charges and 14 others were ordered to lie on the file.

1.4   On 15 June 2001 the professional conduct committee of the General Medical Council determined that Ayling's name should be erased from the Medical Register.

1.5   On 13 July 2001 the Secretary of State for Health announced the setting up of three separate, independent statutory Inquiries, none of which was to be held in public. One of those Inquiries related to Ayling, the second to Richard Neale, a consultant obstetrician and gynaecologist who worked in a number of hospitals in North Yorkshire and the third to William Kerr and Michael Haslam, two consultant psychiatrists who practised in North Yorkshire. We shall refer to them jointly by the name by which they have become known namely, the 3 Inquiries. The 3 Inquiries had broadly similar terms of reference, which required in each case an investigation of how the NHS locally had handled complaints about the performance and/or conduct of the doctors.

1.6 The Secretary of State's announcement indicated that in relation to Ayling, the investigation would be chaired by Dame Yvonne Moores, Chair of the Southampton University Council, its overall purpose being:

> "To assess the appropriateness and effectiveness of the procedures operated in the local health services (a) for enabling health service users to raise issues of legitimate concern relating to the conduct of health service employees; (b) for ensuring that such complaints are effectively considered, and (c) for ensuring that appropriate remedial action is taken in the particular case and generally."

1.7 The Inquiry was asked specifically:

- To identify the procedures in place during the period 1985–2000 within the local health services to enable members of the public and other health service users to raise concerns or complaints concerning the actions and conduct of health service professionals in their professional capacity.
- To document and establish the nature of and chronology of the concerns or complaints raised concerning the practice and conduct of Doctor Clifford Ayling, a former GP from Kent during this period.
- To investigate the actions which were taken for the purpose of (a) considering the concerns and complaints which were raised; (b) providing remedial action in relation to them; and (c) ensuring that the opportunities for any similar future misconduct were removed.
- To investigate cultural or other organisational factors within the local health services, which impeded or prevented appropriate investigation and action.
- To assess and draw conclusions as to the effectiveness of the policies and procedures in place.
- To make recommendations informed by this case as to improvements which should be made to the policies and procedures which are now in place within the health service, (taking into account the changes in procedure since the events in question).
- To provide a full report on these matters to the Secretary of State for Health for publication by him.

1.8 The Secretary of State's announcement made clear that it was not proposed to assess the culpability of Ayling on a case-by-case basis. It went on to say that as the Crown Court's decision had clearly established the misconduct perpetrated by Ayling, the investigation would not be conducted through public hearings although the report would be published in full.

1.9 In January 2001 Harman & Harman, Solicitors in Canterbury, Kent, acting for a number of women, including some who had been indecently assaulted by Ayling, wrote to the Secretary of State indicating that they wished to make representations to any government Inquiry. In March 2001 they wrote again, this time to the Chief Medical Officer, expressing the view that any investigation about Ayling should take place in a public forum. Following the Secretary of State's announcement on 13 July 2001 concerning the establishment of the 3 Inquiries, Harman & Harman commenced proceedings on 23 July 2001 on behalf of their clients seeking judicial review of the decision of the Secretary of State dated 13 July 2001 not to hold an inquiry in public in connection with Ayling.

1.10   On 18 September 2001 the Department of Health sent a letter to Harman & Harman indicating some amendments in connection with the Secretary of State's earlier announcement. These were that interested parties or their representatives would be allowed to attend all of the Inquiry hearings and that a process would be established whereby issues of concern could be raised with the Inquiry Chairman. Additionally, a Queen's Counsel or other demonstrably independent person would be appointed to head the Inquiry in place of Dame Yvonne Moores. Also, the ambit of the Inquiry would be extended so as to cover Ayling's career from 1971 to 2000. The media and members of the public would continue to be excluded from the Inquiry hearings but there was to be no restriction on witnesses talking to the media.

1.11   On 27 September 2001 a former patient of Richard Neale commenced proceedings for judicial review of the decision by the Secretary of State not to hold proceedings in public in connection with the Inquiry concerning Richard Neale. The claims for judicial review by the former patients of Clifford Ayling and Richard Neale were heard together by Mr Justice Scott Baker (as he then was) in February 2002 and he gave his judgment on 15 March 2002. He decided that the decision of the Secretary of State, as amended, to set up each of the Inquiries as private inquiries was lawful and therefore both claims for judicial review failed. Accordingly, the Inquiry was to be held in private but taking account of the concessions made by the Secretary of State in September 2001 (see paragraph 1.10 above).

1.12   On 6 September 2002 the Secretary of State for Health announced that Anna Pauffley QC (as she then was) would chair this Inquiry. He also announced the appointment of two Panel members to support the Chairman. They were:

- Mary Whitty, a former Chief Executive of Brent and Harrow Health Authority; and
- Peter Berman, a solicitor and the Honorary Secretary of the National Association of Lay People in Primary Care, and now Vice Chairman of Taunton Deane Primary Care Trust.

1.13   Pauline Fox was appointed as Secretary to the 3 Inquiries and in October 2001 she established a secretariat to serve those Inquiries. She left the 3 Inquiries in December 2002 to take up another appointment. Colin Phillips was appointed to replace Pauline Fox and he took up post in March 2003. John Miller was appointed Assistant Secretary to the Inquiry. Michael Fitzgerald was appointed Solicitor to the 3 Inquiries; subsequently he was assisted by Duncan Henderson who was appointed Deputy Solicitor to the 3 Inquiries. Eleanor Grey was appointed to be Counsel to the Inquiry and Peter Skelton was appointed Junior Counsel to the Inquiry. Dr Ruth Chadwick was appointed as Commissioning Manager (Experts) to the 3 Inquiries. The role of the legal team was to assist the Panel in the investigation, advise on matters of law and evidence, and to present the evidence to the Inquiry at its hearings. A full list of those who worked on the Inquiry is in Appendix 2.

1.14   The Secretariat was initially located at The Sanctuary, Westminster, London SW1. In September 2002 the Secretariat moved to Hannibal House, a government building at Elephant & Castle, London SE1. The Secretariat was at all times housed in secure accommodation, which was kept entirely separate from other occupiers of the buildings.

Form of Inquiry

1.15   As set out at paragraph 1.5 above, the Secretary of State decided that the Inquiry should be conducted in private but subject to the variations mentioned at paragraph 1.10 above. This form of inquiry became known as a modified form of private inquiry. Some of the challenges faced in operating within the parameters of this hybrid inquiry are listed in Appendix 6.

1.16   It was decided that the Inquiry would be divided into two parts. Part One would comprise the evidence-gathering process and would address paragraphs 1(a) to (c) of the terms of reference.

1.17   Part Two (see paragraphs 1.45 to 1.49 of this Report) would examine what appropriate recommendations could be made for the revision and improvement of the procedures operated in the local health services for the handling of complaints and concerns.

Adversarial or Inquisitorial?

1.18   There is no statutory entitlement for any person to call witnesses, cross-examine or make submissions in an Inquiry of this sort. It was for the Chairman to decide what form the Inquiry should take and it was decided that the Inquiry would be inquisitorial, not adversarial in nature.

1.19   In October 2002 a draft Procedures Paper was produced by the Inquiry, setting out the procedures that were to be adopted following a process of consultation. It was sent to those individuals and bodies who had expressed an interest in the work of the Inquiry. A copy of the Procedures Paper is in Appendix 9. The Procedures Paper detailed how the Inquiry would deal with document-gathering, requests for witness statements, the use to be made by the Inquiry of statements or other documents and confidentiality undertakings. A List of Issues was also distributed with the Procedures Paper for consultation. That document set out the issues that the Panel proposed to explore in its work. It acted as a guide for the preparation of witness statements, and more generally in connection with the Inquiry's work. A copy of the List of Issues is in Appendix 10.

Identifying Participants

1.20   It was decided to recognise those bodies and individuals who expressed an interest in the work of the Inquiry and who came within the ambit of the terms of reference as "participants". A list of the participants and their representatives is in Appendix 4.

1.21   It was decided that participants, and those acting for them, would not be allowed to call or cross-examine witnesses. But those representing participants and witnesses were allowed to re-examine those witnesses whom they represented. Provision was made in the procedures for that re-examination to be time-limited. In practice it was not necessary to enforce the limitation.

1.22   At the end of the oral hearings, representatives of the participants and witnesses who wished to do so were permitted to make time-limited closing submissions, which could be supplemented with written closing submissions.

The General Medical Council

1.23   The Inquiry did not have jurisdiction to inquire into non-NHS bodies such as the General Medical Council (GMC) although it was concerned with the interfaces between the NHS and the GMC or other such bodies. In the event, the Chief Executive of the GMC volunteered a witness statement and gave oral evidence.

Relationship with Clifford Ayling

1.24   The Inquiry wished to engage with Ayling in its work and made efforts to do so. However, for the reasons which are explained in Appendix 7, Ayling chose not to participate in the Inquiry process at a time or in a fashion which would have enabled the Inquiry to take account of his input. Accordingly, the Inquiry did not have his assistance in, for example, commenting upon material submitted to the Inquiry and in respect of which it may have been instructive to have received his views. The lack of any input or cooperation from Ayling into the work of the Inquiry or the evidence it received must always be borne in mind when reading this Report.

Preparations for the Oral Hearings

Preliminary Meeting

1.25   On 6 November 2002 there was a preliminary meeting in Folkestone to which everyone who had expressed an interest in the work of the Inquiry was invited. The purpose of the meeting was to enable the Panel to introduce themselves to prospective participants and also to introduce members of the Inquiry team.

1.26   It gave an opportunity to explain the work of the Inquiry and what was intended for the future, including likely timescales within which the Inquiry would work.

Gathering Witness Statements

1.27   As mentioned above, in order to structure the work in Part One, a List of Issues was produced which reflected the terms of reference.

1.28   The Solicitor to the Inquiry wrote to everyone who might be able to give relevant evidence, asking them to produce a witness statement. Such requests were accompanied by a document which set out those particular matters arising from the terms of reference and List of Issues about which it was thought the witness would be able to provide evidence. In most cases these requests were made through the representatives of the participants. The Inquiry is most grateful for the assistance provided by those representatives in obtaining the witness statements and subsequently providing them to the Inquiry.

1.29   Ultimately a bundle of witness statements was prepared by the Secretariat. In a process more fully described in Appendix 9, copies of witness statements were made available to the participants. The participants and their representatives signed a confidentiality undertaking which acknowledged that it was necessary to keep such material confidential and to use it solely for the purposes of the Inquiry.

Gathering Documents

1.30   Section 2 of the National Health Service Act 1977 under which the Inquiry was established does not give the Chairman power to require the production of documents. Accordingly, the Secretariat wrote to the relevant public bodies seeking voluntary production of all relevant documents. The Secretariat then had the task of managing the considerable amount of documentation that was produced in response.

1.31   The documents were read and assessed by the Inquiry team and bundles of relevant material were produced. Copies of some of the documents in the bundles were made available to participants in the way described in Appendix 9.

Expert Assistance

1.32   The Inquiry has had the benefit of reading reports commissioned by the Inquiry from the experts listed below. Copies of their reports were made available to the representatives of the participants to assist them in their work in connection with the hearings.

i.   *Description of the NHS Complaints Procedures for Committees of Inquiry into the Performance and Conduct of Neale, Ayling, Kerr and Haslam* (Professor Linda Mulcahy, Birkbeck College, University of London)

ii.   *Lessons to be Learned from Complaint Handling in the NHS 1960–2003* (Professor Linda Mulcahy, Birkbeck College, University of London)

iii.   *Cross-Sector Regulation of Poor Performance* (Professor Linda Mulcahy and Steve Banks, Birkbeck College, University of London)

iv.   *Report on the Law Relating to References* (Professor Ian Smith, Clifford Chance Professor of Employment Law, University of East Anglia)

v.   *Report on the Law Relating to Whistleblowing* (Professor Ian Smith, Clifford Chance Professor of Employment Law, University of East Anglia)

PART ONE PROCEEDINGS

Venue

1.33   The hearings began on 29 April 2003 at the Holiday Inn Hotel, Ashford. This was almost two months later than had been envisaged in the preliminary meeting in November 2002. The principal reason for the delay was the need to identify, and make ready for the hearings, suitable premises in South East Kent. Regrettably, no such premises could be found in the immediate vicinity of Folkestone. The Secretariat first identified suitable accommodation in Ashford. Following the submission to the Secretariat of the detailed costings for the works of alteration necessary to the identified premises, it was reluctantly concluded that the costs were so substantial that it would be quite wrong for them to be paid out of public funds. In the circumstances, at a late stage, a fresh search for suitable premises was launched. This resulted in a decision to hold the hearings at the Holiday Inn Hotel, Ashford. A free daily coach was provided for former patients of Ayling to travel from Folkestone to and from the venue. The accommodation at the venue provided a suitable hearing chamber. In layout and presentation, every effort was made to make the room as informal as the circumstances required. Other accommodation was used at the hotel as an office for the secretariat and rooms for use of the participants.

Opening the Inquiry and hearing the evidence

1.34   The hearings began on 29 April 2003, when Eleanor Grey, Counsel to the Inquiry, made her opening statement. That statement identified the matters upon which the Inquiry would need to focus over the period of the hearings. Thereafter opening statements were made by other participants. The first witness was called on 30 April 2003. In total, 68 witnesses were called to give evidence over 27 days.

1.35   The written statements of a further 179 witnesses were put into evidence without the need for them to attend the Inquiry. The oral evidence was completed by 25 July 2003.

1.36   All oral evidence was simultaneously transcribed using a system called Livenote. A transcript of the proceedings was made available to the representatives of the participants as soon as conveniently possible after each day's evidence.

1.37   Closing submissions from the participants were heard on 31 July 2003, supplemented by written submissions at the election of the participants.

1.38   Arrangements were made for representatives of Victim Support to be in attendance on each day of the oral hearings. The Inquiry is very grateful to them for agreeing to provide support for all those attending to give evidence, whether former patients or healthcare professionals.

Powers of Compulsion

1.39   Section 2 of the National Health Service Act 1977, under which the Inquiry was established, does not give the Chairman the power to call witnesses to attend and answer questions. Initially the absence of such powers did not appear to be causing any undue difficulties. However, as the hearings progressed, it became clear that, without compulsory powers, the attendance of certain important witnesses could not be guaranteed. Accordingly, on 14 May 2003 the Chairman wrote to the Secretary of State for Health seeking additional powers under Section 84 of the 1977 Act. This section includes power for the Chairman to compel the production of documents and the attendance of witnesses to give evidence. On 30 May 2003 the Secretary of State indicated by letter that he granted those powers.

1.40   Once it was announced that the Secretary of State had granted compulsory powers to the Chairman, any reluctant witnesses, with one exception, complied with requests to provide a witness statement and attend to give oral evidence. It was necessary for the Chairman formally to exercise the powers on one occasion. The witness then provided a witness statement and attended to give oral evidence, as requested.

Legal Expenses

1.41   An Inquiry such as this does not have any power to order payment of legal costs from public funds or by any other party. However, the Secretary of State indicated that if the Chairman made a recommendation that the legal costs of a participant should be met out of public funds, then it would be sympathetically considered. Such a recommendation was made in respect of the costs of representation of the former patients of Clifford Ayling, represented by Harman & Harman, and in respect of two other witnesses. The Secretary of State accepted those recommendations.

Dealing with Potential Criticism

1.42   As was made clear at the preliminary meeting, if it was considered necessary to criticise the way in which events, including complaints, had been handled in the past, the Inquiry procedures were designed to ensure that persons who might have been affected by such criticisms would be given a proper and fair opportunity to respond. The procedures were established to meet those requirements. However, as was also made clear at the preliminary meeting, there was a further step to ensure fairness.

1.43   It was made clear that no criticism would be made without ensuring that that person first had a proper opportunity to answer the criticism. Wherever it was possible to do so, the witness would be informed by the Inquiry of the nature of the potential criticism before they were called to give evidence. Where that was not possible, for example, because potential criticisms emerged at a time after oral evidence had been given, then they would be given an opportunity to respond before the closing date for the receipt of evidence.

1.44 Notices of potential criticism were sent to witnesses where it appeared that they might be criticised for their conduct in relation to matters covered by the Inquiry's terms of reference. Each witness was given the opportunity to address these points during the course of their evidence. The Solicitor to the Inquiry wrote to those witnesses or their representatives after they had given their evidence to invite any further comments in writing to supplement what had been said in oral evidence.

PART TWO

Preparing for Part Two

1.45 The Terms of Reference required the Inquiry to assess and draw conclusions as to the effectiveness of the policies and procedures in place, and to make recommendations informed by Ayling's case as to improvements which should be made to the policies and procedures which are now in place within the health service (taking into account the changes in procedures since the events in question).

1.46 In responding to the Terms of Reference it was clear to the Inquiry that recommendations were likely to fall into two categories. The first category would be addressed to the particular circumstances concerning Ayling and to the events that occurred in those localities where he practiced within the NHS. The second category would be recommendations with wider potential impact that might affect relevant agencies across the country. The Inquiry has kept in mind that the Neale Inquiry has similar terms of reference and that the Shipman Inquiry chaired by Dame Janet Smith is also currently enquiring into the performance of the functions of those statutory bodies, authorities, other organisations and individuals with responsibility for monitoring primary care provision.

Providing a Framework for Part 2

1.47 In January and February 2003 written submissions were invited from relevant agencies, organisations and individuals with a view to informing our recommendations. Those submissions, together with the reading of the documents and witness statements gathered for Part 1, greatly assisted in identifying the broad issues to further explore in Part 2.

1.48 Professor Charlotte Humphrey of King's College, London and Dr Kathryn Ehrich, an independent research consultant, were appointed to help plan and identify experts for a series of seminars which were held jointly by the Ayling and Neale Inquiries over five days in September 2003. Although the seminars took place in private at the Thistle City Barbican Hotel, London, participants in the Inquiry were invited to attend as observers. The seminars covered the following topics:

- Supporting patients in raising concerns about their care;
- Supporting staff in raising concerns about their colleagues;
- The employment context;

- Sharing information across different bodies about individual conduct and performance; and
- The role of chaperones.

1.49   The participants in the seminars were chosen from those who had made written submissions, and from those not previously involved in the Inquiry but who were identified as having an interest. A full list of those who took part can be found in Appendix 13. The airing of views at the seminars greatly assisted in formulating the recommendations. The Inquiries are most grateful to Ann James CBE, a policy advisor and consultant in public service reform in the UK and abroad, who ably facilitated the seminars, and to all those who took part. The Inquiries are also grateful to those observers who took the trouble to set out in writing their views on the topics discussed.

Closing the Inquiry

1.50   On 31 July 2003 the evidence-gathering process of the Inquiry was formally closed. No material sent to the Inquiry after that date has been considered for the purposes of preparing this Report.

CHAPTER 2
GENERAL INTRODUCTION

2.1   Clifford Ayling came to the east Kent area in 1973, having worked previously in a number of hospitals in and around London since qualification in 1963, including the North Middlesex Hospital from 1971–1973. From 1974 until 1988 he was employed as a part-time clinical assistant in obstetrics and gynaecology, working at the Kent and Canterbury Hospital in Canterbury and the Isle of Thanet Hospital in Margate.

2.2   In 1981 he entered general practice in Folkestone, initially in partnership with Dr Ribet, but from 1983 as a sole practitioner. In anticipation of his eventual retirement at the age of 70 in 2001, in 1998 he joined the partnership of Dr Hossain and other GPs in Folkestone.

2.3   From 1984 until 1994, he was also employed as a part-time clinical assistant in colposcopy at the William Harvey Hospital in Ashford.

2.4   Whilst practising as a GP, Ayling also undertook locum medical sessions in family planning clinics in east Kent and joined the local GP deputising service co-operative, SEADOC.

2.5   In 1998 he was arrested and charged with indecently assaulting former patients. In 2000 he was found guilty on 12 charges of indecent assault, relating to 10 female patients, and sentenced to four years imprisonment. He was found not guilty on a further nine charges. Where we have set out the individual history of patients whose accounts were considered as part of the criminal trial, we have sought to note whether the trial resulted in a conviction or an acquittal.

2.6   The complaints which led to Ayling's convictions for sexual assault related, in broad terms, to inappropriate touching or examinations of women's breasts or gynaecological organs. The earliest incident to be examined in the criminal trial took place in 1991, and most related to events in the general practitioner's surgery, rather than in hospitals. It was a central part of Ayling's defence in the criminal trial that the disputed examinations were medically necessary or justified, and followed guidelines that would be accepted by a responsible body of medical practitioners. The jury's verdict, in relation to the 12 counts on which he was found guilty, implied that they rejected this defence and found that the examinations were conducted for his own personal gratification.

2.7   Once the Inquiry's remit was extended to cover complaints from 1971 onwards, it was inevitable that we would have to examine complaints and concerns which had not been the subject of the criminal trial. Furthermore, it would also be examining events that took place in the hospital setting, which had played little part of the criminal trial. Even in relation to incidents in the general practice setting from 1991 onwards, it was plain that the Inquiry would hear from a great number of witnesses whose accounts had played no part in the criminal prosecution, and in respect of whom Ayling had not been convicted of any criminal offence. Furthermore, the Inquiry's terms of reference required it to look at all complaints and concerns raised concerning 'the practice or conduct' of Clifford Ayling. These broad headings covered matters that had not been in issue in the criminal trial.

2.8 For example, some women questioned Ayling's clinical competence as a doctor. Whilst complaints relating to this issue have been considered when they were voiced in order to assess how the relevant authorities handled them, an assessment of Ayling's clinical competence was not part of the remit of the Inquiry. We are conscious of the fact that judgments formed on the basis of a limited number of incidents, spread over the course of a number of years, could be misleading. This report assesses complaints handling, not the overall pattern of care provided.

2.9 The concerns or complaints which we now heard, in the course of the Inquiry, also varied in their seriousness. Some related to Ayling's manner: some witnesses felt that he could be unprofessional or overly intimate. Others complained that they had not been chaperoned or treated with dignity when examinations were conducted. On their own, complaints of this nature had not led to criminal charges or to trial.

2.10 Other accounts given to the Inquiry echoed, more directly, the themes of the criminal trial, of intimate examinations that were said not to be medically justified. We note that medical practice is not static; practices change. In Annex 1 we describe the developments in clinical practice in the field of obstetrics and gynaecology during the relevant period. In the gynaecological field, we note that over time, a general shift to fewer or less invasive examinations took place. In those circumstances, one interpretation of Ayling's behaviour was that he was simply an 'old-fashioned' or 'thorough' practitioner, who continued to carry out examinations even though many or even most of his peers would no longer regard them as justified. As we have noted, this was a central thread of his criminal defence. In relation to the 12 counts upon which he was found guilty, it was rejected in favour of an interpretation that found the examinations to have been conducted for personal gratification. Ayling was, however, acquitted upon other counts. It was not part of our remit to assess, on a case-by-case basis, whether the examinations criticised during the course of the Inquiry were medically justified or not. We attempted rather to see whether complaints about them were appropriately handled and investigated. Prompt and thorough investigations, conducted at the time, should have been the means of judging the merits of such complaints.

2.11 However, we recognise that one aspect of colleagues' responses to concerns expressed about Ayling's practice was created by this changing context. Some practitioners were aware that Ayling might defend his practices as thorough and question the merits of more recent developments, however much they might personally disagree; others felt inhibited in judging whether or not there were grounds for concern. These reactions were perhaps particularly prevalent amongst general practitioners, who had little or no desire to judge a 'peer'. Furthermore, we note that the women who underwent examinations that other practitioners might no longer consider clinically necessary, were not generally informed, or made aware, that other approaches or other choices existed.

2.12   Because of the number of locations in which Ayling worked, and the overlapping nature of his professional activity, the chronology in our Report is based on those organisations with the responsibility for systems which could and should have identified and taken action on the concerns and complaints generated by Ayling's actions. The 30 years covered by our Report have seen profound changes in the NHS. We have attempted to chart these as simply as possible, and to relate them to the organisational and cultural issues we have identified as key to the Ayling story. In order to tell the story of the complaints and concerns about Ayling and the way they were handled at the time as clearly as possible, we have placed much of the detail relating to the organisations, processes, guidance and responsibilities germane to our Inquiry in a series of Annexes.

2.13   The impact of organisational change within Ayling's employing bodies in the local NHS was important but not singularly significant, given the longevity of Ayling's career in one geographical area. A description of the various reorganisations of the NHS in the East Kent area is given in Annex 2. It is our view that more significance should be attached to the nature of the settings in which he worked – as a single-handed GP, as an unsupervised clinical assistant covering weekend emergencies and in out-patient clinics away from main hospital sites. These areas were not well-monitored or assessed and enabled Ayling to carry out many of his duties in professional isolation.

2.14   It is regrettable that Clifford Ayling, before the closure of evidence, chose not to assist us. Not only did this make it more difficult for us to clarify some of the context, it also deprived him, albeit through his own choice, of the opportunity to tell us in his own words which issues were raised with him at the time, and which were not. That some were not, tells its own story. Appendix 7 describes the attempts the Inquiry team made to engage with Clifford Ayling.

2.15   The Inquiry I chaired has been described as a modified form of private Inquiry. That term discloses the nature of some of the challenges that those working on the Inquiry had in dealing with some very sensitive and confidential issues. It in part also explains why it has taken us so long to complete our work. I am grateful to all those who have put in so much hard and dedicated work to see the task through. Counsel to the Inquiry, Eleanor Grey, ably supported by Peter Skelton, is an inquisitor of the highest quality and we were fortunate to have their abilities available to us. The Solicitor to the Inquiry was Michael Fitzgerald who could not have been more thorough, professional and efficient. He led a legal team that gave us a first class service.

2.16   The Secretariat, initially led by Pauline Fox and then Colin Phillips worked tirelessly and gave us all the support we could ask for. John Miller, the deputy secretary, Kathleen Price, James Malam and Philip Otton in particular dealt calmly and efficiently with a huge amount of written material and enabled the Oral hearings to progress smoothly and efficiently.

2.17 We were also fortunate to be assisted by Dr Ruth Chadwick the commissioning manager for the expert advice we needed who produced work for us that was again of the highest standard. Thanks also to Kypros Menicou, Kathryn Ehrich, Emily Frost and Ann James, CBE for putting together our programme of Seminars on topics we felt needed a more detailed examination.

2.18 Finally I cannot praise highly enough the support and advice I have received from my two panel members, Mary Whitty and Peter Berman. Mary's considerable expertise and industry aligned with Peter's strong analytical skills enabled the report to reach the conclusion I can now forward to the Secretary of State for his consideration.

2.19 I think all of us connected with the report were surprised at how long it took us to complete our task. It took much longer than any of us would have wanted but it was a true reflection of the very extensive input from a wide range of witnesses and experts that had to be amassed, dissected and analysed. We have striven for accuracy and precision in the report and we have tried our very best to reflect both the detail and impressions that we have been given. In particular the Panel (that is Mary Whitty, Peter Berman and I) are aware that organisational responsibilities are changing. Where we refer to them in our report, we mean to refer to the bodies that exercise the relevant power of function. Should errors have crept in, they are mistakes honestly made against a context of overwhelming amounts of written evidence and days of oral testimony.

2.20 The work of our Inquiry would not have been possible without the co-operation of the staff and contractors of the NHS in East Kent, for which we are grateful. We recognise that for many of these we were asking for memories and information dating back many years, and that the effort of recollection and review was evidently difficult and painful for some.

2.21 Most importantly of all, our Inquiry could not have taken place without the contribution of a number of Ayling's former patients who gave evidence to our Inquiry, and whose courage and fortitude in helping our work was deeply impressive. We hope that our report shows them that we recognise that there were errors in the way that their complaints were dealt with at the time and possible solutions for the avoidance of such mistakes in the future.

RECOMMENDATIONS

Introduction

2.22 In reaching our conclusions and determining our recommendations, we are very conscious that the values of patient safety are more evident in the NHS now than at the time Ayling was in practice. Quality assurance principles underpin active attention to clinical performance and patient welfare and are embedded in the expectation of NHS Trust performance.

2.23   However, quality assurance processes within NHS organisations are relatively new and therefore not widely tested in the case of extreme examples of disturbing behaviour such as those described to us as allegedly exhibited by Ayling. Furthermore, many of the various bodies responsible for these processes are also new and, in parallel, significant organisational change has taken place within the NHS.

2.24   Continuing change is likely in both organisations and in treatment settings. In particular, the identification and development of new models of care and the provision of care in novel locations outside the familiar and traditional to staff and patients (such as one-to-one settings or in locations managed outside the NHS) may further challenge the effective application of robust quality assurance systems.

2.25   We therefore concentrate on proposals which we believe would enhance existing policies and procedures in those services provided and commissioned by the NHS, and which have been informed by the conclusions we have drawn from our Inquiry. Our recommendations are drawn together below under topic headings that seem to us to cover the main issues involved when we consider the evidence we have received.

"Sexualised Behaviour"

2.26   In the course of our Inquiry, we heard allegations of a number of disturbing instances where Ayling's behaviour was overtly sexual and broke the boundaries of the trust and integrity patients have the right to expect from their doctor. We have learnt even more of the long history of continuing unease that his approach generated amongst those who worked with him on a regular basis or were treated by him. His approach was described as being overfamiliar to sensitive and intimate examinations which bordered on the unprofessional and was distressing to both recipient and observer. We have adopted the phrase "sexualised behaviour" to describe this.

2.27   In the course of our Inquiry, we have found little if any published guidance for employing or regulatory authorities in either recognising or responding to "sexualised behaviour". We believe that there is an urgent need to address this and ensure that all NHS employers and contracting organisations recognise and respond to such behaviour as vigorously as they would to allegations of sexual harassment.

2.28   A consistent theme of the evidence presented to us was the interpretation placed on what they were told by health care professionals who were in a position at the time to take action on allegations about Ayling's abusive and unacceptable approach to his patients. We recognise the magnitude of the breakdown in belief in professional integrity that to do otherwise would have represented for many of Ayling's colleagues working within the ethical framework of the same profession. In effect, they recast what they heard into explanations which they could find acceptable and in so doing, deceived themselves and failed their patients.

2.29   Today, the index of suspicion about motivation for questionable behaviour in public services is very much higher than it was when Ayling was in practice. However, there is no employing, educational or regulatory organisation within the modernised NHS with specific responsibility for dealing with "sexualised behaviour" amongst health care professionals.

2.30   We therefore recommend that the DH convene an expert group under the auspices of the Chief Medical Officer to develop guidance and best practice for the NHS on this subject. The group should include the NHS Confederation, the RCOG, the RCGP (and other Colleges as appropriate, such as the Royal College of Psychiatrists), the NCAA, the CRHP, the GMC and representatives of undergraduate and postgraduate medical education. The group should take advice from experience of dealing with "sexualised behaviour" elsewhere in the public sector such as educational services and from health care systems in other countries such as Canada.

2.31   In parallel with this, we recommend that local policies within all NHS Trusts for reporting staff concerns (whistleblowing) should specifically identify "sexualised behaviour" as appropriate for reporting within the confidence of this procedure.

Listening and Hearing

2.32   Another clear message from what we heard in the course of our Inquiry was the tentative way in which patients expressed their anxieties about Ayling's behaviour and conduct. Many patients, in raising their concerns with other and trusted health care staff, were seeking to validate their concerns – they sought reassurance that what they had experienced was wrong and they were right to feel violated by what they said had happened. We would describe these as "proto-complaints".

2.33   Since Ayling was in practice, PALS have been established within each NHS Trust which we believe would now offer a confidential and safe haven for the discussion and articulation of "proto-complaints". But for PALS to provide such a service for the sensitive and intimate concerns we heard of during the Inquiry, we recognise that investment in PALS will be required.

2.34   We therefore recommend that accredited training should be provided for all PALS officers in this potential aspect of their work, and that SHAs should require confirmation from each NHS Trust in their area of the completion of such training within the next 12 months.

2.35   During the course of our Inquiry, we learnt that the visibility and accessibility of PALS in primary care settings was an emerging concern.

2.36   We therefore recommend that the Modernisation Agency develop a model of best practice and, if appropriate for them so to do, the patients' forums could monitor the effectiveness of service provision against this model. The implementation of this model and associated performance measures should be a formal component of CHAI's reviews of PCTs.

Complaints Procedures

2.37 We describe in our Report the substantial reviews of the effectiveness of NHS complaints procedures over the years covered by our Terms of Reference. These are about to be revised again to strengthen the independence and scrutiny of complaints investigations.

2.38 From what we learnt during our Inquiry, we particularly welcome the emphasis on supporting patients in making complaints that the setting up of ICAS represents. We were struck by the experience of two patients who complained formally about Ayling and who spoke to the Inquiry. These two had successfully navigated the procedures in place at the time with the help and support of friends and relatives, and we hope that ICAS will provide such support for every patient who needs and wants help to see a satisfactory response to concerns about their care. But we cannot come to any firm conclusion on this in light of the novelty of the service.

2.39 We recommend that the same training for ICAS staff in handling concerns and complaints of an intimate and sensitive nature as that we have recommended for PALS staff should be provided, and that this should form part of the service specification for ICAS. We also believe that satisfaction surveys should be built into the work of ICAS on completion of their work with each complaint so that their performance can be routinely monitored and a cycle of continuous improvement be established.

Tracking Repeated Complaints and Concerns

2.40 We comment in our Report on the way in which each episode of concern about Ayling that was formally expressed was dealt with on an individual basis. We also comment on the consequence of an absence of an inquisitorial approach to less formally expressed concerns. The cumulative effect of these was that first, very few written records were apparently kept and secondly, connections either within an employing organisation or across organisations were not made. In consequence, a number of opportunities to take more decisive and long-term action were missed.

2.41 During our Inquiry we discussed the need to track repeated complaints and concerns about an individual practitioner. Whilst there are now many relatively new and emerging organisations, structures and processes for assessing and appraising the competence and performance of clinicians in order to determine remedial action, we were unable to identify any single body where an overarching pattern of concern throughout the career of a clinician in a number of locations might be identified. Indeed, we learnt of some anxiety that the plethora of overlapping approaches now available might cause confusion amongst those seeking to invoke the support they are designed to provide. However, dealing with concerns and complaints about a practitioner is an employment issue.

2.42 We recommend that all NHS Trusts and health care organisations such as deputising services directly employing staff should require them (and particularly part-time staff) to make a formal declaration of any other concurrent employment, not only for obvious health and

safety reasons but also to ensure a record is kept of other organisations with an interest in the individual's performance. Failure to make such a declaration should be a disciplinary matter. This requirement should be appropriately adapted for PCTs to be kept informed of other professional employment undertaken by GPs.

2.43   In our discussions about maintaining a record of recurrent complaints and concerns, we were conscious of the requirements of the Data Protection Act (DPA). In framing the following recommendations, we believe that the implementation of these would be consistent with the principles of the DPA.

2.44   First, we recommend that copies of any written records regarding complaints and concerns and the outcome of these which name an individual practitioner should be placed on that practitioner's personnel file, to be kept for the length of their contract with that organisation. This should be made known to the practitioner concerned.

2.45   Secondly, we recommend that the regular reports on patient complaints and concerns made to NHS Trust Boards and other corporate governance bodies should be structured to provide an analysis not only of trends in subject matter and clinical area but also to indicate whether a named practitioner has been the subject of previous complaints.

Sole Practitioners

2.46   Much of the concern about Ayling's behaviour and practice was well known in the various health communities in which he worked. We review in our Report the likelihood in today's NHS of such concerns being expressed more formally through a range of routes. We also acknowledge that the NHS today is one in which practitioners increasingly work in multi-disciplinary teams, with cross-cover for patient activity and peer support. This itself has a self-regulating benefit in performance and behaviour. Furthermore, critical attention is being paid to poorly performing doctors. However, isolated practitioners still exist where there is no immediate mentoring, either formal or informal. Many such isolated practitioners work in non-hospital settings such as general practice.

2.47   We appreciate that there will always be single-handed general practitioners and that it is not DH or Government policy to encourage all practitioners to work in group settings,

2.48   We therefore recommend that PCTs should develop specific support programmes for single-handed practitioners, to be agreed with the practitioner concerned and the PCT's StHA. Such programmes should pay critical attention to managing the risks of clinical and professional isolation associated with single-handed practice. Implementation should be monitored by the StHA and form part of the regular CHAI review of the PCT.

2.49 Additionally, PCTs should pay particular attention to developing and supporting the independence of practice managers in single-handed practices, including the acknowledgment and resolution of potential conflicts of interest which may arise where the manager is the spouse or a close relative of the practitioner. This too should be the subject of monitoring and review by StHAs and CHAI.

Chaperones

2.50 The role of a chaperone was raised at many points in the course of our Inquiry, and led to much discussion as to the expectations and availability of a chaperone in sensitive and intimate examinations, particularly in primary care settings.

2.51 We found no common definition of the role of a chaperone. Four differing roles were described to us:

- a chaperone provides a safeguard for a patient against humiliation, pain or distress during an examination and protects against verbal, physical, sexual or other abuse
- a chaperone provides physical and emotional comfort and reassurance to a patient during sensitive and intimate examinations or treatment
- an experienced chaperone will identify unusual or unacceptable behaviour on the part of the health care professional
- a chaperone may also provide protection for the health care professional from potentially abusive patients.

2.52 A further definition is that of the Association of Police Surgeons, which describes a chaperone as someone who "supports and befriends the victim".

2.53 We were told that the Royal Colleges of General Practitioners (RCGP) and of Obstetricians and Gynaecologists (RCOG) have both undertaken work on chaperoning, coming to different conclusions as to the purpose and value of a chaperone's presence, perhaps not unsurprisingly given the different clinical and treatment locations in which their members work. We were also made aware that the issue of chaperoning was of concern to other health care workers such as midwives, and in other clinical disciplines such as genito-urinary medicine. Technological solutions to the dilemmas around the role, use and availability of chaperones were described to us. The impact of the presence of a chaperone on the openness with which both a patient and a health care professional might share sensitive and confidential information was pointed out to us.

2.54 From the evidence offered to us and our subsequent discussions, we believe that there is a distinction between the passive and active role of a chaperone. A passive chaperone is a witness of the conduct of a clinical examination so, for example, technology could provide a "virtual' chaperone. An active chaperone has a defined role in the examination and treatment of a patient as part of the clinical team.

2.55   In considering the use of a "virtual" chaperone to record both visually and audibly the conduct of a clinical examination, we were attracted by the independence, objectivity, availability and potential ubiquity of a relatively low cost solution to the problem of providing chaperones. But we were equally aware of its disadvantages – it would not offer personal support, and nor could it intervene if an untoward incident took place.

2.56   We therefore concluded that the value of a chaperone rested with an "active" chaperoning model, and the presence of a chaperone at a consultation must be the patient's decision but routinely offered by a health care professional. However, a number of concerns were identified to us about this: that it may be the healthcare professional's wish for a chaperone to be present, that raising the issue of the presence of a chaperone may create tension between the patient and the health care professional and the way in which the question is raised may dictate the patient's response. Additionally, the most vulnerable patients (for example, because of age or culture) may be those less able or willing to express a preference for a chaperone, and the presence of a chaperone should be clearly confined to that part of a consultation involving a clinical examination and treatment.

2.57   In the absence of any common understanding across the NHS of the purpose and thus the appropriate use of chaperones, we feel that our recommendations on this subject must apply to the variety of settings and circumstances in which care is provided and the degree of risk to patients and health care workers. This is a matter of risk management policy which should be discussed, determined and implemented locally within each NHS Trust.

2.58   We recommend that no family member or friend of a patient should be expected to undertake any formal chaperoning role. The presence of a chaperone during a clinical examination and treatment must be the clearly expressed choice of a patient. Chaperoning should not be undertaken by other than trained staff: the use of untrained administrative staff as chaperones in a GP surgery, for example, is not acceptable. However the patient must have the right to decline any chaperone offered if they so wish.

2.59   Beyond these immediate and practical points, there is a need for each NHS Trust to determine its chaperoning policy, make this explicit to patients and resource it accordingly. This must include accredited training for the role and an identified managerial lead with responsibility for the implementation of the policy. We recognise that for primary care, developing and resourcing a chaperoning policy will have to take into account issues such as one-to-one consultations in the patient's home and the capacity of individual practices to meet the requirements of the agreed policy.

2.60   Finally, reported breaches of the chaperoning policy should be formally investigated through each Trust's risk management and clinical governance arrangements and treated, if determined as deliberate, as a disciplinary matter.

Local Medical Committees

2.61   In our Report we draw attention to the ambiguous role played by the Kent LMC in the Ayling story, and the consequences of this on early and decisive remedial action.

2.62   We believe that in the new arrangements for assuring service quality and patient safety, LMCs can no longer undertake the role the Kent LMC played over the period Ayling was in practice. This role was perceived by local GPs as a "safe haven" for troubling knowledge and a body to whom responsibility for further action could be entrusted. This is inappropriate today.

2.63   **We therefore recommend that LMCs clarify their role in relation to supporting GPs to make it explicit that acting on the receipt of information about a GP which indicates patient safety is being compromised is not part of their role, and ensure that this is embedded in professional guidance from the GMC and medical defence organisations.**

2.64   **We further recommend that if LMCs are the recipient of concerns about a practitioner's clinical conduct or performance, this information should be immediately passed on to the relevant PCT or professional regulatory body for appropriate investigation. This should be made known to their constituents. We believe that not doing this would leave professional members and staff of a LMC in the potential position of having failed to meet their own professional obligations.**

Criminal Investigations

2.65   Three particular concerns were brought to our attention about the progress of the latter stages of the Ayling story which we believe merit further attention. These relate to the continuing responsibility of the NHS when potentially criminal action on the part of a health care professional has been identified. We were told that East Kent Health Authority staff felt overwhelmed by the size and complexity of the emerging case against Ayling and that patients felt unsupported and ill informed by the NHS during a protracted investigation by the Kent Police.

2.66   The first of these concerns was the absence of a source of expert advice and support for the East Kent HA in dealing with a high profile and, to them, novel situation involving potentially criminal activity over a number of years on the part of one of their general practitioners. Whilst handling incidents of deliberately criminal, reckless or negligent behaviour by a health care worker will be rare for individual health care organisations, across the NHS there will be a body of experience and developed good practice in dealing with these which should be made immediately available to those confronted with such a situation for the first time.

2.67 The second of these concerns is the lack of a clear agreement between the criminal justice system, the NHS and the GMC as to the investigatory responsibilities of each. By default, in the Ayling case it was accepted that the Police inquiries and the preparation of their case for the Crown Prosecution Service (CPS) should supersede investigation and action by employing and professional regulatory bodies since each was reliant on the same witnesses and there was a concern that the rehearsal of evidence in other fora could have had an adverse effect on criminal proceedings.

2.68 We are aware that within the Department of Health there now exists a unit that is building up the necessary expertise. It will be important to ensure that such a body of knowledge is properly accumulated and disseminated so that all NHS Trusts know the advice is available.

2.69 We are also aware of work currently being undertaken by the Department of Health, the Police and the HSE to develop a Memorandum of Understanding for the effective investigation of serious incidents. The steering group for that work should take our recommendations into account. Once the Memorandum is completed, it should be made widely available.

2.70 The third concern was the inadequacy of information and support offered to patients by the NHS during the Police investigations of the allegations against Ayling. Formal communication with patients was marked by long gaps and a lack of connection with previous communications. Informal support beyond the immediate help-line set up in the autumn of 1998 was not continued, and patients compared this adversely with the victim support service offered by the Kent Police.

2.71 We recommend that there should be set out in a Memorandum of Understanding (such as that which exists between the GMC and the NCAA) between the NHS, professional regulatory bodies such as the GMC and the CPS a clear agreement as to the responsibilities of each organisation in the investigation of potential criminal activity by health care professionals. This should then be promulgated to the NHS and built into the guidance suggested below.

2.72 We therefore recommend that SHAs work together with the Department of Health to produce guidance for PCTs and other NHS Trusts in handling such incidents, particularly since the latest reorganisation of the NHS has created a large number of relatively inexperienced PCTs with responsibility for GP contracts.

2.73 We further recommend that part of the guidance we have suggested SHAs and the Department of Health develop for the NHS should specifically address a patient's communications strategy and the involvement of local victim support services.

CHAPTER 3
THE CLIFFORD AYLING STORY

A) HOSPITAL PRACTICE – 1971 TO 1988

Kent & Canterbury and Isle of Thanet (Margate Wing) Hospitals

Introduction

3.1   This section of the Report deals with Ayling's career as a hospital doctor, primarily in east Kent.

3.2   From his qualification in 1963 until 1975, Ayling was employed in a number of surgical training posts at Senior House Officer and Registrar grades in hospitals in north and south London as well as the Isle of Thanet and Canterbury Group of Hospitals. However, by 1975 he had apparently ceased to apply for any other training posts, in particular Senior Registrar posts which would have been the next step in a career in hospital obstetrics and gynaecology and which could have led to his appointment as a consultant in that specialty.

3.3   In 1975 Ayling returned to east Kent and was appointed as a part-time clinical assistant in obstetrics and gynaecology at the Kent and Canterbury (KCH) and Thanet District Hospitals. He continued working sessions at that grade until 1988. (Details of the position clinical assistants occupy in the NHS and their role and responsibilities are set out in Annex 3). The appointment was reviewed annually. Clinical assistant posts were not recognised as training posts and therefore not subject to formal professional supervision. In addition, the numbers of junior staff (i.e. registrars and senior registrars) in obstetrics and gynaecology to support the consultant staff at KCH and Thanet were considered inadequate by the consultants.

3.4   Ayling therefore provided essential emergency cover as well as routine out-patient care which enabled obstetric and gynaecology services to be maintained on a number of hospital sites, whilst working without consultant supervision. In 1982, he entered full-time general practice but did not relinquish any of his agreed clinical assistant sessions.

3.5   During this time, a number of nursing and midwifery staff came to hold serious concerns about Ayling's behaviour and clinical management. Some of these were expressed contemporaneously; others were brought to the Inquiry's attention through the process of inviting witnesses to make statements and give evidence in person.

3.6   The Inquiry has heard of one formal complaint made by a patient during the period from 1975 to 1986, alongside concerns raised informally by a small number of other patients who spoke to members of staff. In 1987, what is known in the NHS by the term a "serious untoward incident", led to the decision not to renew his contract as a clinical assistant in obstetrics and gynaecology. Although Ayling was known to be a general practitioner, the circumstances under which his contract was not renewed and the fact of this termination were not conveyed to the Kent Family Practitioner Committee (FPC).

3.7   He was however re-employed for a further year as a clinical assistant in colposcopy until this was terminated as a result of an anonymous patient complaint in 1988. Again, the Kent FPC was not told of this.

3.8   Because Ayling was working as a clinical assistant and therefore accountable to a consultant, we explore in particular the evidence of two of the four consultants for whom Ayling worked (the two others are now deceased) about their actions in response to concerns and complaints of which they were aware at the time, and their response to the evidence presented by other health care staff to the Inquiry.

Ayling's Training and Early Career

3.9   Clifford Reginald Ayling was born on 1st November 1931. He first qualified with an engineering degree from the University of London in 1955 and worked as a telecommunications engineer with Marconi from 1955 to 1960. Ayling started medical training at University College Hospital, London, when he was some 27 years old. He qualified in 1963 with M.B., B.S. at the age of 32. He became a Diplomate of the Royal College of Obstetricians & Gynaecologists (RCOG) in 1967 and subsequently a Member in 1970 and a Fellow in 1985. Evidence given by Ayling during his criminal trial refers to him obtaining a certificate and diploma in family planning in the 1960s. We have in our possession a certificate issued by the Family Planning Association on 9th November 1969 confirming that he was trained in contraceptive planning techniques. He was said to be suitable for employment as a Medical Officer at a Family Planning Association Clinic.

3.10   Ayling's early career history may be summarised as follows:

1950-55	Student Apprentice	Marconi Telegraph & Wireless Co
1955-60	Telecommunications Engineer	Marconi Telegraph & Wireless Co
1963	HS Surgical Unit	University College Hospital (London)
1964	HP to Dr McGown	Oldchurch Hospital
1965	HS in Obs & Gynae	Oldchurch Hospital
1965	SHO Gynae	Royal Northern Hospital
1966	SHO Surgery	Joyce Green Hospital
1967	Registrar Obs & Gynae	Beckenham Hospital
1969	SHO Haematology	Lewisham Hospital

1969	Registrar Obs & Gynae	Redhill & Crawley Hospital
1970	Registrar Obs & Gynae	North Middlesex Hospital
1973	Registrar Obs & Gynae	Thanet District Hospital
1974	Lecturer Obs & Gynae	The London Hospital Medical School
1975	Clinical Asst Obs & Gynae	Canterbury & Thanet Hospitals

The North Middlesex Hospital

3.11   Under our Terms of Reference, we begin in 1971. Ayling was employed as a Registrar in Obstetrics & Gynaecology at the North Middlesex Hospital, having held the post since 1970. Little is now known about this period of Ayling's hospital practice. However, one of his former patients, Patient A, has brought her experience to our attention.

3.12   In early 1971 Ayling delivered Patient A's first child by Keillands forceps at the North Middlesex Hospital. The delivery was highly traumatic and during its course Patient A suffered significant soft tissue injuries, which later required surgical repair. According to Patient A's evidence to the Inquiry, these physical difficulties were exacerbated by the effect of Ayling's manner towards her. Patient A told us how she noticed that he had an erection during the course of a pre-natal examination. She says Ayling described his arousal as "an occupational hazard".

3.13   Some weeks after the delivery Patient A wrote in strongly critical terms to Mr John Brace, her consultant at the North Middlesex Hospital, asking for an explanation of what had 'gone wrong'. Mr Brace subsequently invited her to come and see him, although neither he nor Patient A can recall whether such a meeting took place and there is no note of it within her medical records. Like many other patients at that time, Patient A was unaware of the procedures which should then have been in place, following guidance issued to the NHS in 1966, for raising a more formal complaint about the treatment she had received.

3.14   It is not the purpose of our Inquiry to determine whether the care provided by Ayling to Patient A was acceptable or not. However, it is clear from Patient A's letter that her treatment raised serious questions about Ayling's practice as an obstetrician, particularly in the use of forceps; and her evidence to us raised further issues about his attitude towards female patients. In this respect Patient A's evidence, which occurred towards the very start of Ayling's work as a hospital clinician, foreshadows that of many subsequent patients. As will be shown below, there were persistent concerns about Ayling's practice throughout his career – and on very few occasions were those concerns fully investigated or properly followed through. Not having received Ayling's co-operation in our Inquiry, we have not been able to take his views on the events, nor even to know if some of them were brought to his attention at the time they occurred.

Initial Employment in Canterbury and Margate

3.15   By 1972 Ayling was apparently experiencing some frustration at being unable to progress upwards from the post of Registrar. A consultant to whom he wrote for advice commented that:

> "the Senior Registrar post is providing the modern bottleneck … the establishment in Senior Registrarships is very tight and related to the expected number of consultant vacancies".

3.16   Ayling obtained another position as a Registrar in Obstetrics & Gynaecology with the Isle of Thanet & Canterbury Group of Hospitals. The post commenced on 16th April 1973 and was subsequently renewed for a further year.

3.17   On 13th July 1973, only a few months after Ayling's appointment as a Registrar, Mr William Patterson and Mr Peter Fullman both took up their posts as Consultants in Obstetrics & Gynaecology at Thanet and KCH, increasing the number of consultant obstetricians and gynaecologists in the Canterbury and Thanet Health District from two to four. There is a more protracted description of their dealings with Ayling later in this section. Ayling had by that stage been working in training posts in obstetrics and gynaecology for some eight years. Mr Patterson told the Inquiry that Ayling had not fully completed his training in some of the standard surgical procedures such as vaginal hysterectomies and repairs. It is not clear whether Ayling's inability to progress further within the profession was due to deficiencies in his clinical ability or performance or the strength of the contemporaneous competition. Either way, his hospital career never progressed into the grade of Consultant, and from 1974 until his employment was ended by the William Harvey Hospital in 1994, Ayling remained a Clinical Assistant in Obstetrics & Gynaecology.

The London Hospital

3.18   Ayling left Thanet and KCH in order to take up an appointment as a Lecturer in Obstetrics & Gynaecology at the London Hospital Medical School commencing on 1st July 1974. He was appointed an Honorary Clinical Assistant at the Hospital at the same time.

3.19   We do not have any evidence relating to Ayling's clinical work at the London Hospital. However, we have been supplied with the two letters that accompanied the cessation of his employment in 1975. The first records a decision not to renew his lecturer's post for a further year, without giving any reasons. The second is a personal letter of career advice to Ayling from the Dean of the London Hospital. It suggested that he looked for academic posts, where his background in engineering could be of assistance to the NHS.

3.20   The Dean of the London Hospital is now deceased. Therefore we have been unable to discover, with any acceptable degree of reliability, the intent behind that letter; and whether it indicated any degree of concern over Ayling's clinical skills or whether it should be read only as a positive endorsement of academic career ambitions.

The Kent & Canterbury Hospital and the Isle of Thanet District Hospital

3.21   Ayling followed the suggestion from the Dean of the London Hospital and applied for further academic posts, but without success. Instead he worked briefly as a Locum Consultant in Obstetrics & Gynaecology in the Canterbury & Thanet Health District from 28th July 1975 to 10th August 1975.

3.22   At that time, the Obstetrics and Gynaecology Department of the Thanet District Hospital was largely based in the Margate Wing of the hospital, and consisted of an antenatal clinic, a delivery suite and two obstetric wards which provided both antenatal and post-natal services. An outpatient colposcopy service was based in the gynaecology and female surgery ward at the Margate Wing and there was a further gynaecology ward at the Ramsgate Wing, which closed some time after 1983. The number of deliveries at the Thanet Hospital was approximately 1,400 per annum: contemporaneous guidance from the RCOG would have classified it as a relatively small obstetrics unit, the ideal size of a unit being one handling approximately 2,500 deliveries each year. In the early 1970s, neonatal units were established – a special care baby unit (SCBU) at Margate and a neonatal intensive care unit (NICU) at KCH.

3.23   The maternity unit at KCH was a slightly larger unit than that at Thanet, delivering approximately 1,800 babies per year. It was the unit to which more complex cases were likely to be referred because of its neonatal facilities.

3.24   The Inquiry was told that *"Thanet for historical reasons was incredibly short of junior staff...Thanet had the greatest number of clinical assistants in the Region"* and *"it did make a great deal of use of clinical assistants"*.

3.25   Mr Fullman recollected: *"We were very, very thin on the ground and stretched over an enormous area"*. The consultants worked approximately 60 hours per week with another 10 to 20 hours on call, and their junior staff worked similar timetables to the extent that government regulations allowed.

3.26   On 15th July 1975 Ayling wrote to one of the four consultants, Mr Dwyer, asking to be considered for the post of Clinical Assistant in the Obstetrics & Gynaecology Department of the Thanet District Hospital, Margate Wing, stating, *"As I am known to you and your colleagues I trust that it will not be necessary for me to append my Curriculum Vitae, etc"*. On 30th July 1975, he was offered a part-time post in the Thanet and Kent & Canterbury Hospitals commencing on 1st September 1975. The position was for a year in the first instance and was then subject to annual review.

3.27   The part-time post filled by Ayling across the two hospitals was, according to Mr Fullman *"really to replace a registrar post which we were not allowed to have by the Regional Health Authority"*.

3.28   Until 1977, the junior medical staffing at Thanet Hospital in obstetrics and Gynaecology consisted of a registrar, a senior house officer (SHO) and a pre-registration house surgeon (HS). Two further SHO posts were added with the introduction of GP vocational trainees in 1977 and a second registrar post was created in 1983. However, funding for a second SHO post was refused by the SE Thames Regional Health Authority (RHA). and such a post was not established until after Ayling ceased to work as a clinical assistant in 1987. The paucity of staff at Thanet led to a number of occasions when the maternity unit had to close

3.29   At KCH, the junior medical staffing was supplemented by an arrangement with a hospital in Melbourne that provided experienced registrars to work in Canterbury before they returned to work in Australia. These posts were supernumerary to the funded establishment and thus escaped the concerns held by the RHA about career hierarchy and, according to Mr Fullman, *"were an absolute gem as far as the registrar cover in the hospital was concerned."*

3.30   Ayling continued to be employed as a Clinical Assistant until 30th June 1987. The employment contracts for clinical staff (other than consultant staff) were issued by the Canterbury and Thanet District Health Authority but the management of those contracts, their renewal and the discipline of the employees to whom they related was left to the individual hospital units. In the event of a decision by a unit to issue a final warning or to dismiss an employee of the District, there was a right of appeal to the DHA Consultant witnesses emphasised that it was for the hospital management to discipline and dismiss staff but in the case of a clinical assistant's contract, the Medical Staff Committee (to which all consultant medical staff belonged) retained the right to approve the renewal of a contract, guided by the recommendations of the consultant(s) under whom the assistant worked.

3.31   Ayling's original contract was to provide three sessions at Kent & Canterbury Hospital and three at Thanet Hospital. These sessions were for "on call" work which meant that junior medical staff or nursing staff would contact Ayling for advice or ask him to see a patient if they were concerned about her and her consultant was unavailable. Apart from two weekday afternoons (Thursday and Friday) which Ayling worked alternating weekly between the two hospitals, he also provided weekend cover. Ayling alternated each weekend between the two hospitals, at Kent & Canterbury he was "on call" for Saturday and Sunday nights from home whilst at Thanet, he was resident at Margate from 9am Saturday until 9am Monday.

3.32   In April 1977 payment for two additional sessions was made in recognition of his "on call" work, thus bringing the total number of contracted sessions up to eight.

3.33   Ayling also acted as a locum consultant when consultants were on annual leave. One of those consultants, Mr Patterson, has stated that when this happened, he selected the procedures that he thought that Ayling was competent to perform, leaving the more complex to await his return.

3.34   In his criminal trial Ayling stated that his post as a clinical assistant was a *"special job, in which I used doing [sic] some clinical work during the day. But mostly it was on call work"*. In a letter of application for a post at the William Harvey Hospital (discussed in detail later in the Report), Ayling stated that the Clinical Assistant's job was to enable him to "undertake research in radio-telemetry". However, a research grant made in 1976, for *"Development of a Transmitter for Use in the Labour Ward"*, was not continued after March 1977. Ayling suggested that domestic commitments had prevented him from making the hoped-for progress on this project.

3.35   Over a number of years a substantial amount of unpaid sessions came to be added to this programme by Ayling. Mr Patterson told the Inquiry that by the early 1980s, when Ayling had started work as a full-time GP principal, there was concern that he was stretching himself too thinly and that this might be affecting his clinical competence.

3.36   We have also seen correspondence relating to health concerns, dating from July 1979. Ayling's medical advisor suggested that he was suffering from over-work and that the present pattern of being "on call" every weekend was most unsatisfactory. He suggested that Ayling should replan his life in order to give himself more relaxation. In October 1979 Ayling wrote to the District Administrator outlining his workload and noting that he had been *"strongly advised to work within the terms of my contract"*. In addition to the eight sessions noted above, he wrote that two further sessions had been undertaken *"in order to start an Ultra Sound Obstetrics Service and to maintain the Friday morning ante-natal booking clinic for which there is undoubtedly a need"*. He had also assisted in the training of radiographers.

3.37   The response of the Chairman of the Medical Executive Committee to the Chairman of the Obstetric, Gynaecological and Paediatric Division at KCH, was that *"there is no way in which the District can fund these extra sessions. I therefore suggest that he confines himself to the work that he was originally contracted to do"* – that is, the eight paid sessions.

3.38   Mr Patterson told us that despite the concerns that Ayling was covering too many sessions:

> "in practice there was little we could do because we were so short of obstetricians at Margate. For a long time in the 70s and 80s this shortage threatened the viability of the unit. Ayling helped to prop it up."

3.39   It is clear from his comments that Ayling's availability, especially to cover weekends made him indispensable within the overstretched units at Thanet and KCH. This view is consolidated by the documentary evidence relating to Ayling's employment.

3.40   It is also supported by Mr Fullman's evidence to us that the Regional Health Authority had blocked the consultants' attempts to obtain another registrar post, on the basis that such posts were stepping-stones to consultant posts and should not be filled without a clear pathway of promotion. At one point, the consultants were so desperate for another registrar that they telephoned Mr Roger Gale, MP for Thanet North, and asked him to intervene. He travelled to Kent to interview them and then raised the matter in the House of Commons. About six months later a further registrar post was created at Thanet Hospital.

Staff Concerns and Complaints

3.41   This section is concerned with the evidence relating to Ayling's practice at the Thanet and Kent and Canterbury Hospitals from 1975–1988. It has been one of the more difficult periods for the Inquiry to assess. To fulfil our Terms of Reference, we asked for staff to report what knowledge they had of complaints or informal concerns about Ayling, whether made by staff or patients. Significant numbers of staff responded by telling us of their memories. In doing so, they were looking back over events that occurred many years ago, and limited contemporaneous material was available to assist them. In some cases, this was because no records had ever been made. In others, it appears that records were later destroyed. However, we accept that staff's memories of these years were genuinely and honestly held, and that they told us of views which they had genuinely held at that time.

3.42   Inevitably in an Inquiry such as this, we heard little or nothing from those who had no recollection of concerns being expressed, and who held none themselves. Thus, even before allowing for the effect of the passage of time on witness availability and memory, our Report does not, and could not, paint a complete and full picture of the views held by staff. But we did not seek, and were not required by our Terms of Reference, to assess either Ayling's overall conduct, or how he behaved on particular occasions. Such an exercise would have been impossible and inappropriate, given (for example) the fact that Ayling did not contribute to this Report and his comments on the episodes detailed below have not been obtained.

3.43   Equally we were not asked to assess Ayling's clinical competence by any objective standard. We did need to look at the facts where questions and concerns were raised by staff and patients, to establish whether a legitimate concern had been raised; but we make no attempt to marshal what incidents there are to form any quantative assessment of Ayling's clinical practice. Similarly we were not asked to undertake any quantative judgement of those staff and patients who were satisfied with, or were silent about, the care afforded them by Ayling. This Report assesses complaints handling, not the overall pattern of care provided.

3.44   Rather, our remit was to investigate how the NHS handled – or failed to respond to – the expression of any concerns. In looking at this, we considered that the fact that other members of staff would have been supportive of Ayling, or that he himself would have denied that incidents we have heard described took place, or that anything untoward happened, did not invalidate our work. If a staff member or a patient express a concern, it must be fully and properly investigated. The fact that another member of staff – or even large numbers of staff members – do not share the concern is no reason not to take it seriously. Judgments upon the weight of the evidence gathered come at the end, and not the beginning, of a process of investigation.

Thanet District Hospital

3.45   We heard evidence from some midwives at Thanet that concerns about Ayling's obstetric performance and his conduct towards female patients were widespread within the medical and midwifery hierarchies throughout his employment as a clinical assistant.

3.46   Despite this, it was difficult for us to identify specific occasions on which a member of staff expressed concerns about Ayling to a senior manager or clinician. With the exception of the 1984 midwife's statement (reviewed later in our Report) there appear to be no written records of staff complaints.

3.47   That is not to say that no concerns were expressed. We accept that they were. Rather it is indicative of the contemporaneous culture within the profession to rely upon informal mechanisms for raising concerns about a colleague. Though understandable, the effect of this was the lack of accumulated information about Ayling's practice and behaviour; information which should have led to a formal investigation and – if the allegations were upheld by such a process – the earlier cessation of his career as a doctor. We have referred elsewhere in our Report to the damage caused by the failure to gather and document information that would have enabled an earlier intervention to investigate formally Ayling's activities.

3.48   From the evidence given to us it is apparent that the complaints about Ayling focused on a number of persistent themes. These were as follows:

Length and Frequency of Internal Examinations

- Witnesses told us that that Ayling took too long carrying out internal examinations on female patients or would perform noticeably more examinations than other doctors. To some he was known as *"Fingers Fred"* or *"Fingers Ayling"*.
- Witnesses were divided as to whether these examinations were simply unnecessary or performed for other, possibly sexual motives. Several had no such perception. Others were more critical and suspected that at times Ayling derived some form of gratification from the examinations he carried out.

Frequency of Breast Examinations

- Staff also told us that Ayling carried out breast examinations with excessive frequency. This perception was corroborated in the evidence of a patient, who told us that she had asked a nurse *"does he have to do that"*, but had been told only that Ayling was a doctor and therefore knew what he was doing.

Inappropriate Personal Remarks or Innuendo

- Many witnesses recollected that Ayling made remarks containing inappropriate sexual innuendo during internal examinations or intimate procedures. There were repeated accounts of Ayling commenting that he would sew a patient up *"nice and tight"* when performing an episiotomy.

- In general it was felt that patients and their partners did not react adversely to such comments, although in some instances the midwives themselves considered the sexual content of the jokes and innuendoes to be obnoxious and disrespectful. One midwife chose to challenge Ayling directly about his remarks. However, she noticed no change in his practice. Another was so shocked that when she subsequently became a patient at the Hospital she insisted that he did not perform surgery on her.

Rough or Inconsiderate Care

- Several midwives reported that Ayling was excessively rough or heavy-handed when delivering babies or performing internal examinations. In some instances, this led to oral complaints from patients about his physical manner.
- We have been told that Ayling was also known to perform more extensive episiotomies than other obstetricians and to opt for forceps deliveries when a Caesarean section would possibly have been more appropriate. One witness described his use of Keilland's forceps as *"adventurous"*; a criticism which echoes a former patient's experience at the North Middlesex Hospital in 1971.
- According to another witness, the midwives would groan when Ayling appeared on the ward. She personally called him *"Butcher Ayling"*. This was not because she had seen him butcher a patient but because she thought that he was more suited to that occupation than working in a hospital.
- Another midwife considered that when Ayling *"had the bit between his teeth"* during deliveries he found it very hard to let go. He would achieve what he wanted by whatever means he saw fit – including sometimes, in her view, by brutalising the woman concerned.

Perinatal Morbidity

- Dr David Cook, the senior paediatrician at Thanet District Hospital, told us that over time he and his colleagues noted that when compared with other obstetricians a higher proportion of the babies delivered by Ayling appeared to have undergone traumatic forceps deliveries. They would have forceps marks or bruising, and typically would be a bit concussed for a day or two and subsequently somewhat irritable. He also noted similar problems following ventouse deliveries. It should be noted that the Inquiry did not undertake a systematic comparison of Ayling's complication rates with other practitioners to substantiate these impressions.
- Dr Cook's recollection was that these were temporary problems – he could not recall any babies suffering long-term problems as a result of Ayling's care nor was there any concern that there was a higher death rate associated with his interventions. His impression was that the reason for this higher morbidity was that Ayling was *"keen to get the baby out vaginally and was reluctant to resort to Caesarean sections"*. Various informal discussions about Ayling's performance were said to have taken place between the paediatricians and the obstetric consultants over a period of years. The paediatricians did not feel that

Ayling was a very gentle obstetrician and queried his employment. Dr Cook was left with the impression that the obstetricians took their complaints on board but felt that Ayling was doing a reasonably satisfactory job and offered residential cover that would be difficult to replace.

Avoidance of Ayling's Care

- We heard from a number of female members of staff who commented that they took steps to ensure that Ayling would never be involved in their care when they were admitted as patients. One midwife stated that although Ayling was very nice to her in offering his sympathies she would not have allowed him to carry out an examination on her or to touch her in any way.
- Staff also commented that patients themselves expressed an unwillingness to be seen by Ayling, in part due to his keenness to do vaginal examinations. Several midwives reported being asked by patients to make a clear note to that effect in their medical records.

Staff Complaints

- We received evidence from midwives who said that they had repeatedly complained about Ayling to their managers. One nurse in an Outpatients Department remembers reporting concerns about Ayling's examinations to her Sister, and that many of her colleagues did the same. She could not say whether the matter was taken up with senior managers, but she was finally told to stop complaining, as nothing would be done. Her understanding was that the doctors would unite and support Ayling. She felt that the culture of the time was that doctors were unapproachable and it was felt that Ayling would defend his conduct on the basis that detailed or thorough examinations were necessary to ascertain the cause of a patient's problem.
- Many of the concerns about Ayling's inappropriate conduct emanated from the Antenatal Clinic at Thanet, which was managed for many years by Sister Penny Moore. She and several members of her nursing and midwifery staff told us that they had serious concerns that Ayling performed unnecessary and excessively lengthy vaginal examinations. One particularly serious incident, which is said to have occurred in 1980, led Sister Moore to ban Ayling from the Antenatal Clinic and to speak directly to a consultant about his conduct. Details of that incident are discussed in more detail below.
- We were also told that in the late 1970s the midwives wrote a petition or letter stating that they could no longer work with Ayling and that he was harming patients. No copy of this petition is still in existence although one midwife, Jennifer Cook, remembers signing it.
- The petition was said to have gone to the Senior Nursing Officer, Mrs Pat Elworthy, and may also have been sent to one of the four consultants. However, there is no record of it within the documentation kept by the Hospital and neither Mrs Elworthy, nor Mr Patterson and Mr Fullman have any recollection of it. Although we accept that such a petition was composed, we were therefore unable to determine whether or not it was ever in fact sent.

Kent and Canterbury Hospital

3.49   We received more limited evidence of concerns about Ayling's conduct and performance from the midwives, nurses and other healthcare staff at KCH. One explanation for this is that Ayling may have behaved differently at KCH than at Thanet. However, this is highly improbable given the consistency of patient and staff concerns about Ayling both at Thanet and other hospitals throughout his career. In our view the more plausible explanation is a combination of two factors.

3.50   First, Ayling spent more time at Thanet than at KCH because of the residency requirement of his weekend "on call" at Margate. Possibly this was a reflection of the Australian registrar arrangement at KCH so Ayling's services would have been needed more frequently at Thanet than KCH. Therefore staff at the latter institution had fewer opportunities to reach firm conclusions about his performance. Secondly, the midwifery staff at Thanet appear to have formed a strong collective view of Ayling relatively early on in his career, as demonstrated by their composition of a petition in the late 1970s. Therefore information about his approach to female patients was more widely disseminated among the healthcare staff at Thanet than at KCH, where no strong consensus about Ayling's behaviour appears to have been reached.

3.51   Despite the apparent differences in volume and severity of complaints, there are noticeable qualitative similarities between the evidence of the midwives at KCH and those at Thanet.

3.52   One sister at the KCH, who worked with Ayling during the 1980s, commented that she found him rather obsequious. He had a reputation as something of a *"butcher"* and could be quite aggressive with regard to some of his procedures. He seemed to pull quite hard when using forceps and performing ventouse deliveries; although she felt that some doctors do make hard work of things that others appear to undertake easily. Furthermore, she added that, despite Ayling's reputation, at times he would *"bail us out and do something brilliant"*.

3.53   More significantly the sister recalled that while some male obstetricians were occasionally allowed to see a patient without a chaperone, there was a general feeling that Ayling could not be left alone with women. She also remembered that on occasions he would say unsuitably lewd remarks such as *"stitch her up tightly"*. However, comments did not appear to upset women or their partners and she was surprised when the sexual allegations emerged in the 1990s.

3.54   Another midwife, who briefly worked with Ayling at the KCH from April 1986, remembered that there was a general feeling among the midwifery staff that Ayling was heavy-handed with patients when performing instrumental deliveries. She also commented that he did not mix well with other professionals.

3.55   Dr Scott, a Registrar on the GP vocational training scheme in the mid-1980s remembers Ayling as a solitary character who did not socialise with other staff. He recognised that there was a tension between Ayling and the

KCH midwives, caused by a feeling that he *"had a tendency to intervene in labour more than other doctors and more than some midwives felt necessary"*. However, he commented that such a view was not uncommon within maternity units. There was also a general atmosphere of awareness amongst midwives that if Ayling was called in to assist a delivery, it would lead to a quick decision to conduct a forceps delivery. He does not recollect other concerns about his practice.

3.56   Another midwife and ward sister who started work at the hospital in 1985 told the Inquiry that she worked with Ayling on the labour wards. She remembered having an easy working relationship with him; she found him pleasant and undemanding. She was not aware of any concerns that he might represent a sexual threat to anyone, and as ward sister would have expected to be told if that had been a worry. In any event, Ayling (like other doctors) would generally have been accompanied by a midwife when seeing patients. Professionally, she remembered that his deliveries by forceps or caesarean were rather more 'messy' than those performed by other doctors; further his episiotomies were larger than the average. There was a general feeling that Ayling did more forceps deliveries than others, but no audit was carried out to substantiate that impression. Although she remembered babies being delivered by Keillands forceps that looked rather 'bruised and battered', she stressed that higher numbers of difficult forceps deliveries had been carried out in those years, and superficial trauma was generally associated with the use of these forceps. In general terms, she did not doubt Ayling's competence. Dr Appleyard, a consultant paediatrician who took up his post at KCH in 1971, and set up the neonatal unit there, worked with Ayling. He was more guarded than Dr Cook in his recollections of Ayling's performance. He noted that when he first arrived in East Kent, the perinatal mortality in Canterbury was higher than the national average. However, over time the mortality figures improved as they built up their neonatal team. As outcomes improved over time, it became apparent to him that Ayling's individual performance was not as good as other obstetricians in training on the Obstetric Emergency rota. He felt that it was not that Ayling's performance was bad; it was simply that it did not improve in line with other staff.

Mr Patterson and Mr Fullman

3.57   Mr Patterson and Mr Fullman had first come across Ayling during his employment as a Registrar at Thanet and KCH between April 1973 and June 1974. Ayling had then spent a year at the London Hospital before returning to Kent to take up the post of Clinical Assistant.

3.58   Although Ayling was formally accountable to the four Consultants (Mr Patterson, Mr Fullman, Mr Ward and Mr Dwyer), in respect of his care of their patients, in practice it appears that from the commencement of work as a clinical assistant he worked without formal, or effective, supervision. Although an element of a clinical assistant post was seen as an informal training opportunity for the individual concerned, in Ayling's case he covered for the very doctors who should have monitored his work and performance. There was in fact no system in place to monitor his general performance or behaviour towards patients. This is not a criticism of the then management. It is simply a reflection of the culture and systems of the time and the anomalous position that clinical assistants occupied. Indeed it may be taken to reflect a more general difficulty at the time, namely that there was a lack of clinical audit and supervision among all grades of doctor. So the practical effect of Ayling's autonomy as a specialist practitioner was that those responsible for his work, namely his consultants, gained little first-hand experience of his competence. They were reliant on junior colleagues, the nursing and midwifery staff and patients themselves to express any concerns about Ayling's practice.

3.59   Mr Patterson and Mr Fullman remained close colleagues throughout their time at Thanet and KCH and though they routinely worked at different hospitals, they would meet frequently and informally to discuss matters of mutual concern. Despite their friendship and professional proximity, there were pronounced differences between their recollections of Ayling's performance and behaviour.

3.60   Mr Patterson was a thoughtful and reflective witness. He readily acknowledged that he had known of Ayling's reputation for heavy-handedness. In his own words, he felt Ayling was *"not the tidiest of operators"* and there was frequently a lot of blood lost during his procedures. He also accepted that as one of Ayling's supervising Consultants, he was ultimately responsible for the quality of his obstetric performance. He concluded his oral evidence by saying that he had *"to accept that a lot of criticism is levelled at [him, Patterson] and some of it sticks"*. Mr Patterson expressed genuine abhorrence at the accounts given by the midwives of Ayling's inappropriate comments and approach to female patients during his years as his clinical assistant. His general position was that many, if not all, of these events should have come to his attention at the time. However, he strongly denied having received any specific complaints from midwives about sexualised conduct by Ayling. His conclusion was that to some extent at least *"there was almost a conspiracy of silence"* over sexual issues which had acted as a bar to information being passed between the midwives and the doctors. He felt that it was possible that midwives had not expressed themselves explicitly and that if they had explained matters in coded language then he had not read their code.

3.61   In contrast to this, Mr Fullman was a defensive witness whose principal concern, we consider, was to minimise his personal responsibility for Ayling's actions. His reaction to the majority of specific incidents about which he was questioned was that he knew nothing of the event at the time and therefore could not be criticised for any lack of action on his part. He also maintained that he had no general knowledge of the underlying concerns about sexualised behaviour by Ayling.

3.62   Given the weight of the evidence we received, we were unable to accept these aspects of Mr Fullman's evidence and where his account differed from those of other witnesses such as Mr Patterson or Sister Moore, we concluded that the latter were the more accurate and should be preferred. Despite Mr Fullman's denials, it was clear to us that he shared a significant proportion of the responsibility for the failure to acknowledge and investigate Ayling's actions further than he did.

The Incident at Thanet Antenatal Clinic in 1980

The Evidence of Penny Moore

3.63   Sister Penny Moore told us that during the early part of 1980 she became directly involved in a serious incident involving Ayling in the Antenatal Clinic at Thanet. The sensitivity of this episode is such that we must be circumspect in our description of it, in order to avoid any risk of identifying individuals concerned. We should also point out for the record that whilst Penny Moore told us that she did make contemporaneous notes of the incident, she destroyed them well before being asked to give evidence to us. We therefore did not have the benefit of reviewing those notes. She also had to rely on her recollection of the events from her memory of it. We have no evidence that the information given to us was brought to Ayling's attention at the time.

3.64   According to Penny Moore's account she was called urgently by a nurse chaperone at a post-natal examination and, on entering the room, she found Ayling masturbating while carrying out a vaginal examination on a young woman. Her immediate response was to pull Ayling forcibly away from the patient and order him to leave the Clinic. Though herself traumatised, she then traced the patient's consultant, Mr Fullman, and asked him to come immediately to the Hospital.

3.65   Penny Moore told us that on Mr Fullman's arrival she explained that Ayling had assaulted a patient and described exactly what she had seen. She recalled Mr Fullman's reaction was not one of "shock horror" but of "very professional" sympathy for her experience. She offered to fetch the nurse chaperone but Mr Fullman said that this was not necessary because he believed what she was saying.

3.66   Penny Moore then told Mr Fullman that she did not want Ayling at the Clinic again. In response, he told her that Ayling would be referred to a psychiatrist. The impression she had was that this was a very quick decision, as if the possibility had already been in his mind before. She also said that she wanted to speak to Mr Patterson about it but Mr Fullman said that he would do so himself. The question of Police involvement was not raised.

3.67   Penny Moore told us that she heard nothing more, either from the consultants or from her nurse managers, whom she described as somewhat ineffective. She presumed Ayling was getting psychiatric treatment. She made it clear that her overwhelming priority at the time was to keep Ayling out of her Clinic *"to protect her Mums"* and was devastated to learn much later on of the consequences of no disciplinary action being taken over this incident.

3.68   Some time after the incident had occurred Penny Moore discovered that Mr Patterson was re-introducing Ayling to the Antenatal Clinic. According to her evidence she challenged Mr Patterson directly about this in front of Ayling and was told not to question a Fellow of the Royal College of Gynaecologists [that is, Ayling]. Her response was to insist that she would chaperone Ayling herself and that her colleague, Julie Miller, would manage the Clinic. There was no response from Ayling.

3.69 In his evidence, Mr Fullman agreed that the incident Penny Moore described was extremely serious and amounted to a criminal offence. He did not seek to debate whether or not the incident had occurred, but instead maintained that he had known nothing about it at the time and that Penny Moore had never spoken to him about it. He also denied speaking to her about a psychiatric referral and assumed that Penny Moore's understanding of this stemmed from a separate incident of the same year (see below). He maintained that he was unaware that Ayling had been banned from the Antenatal Clinic.

3.70 Mr Patterson was also asked about his recollection of this incident, which he accepted amounted to criminal conduct. He also denied hearing about it at the time and was certain that if Mr Fullman had agreed to speak to him about it he would have done so. The only explanation that he could think of was that Penny Moore had spoken to one of the other consultants, Mr Ward or Mr Dwyer (who supervised the Antenatal Clinic at Thanet). However, he would have expected the recipient of such a complaint to have discussed it with all three other consultants. Both Mr Ward and Mr Dwyer are now deceased.

3.71 In relation to Ayling's apparent reintroduction to the Clinic, Mr Patterson went on to say that as he was unaware of the original incident, he saw no problem having Ayling there with him, probably as a locum. He accepted that he may have rebuked Penny Moore for questioning a Fellow of the Royal College, but said that he was simply exercising his authority as a consultant and was referring to the fact that Ayling was an experienced doctor.

3.72 Mr Patterson ultimately accepted that he must have been extremely naïve not to have seen the implications of such an extraordinary outburst by a Sister who had actually barred a doctor from her Clinic. He did say that he thought that this might have been because Penny Moore disliked Ayling. However, he also accepted that Ayling normally defended himself vigorously and the fact that he kept quiet on this occasion should have alerted him to a real problem. Mr Patterson concluded his evidence on this incident by saying that, if Penny Moore was correct, *"then we are culpable"*.

Conclusions

3.73 We are satisfied, first, that Penny Moore did witness an incident in the Antenatal Clinic in 1980, which raised extremely serious questions about Ayling's conduct; and secondly, that Penny Moore reported the incident directly to Mr Fullman shortly after it occurred. She was adamant in her response to questions on this particular point.

3.74 We bear in mind that the incident which Penny Moore told us that she had seen concerns a matter on which Ayling has not commented and we heard no evidence from him on this matter. We have no doubt that he would deny that the incident took place and assert that the witness must be mistaken. It is not our task, and we do not seek, to make findings on what actually took place.

3.75   However, in our view the incident reported by Penny Moore clearly
        warranted an immediate investigation and action at the highest level,
        including – if substantiated – dismissal and referral to both the Police and
        the General Medical Council. This could well have ended Ayling's career
        twenty years before he finally ceased to practise. We deplore that fact that
        no such investigation was undertaken.

3.76   In relation to the failed reintroduction of Ayling to the Antenatal Clinic, we
        must agree with Mr Patterson that he was naïve not to have questioned
        Penny Moore further. Had he done so, the reason for her refusal to allow
        Ayling to return would have been discussed openly and a proper
        investigation could have been carried out, if somewhat belatedly.

The 1984 Complaint By Delphine Bentley
3.77   In August 1984 a further incident took place that led to a written complaint
        by a member of staff – a copy of which has been provided to the Inquiry.

3.78   Delphine Bentley, a midwife at Thanet, made a formal statement
        complaining about the way in which Ayling had acted during the delivery
        of a particular patient's baby. According to Ms Bentley, Ayling was
        panicking during the course of labour, shouting at the patient to open her
        legs. He performed an episiotomy without first infiltrating the perineum
        with anaesthetic; and then, following the birth, he made a lewd remark
        about stitching the patient up *"nice and tight"*.

3.79   Although the complaint was in writing, it would appear that it resulted in
        no action of any kind. Senior midwives of the time have no recollection of
        it. Ms Bentley acknowledged that not only had she complained about the
        incident, but that Ayling too had reacted by putting in a complaint about
        her behaviour, as well as that of two other midwives. She heard nothing
        further about this, and was not contacted about it. But if she is right about
        the complaint and cross-complaints, this may provide one explanation of
        the apparent lack of action.

3.80   The midwives thought that Mr Patterson would have heard about the
        incident through the standard networks of communication between the
        midwifery sisters and consultants. However, he told us that he had not
        heard of the incident at the time and was *"shattered"* to learn of it.
        He would have been troubled principally by Ayling's panic. The
        episiotomy without anaesthetic should not have been done and he thought
        that the comment about the way in which the patient would be sutured
        was obscene.

3.81   Mr Fullman maintained that he heard nothing of this complaint or of
        anything in similar vein. He would not agree that there might have been
        cultural factors, which may have prevented midwives from talking to
        consultants about complaints relating to doctors. He said that there had
        been a system in place of the senior midwives being able to ring the
        consultants directly if they were unhappy about the care or treatment a
        patient was receiving. Insofar as Mr Fullman endeavoured to persuade us
        that there had been no shortcomings in the culture and organisation of the

time, which might have prevented complaints from being dealt with adequately, he signally failed.

3.82   Mr Patterson also observed that there was a more general difficulty of communication between consultants and midwives, largely because, "the nursing structure seemed to have a cut off point at a level above ordinary midwives. They did not have true managers." This observation resonates with both other evidence we heard and also with our perceptions of the characteristics of those individual senior midwives during the 1970s and early 1980s. It is meant as no criticism of them to observe that their primary strength and skill lay in the area of specialist nursing and patient care. Matters associated with management, including the processing of complaints, would have been less familiar territory. They were not dealt with then in the same systematic way that they would be handled today.

Conclusion

3.83   It appears to us that the serious failure of the senior staff and management at Thanet and KCH to recognise and address concerns about Ayling's conduct resulted from inadequate communication within the professional hierarchies. These failings should be viewed against the background of a severely stretched service, under-resourced and with insufficient clinicians to cover the service. Mr Patterson did not agree that the physical safety of patients had been compromised, but he did accept that their emotional well being had been put at risk by continued reliance upon Ayling's availability to cover service requirements. It seems to us that that must be right. Properly addressing the concerns would also have enabled a response to be sought from Clifford Ayling himself.

Patient Concerns and Complaints

Introduction

3.84   The main part of this section concentrates on the accounts given by those patients who did raise concerns or complaints with members of staff. We should also record, however, that we also heard from some former hospital patients who had distressing experiences, but who acknowledged that they did not complain at the time. For example, one patient spoke of her recollection of an unchaperoned examination, which took place in 1974. A painful internal examination was conducted, without adequate explanation. Another spoke of a painful and distressing examination, this time conducted in the presence of a nurse chaperone, but one who was standing back from the patient. Neither felt able to complain, but tried rather to tell themselves that they were overreacting. The barriers to raising such concerns are discussed later in our Report.

Patient B

3.85   In 1977 a baby tragically died during the course of a difficult forceps delivery by Ayling at Thanet Hospital. Following the child's death the pathologist identified the cause as lack of oxygen associated with the trauma of an assisted delivery. A perinatal meeting was convened by Mr Patterson, as the consultant obstetrician responsible for the patient, to discuss the case. This was attended by Ayling, Mr Patterson, the junior doctors and possibly by Dr Cook. It is not clear whether Mr Fullman attended, although Mr Patterson believes he would have discussed the issues raised with him in a less formal setting. At the time, it was not the practice to keep minutes or other records of such meetings, as informality was believed to encourage frank discussion. However, Mr Patterson told us that the meeting in its review was critical of the management of the delivery.

3.86   Whatever the outcome of the meeting, it is clear to us that the death of a child in such circumstances raised serious issues about Ayling's ability to make appropriate clinical decisions in the course of difficult deliveries. Mr Patterson accepted this conclusion. Putting the case alongside the concerns voiced about Ayling's use of forceps being *"heavy-handed"*, he agreed that there was the beginning of a pattern of someone who was not appropriately skilled to perform his obstetric duties.

3.87   However, we must again note the absence of any systematic audit of Ayling's practice, either then or now. The evidence concerning one incident – albeit a serious and deeply tragic one – is not enough of a sufficient base for judgments to be made upon clinical competence. Rather, the point we draw out is that the discussion at the perinatal review meeting was not followed up by a systematic attempt to supervise Ayling's practice and, if necessary, offer further training. Dr Patterson told us that he witnessed a number of forceps deliveries, which were acceptable. But *"we couldn't supervise all his forceps deliveries, and these would just come out of the blue, this sort of case"*. As we have noted before the pattern of Ayling's sessions worked against effective consultant supervision. Nor was it until 1992 that the national Confidential Enquiry into Stillbirths and Deaths in Infancy (CESDI) was established as a routine reporting and review process from which lessons could be drawn for individual and wider obstetric learning. At the tine of this incident, the only external scrutiny and review of what happened and why would have been via the coroners' system.

3.88   We must record our disquiet that no attempt was apparently made to offer Patient B any explanation or feedback at the time. Whilst we acknowledge the culture of defensiveness amongst health care staff in relation to serious untoward incidents like this, which was in place in the late 1970s, we deeply regret that it was only in the course of our Inquiry that the parents learned of the cause of their child's death.

Patient C

3.89   Patient C was Mr Fullman's patient at the Kent & Canterbury Hospital in April 1980. A few weeks later her husband wrote a letter of complaint to him about the conduct of the delivery of their baby two months previously. In addition to expressing criticisms about how the labour had been handled generally by staff, and concern about Ayling's clinical judgements, the letter stated:

> "At best I would describe Dr Aileen's [sic] attitude, approach and general behaviour as being brutal, if not actually bordering on the sadistic. He almost seemed to derive pleasure in the way he, very, very roughly, did the internal examination on my wife and his callous and unfeeling attitude did nothing to endear anyone to him."

3.90   Mr Fullman told us that he had been shocked at the contents of the letter. He agreed that *"sadistic"* connoted something sexual and he said that he remembered feeling that the letter suggested that the examinations had been conducted for Ayling's pleasure, rather than to assess Patient C's progress in labour. At one stage, he said that thought Ayling's actions constituted a *"serious assault"*. He later retracted that statement but reiterated that he considered his conduct *"twisted and perverted"*.

3.91   Patient C and her husband met Mr Fullman at KCH to discuss their complaint. He suggested two possible lines of investigation to them: an administrative inquiry initiated by the hospital secretary or a referral for assessment and review under the procedure known colloquially as "The Three Wise Men" (details of this are set out in Annex 4). The second option was a less formal mechanism for investigation, but in Mr Fullman's opinion it was more appropriate because he felt that Ayling's behaviour *"perhaps reflected some form of psychiatric illness and he needed to be assessed and perhaps treated rather than just being investigated"*.

3.92   Mr Fullman subsequently interviewed Ayling, together with his two colleagues, Mr Dwyer and Mr Ward. They told him that the complaint raised serious allegations and that they were going to refer him to "The Three Wise Men". Mr Fullman made the telephone referral and was himself seen by them. He could not recollect the nature of their discussions but knows that he passed over Patient C's letter of complaint.

3.93   Thereafter Ayling was interviewed by "The Three Wise Men" on at least one occasion. He was also referred to a Consultant Psychiatrist, Dr Aaronricks, although in fact the referral appears to have been made by Dr Alan Bussey, the Area Medical Officer, to whom the resulting report was addressed. Dr Aaronricks saw Ayling on 25th July 1980. He expressed the following conclusion:

> "Dr Ayling does not suffer from mental illness of such form as would bring him within the scope of the Mental Health Act 1959. There is no evidence of specific or definable psychiatric disorder; I can find no psychopathology specifically needing to be acted out in a manner, which might be interpreted as covertly or overtly sexual. In my view, psychiatric factors can be excluded from the consideration in the state of affairs in which he now finds himself."

3.94   According to his evidence, Mr Fullman remained ignorant of the fact that Ayling had been referred to a psychiatrist or the outcome of "The Three Wise Men" investigation. He simply assumed that the matter had been investigated fully and that a conclusion had been reached. Further, he did not view it as any part of his responsibility to acquaint either himself or Patient C and her husband with the outcome of the investigation into their complaint.

3.95   We find that given Mr Fullman's recognition of the serious nature of the complaint, it is lamentable that he did not acquaint himself with the outcome of "The Three Wise Men"'s investigation or take any steps to speak to them to assure himself that it was appropriate for Ayling to remain his Clinical Assistant. It is also highly unsatisfactory that, having encouraged the patient and her husband to choose an informal procedure for investigation, he did not provide them with any explanation or reassurance that their complaint had been properly dealt with. If the formal complaints procedure had been used, there would have been an entitlement to a response from the hospital.

3.96   It should be noted that Ayling himself hotly disputed the substance of Patient C's complaints about his examination technique at the time, and denied improper conduct or motives. He wrote to the Medical Defence Union (MDU) on 7th September 1980 stating that, having made some enquiries *'it appears that my techniques are not inferior to others'* and suggesting that other colleagues should more properly be criticised. He reported that "The Three Wise Men" were recommending that he should not be offered any more locum consultant posts, but that nothing had been stated openly. The advice he received was to speak to the Area Medical Officer, Dr Bussey.

3.97   Whether Ayling followed the MDU's advice is unclear and there is no other material in our possession to suggest that any such recommendation was either made or put into practice. However, it was at about this time that he arranged to enter into partnership with Dr Ribet. As a result of this, Ayling wrote to the MDU that he was withholding his letter to "The Three Wise Men" at least *"for the moment"*. Instead, he began to renegotiate his hours as a Clinical Assistant in order to take up the opportunities of general practice.

Patient D

3.98   Patient D saw Ayling on two occasions following an emergency procedure at Thanet Hospital in July 1981. She remembered that he made sexualised and inappropriate comments about her body as he was examining her post-operatively. He then made efforts to remove a drain forcibly from her abdomen, *"yanking"* at it for a period of time. Eventually the drain broke and she was left in considerable pain. Sometime later, Patient D had an operation to remove the drain. When she awoke from the anaesthetic, she found that the bedcovers had been pulled down, she was completely naked and Ayling was standing beside the bed, looking at her body.

3.99   Patient D and her parents subsequently saw Mr Patterson to complain about the treatment she had received. Mr Patterson's contemporaneous response was markedly defensive of Ayling and of his actions. In a letter written to Patient D's GP, he said this about the attempt made by Ayling to remove the drain, *"I assured [Patient D and her parents] that what was done was basically for the patient's own good"*.

3.100   In his oral evidence Mr Patterson apologised to Patient D for the way he responded to her at the time. He stated that it did not occur to him that what he was hearing from Patient D amounted to a complaint about Ayling's sexualised behaviour; although he acknowledged that he had warned Ayling about the dangers of comments being misinterpreted when a patient was coming round from the anaesthetic. Mr Patterson also agreed that there had been no clinical justification for Ayling looking at Patient D naked and that he himself had been naïve in thinking that the patient had been mistaken in believing she had heard sexualised comments. These comments are a telling illustration of a more general failure of the clinicians at the time to comprehend or accept the deviant nature of the behaviour being alleged against Ayling towards some of his patients.

Patient E

3.101   Patient E's second child was delivered by Ayling at KCH in July 1986. She told us that Ayling's overall management of the delivery was chaotic and that he was rude both towards her and his junior staff. She was left with the uncorroborated impression that he had been drinking. Ayling was also said to have been rough and discourteous during his post-operative examination of her. Patient E told us that Ayling performed this examination without a chaperone and without wearing gloves; and that during its course he peremptorily removed a gauze swab, that had wrongly been left in place following delivery, from inside her, leaving her traumatised and needing comfort from the nursing staff.

3.102   Patient E was Mr Fullman's patient. She stated that the nursing staff encouraged her to complain about her treatment and that she did talk to Mr Fullman later in the week, telling him how awful her treatment had been and that Ayling himself was a disgusting man. Although Mr Fullman had been very sympathetic and had apologised for the way she had been treated, he did not say that he would take the matter further.

3.103   For his part, Mr Fullman had no recollection of Patient E or of her complaint. He specifically rejected any suggestion that he had been told about the gauze swab or of Patient E's suggestion that Ayling had been drinking. He also assumed that she was satisfied about the treatment she had been given, on the basis that she had not taken matters further.

3.104   Exactly what Patient E told Mr Fullman in July 1986 cannot now be known. However, it is clear to us first, that she made a strong oral complaint about Ayling's conduct and performance; and secondly, that she was not offered any advice or support as to how to pursue her complaint formally by any member of staff. It is also clear that no steps were taken to record her concerns or to investigate whether her complaints would be supported or corroborated by staff members involved in her delivery and care.

The Caesarean Section – 1987

3.105   The termination of Ayling's employment as a clinical assistant at KCH and Thanet in June 1987 was precipitated by a serious untoward incident that took place in the early part of that year. The episode concerned a patient who did not make a contemporaneous complaint and who has not since come forward to give evidence to us. Therefore we have to be particularly careful to maintain patient confidentiality. As a result, we will discuss the details of this case in broad terms only.

3.106   In summary, in the first quarter of 1987 Ayling performed a Caesarean section at KCH to deliver a premature baby. During the course of the delivery, Ayling cut into the baby's abdomen so seriously that a surgical repair was necessary. The surgical repair was successful.

3.107 Following this incident, a decision was taken to convene a meeting of the senior clinicians and hospital management to discuss Ayling's future. For reasons which are obscure, that meeting did not take place until several weeks after the incident itself – a delay which we consider highly regrettable given the seriousness of the issue and the fact that Ayling was continuing to practise obstetrics. We have received other evidence that investigation of complaints was not done as appropriately or as contemporaneously as good practice would demand.

3.108 There is some dispute as to the nature of the discussions about Ayling during the meeting. Mr Patterson told us that there was a general discussion about Ayling's competence and that the decision to terminate his employment was arrived at on the basis of a history of problems culminating in a single serious surgical error. He commented that by 1987 there were concerns that Ayling's method of delivering babies was heavy-handed and that these would be discussed with him during the course of perinatal meetings. Mr Fullman, maintaining that he was ignorant of any concerns about Ayling's performance, told us that the discussion focussed only on the single incident, which in itself was sufficient justification for dismissal.

3.109 We unhesitatingly prefer Mr Patterson's account and accept that some discussion of Ayling's overall practice must have taken place at the meeting. We are reinforced in this view by a note made by Cathy Bolton, then the Special Project Manager of the East Kent Health Authority (EKHA), of a conversation she had with Mr Patterson on 10th October 2000. The note records:

> "[Mr Patterson] can't remember the dates but does recall that the obstetrician and gynaecologist consultants had a meeting about Ayling and decided that he should not continue to work for them as his work was not of the quality that they wanted in the obstetric and gynae department. There had been some difficult deliveries which Dr Ayling had been involved in, which on review of the actions taken, did not appear to be in the interests of the patients. All four consultants attended: Mr Patterson, Mr Fullman, Mr Morris and Mr Milligan…

> "They had been receiving complaints, both from patients and staff, about 20 per cent and 80 per cent respectively, about Dr Ayling's work. By complaints he means often verbal comments, rather than written complaints. The sort of comments from patients were: painful vaginal examinations; rough with patients; attitude. Comments from staff were: he was rough with patients, attitude to patients, not always the kindest of men, he was not gentle when he examined women, always determined to get the baby out. His memory is not that good, but he thinks that there may have been one or two incidents that brought it to a head and resulted in the consultants' meeting. Their decision was based on a culmination of comments from staff and patients and one or two bigger incidents. He is not aware and does not recall any of the complaints being of a sexual nature."

3.110 The decision was taken not to renew Ayling's employment and he was sent a letter giving him notice that his contract with the KCH would not be renewed when it expired on 30th June 1987. No reasons were given; and no explanation for the lack of notice. On the same day a similar letter was sent from the Unit Personnel Officer of the Thanet Hospital, also advising Ayling that his contract would not be renewed as from 30th June 1987. However, this letter added that:

> "Dr Voysey [the Unit General Manager at Thanet] is actively examining the prospect of establishing a new clinical assistant post (one session per week) for colposcopy. If this can be set up and funded, you will be offered the appointment".

3.111   Ayling's response to the letters was to instruct solicitors, who protested about the decision and initiated proceedings for wrongful dismissal. Several months later the Canterbury & Thanet Health Authority agreed to settle the claim and to pay a sum in "full and final settlement".

3.112   On 10th September 1987, within only a few months of the decision not to renew Ayling's contract, Mr Patterson wrote to Dr Voysey complaining about the loss of his assistance in the Colposcopy Clinic and asking that he be re-employed to undertake a weekly session. Mr Patterson took the view that Ayling was an *"an extremely good colposcopist"*; and the reasons for the decision not to renew his contract as a Clinical Assistant in obstetrics and gynaecology had nothing to do with his competence as a colposcopist.

3.113   We were told that, unaware of concerns amongst the midwifery and nursing staff about Ayling's behaviour being sexualised, Dr Voysey acceded to Mr Patterson's request and Ayling returned to Thanet, for a weekly session. In retrospect this was an unfortunate decision – but one which appeared necessary at the time for reasons of service expediency. We add that, at this remove, we were unable to see contractual documents evidencing this arrangement. It appears that it restarted informally, and was ended on a similar basis shortly thereafter, as we relate.

3.114   Dr Voysey told us that during the summer of 1988 she was asked to see a woman who had seemed, to her secretary, to be upset. She had refused to give her name and wished to see Dr Voysey privately. By the time they began their discussion she had ceased to be agitated and was determined about what she had to say. She said, quite calmly, that she had been escorting her 18 year-old daughter to the Colposcopy Clinic; that Ayling had been sexually aroused and that he had rubbed himself against her daughter's bottom.

3.115   When Dr Voysey asked the woman for her name so that she could begin to record what she had said, the woman refused. She said that her daughter was completely unaware of what had happened and that if she were to know, then she would never trust a doctor again and would not visit a Colposcopy Clinic again. Dr Voysey was sure that she would have explained the various options: that they could go to the Police, to the GMC or they could have discussed the matter with Mr Patterson. However, the woman did not wish for any of those possibilities to be pursued. She thanked Dr Voysey for listening to her and she left.

3.116   Dr Voysey did two things to further investigate the matter. She went down to the Colposcopy Clinic to assure herself that the events described were physically possible. She also talked with two of the nursing staff, who were reticent about speaking to her but whose attitude implied that they were not surprised.

3.117   In her written statement, Dr Voysey encapsulated the dilemma in which she found herself.

> "I remember spending some time considering and re-evaluating the situation. I had an anonymous complainant who might well withdraw her allegations if pressed, no witnesses and a growing conviction that her allegations were justified. Rightly or wrongly I felt bound to respect the patient's privacy. I was afraid that, if I took any action which revealed her identity, her mother might well deny that our conversation had ever taken place. So although I realised that this might not be a solitary occasion, I could see no way out of my dilemma. I thought that if I reported the complaint on no credible evidence, I might be accused of defamation of character. The thinking, climate and culture at that time were completely different to what they are now, making it far more difficult to level accusations against any member of staff."

3.118   Dr Voysey also went to see Sir John Cadell (now deceased) and gave him the full story. They discussed the options open to them – including referral to the Police or the GMC. He agreed with her that without written confirmation of the complaint those avenues were not open to them – a conclusion that we consider reasonable in the circumstances.

3.119   The decision was therefore taken to discontinue Ayling's employment and having found out that Ayling's contract was due to expire in a matter of weeks, Dr Voysey gave instructions that it should not be renewed. She gave the reason that clinical assistant posts were supposed to be training posts for GPs and that Ayling did not fit the criteria. That was the explanation she offered to Mr Patterson, saying nothing of the incident or the true reasons behind the non-renewal of the contract, because she did not think that she would be believed.

3.120   According to Dr Voysey, Ayling's reaction, upon learning that his employment was to be discontinued, was to be angry and threatening towards her. He arrived in her office late one evening when the block was otherwise empty, shouting and yelling, *"Why are you doing this to me? This is totally unfair and unjust"*. Dr Voysey responded, *"Cliff, shut up. Don't go along this line because if you do I'll get enough evidence to get you struck off"*. She told him why she had taken the action she had; that she had had a complaint, of which she gave details, from someone who did not wish their identity to be known; that she was inclined to believe the complaint; and that she thought it dreadful. At that point, Ayling *"went quiet and left"*. This response confirmed her belief that the complaint was true. Again, we record that we do not have Ayling's comments on this evidence.

3.121   Dr Voysey knew nothing of Ayling's other employment at the time. In particular, she did not know that he was and had been working at the Colposcopy Clinic at the William Harvey Hospital in Ashford since 1984.

She had not made any enquiries to discover whether Ayling was employed elsewhere and had not done so because she had *"just thought that he was unemployable"* as a result of his advancing years. In retrospect, it is unfortunate that Ayling was not simply asked where else he was working.

Conclusion

3.122   If there is a criticism to be made of Dr Voysey it is that she did not discuss the information she had been given and the dilemma in which she found herself with Mr Patterson. Ayling was his Clinical Assistant, working under his authority and at his request. Dr Voysey was a clear and compelling witness who would have had little difficulty in conveying the strength of her feelings about the episode. It may have been the case that, having rid the hospital of Ayling, she was keen to draw a line under a most unsavoury incident. It is possible that she found discussion of it with others distasteful in the extreme. It could be that she genuinely did not think she would be believed and therefore thought it best to take no further action. Whatever the position, in retrospect, we consider it unfortunate that the opportunity to inform Mr Patterson about Ayling's conduct was missed. However, at the time, Dr Voysey's action was understandable and an option available to her that she regarded as viable.

3.123   Although Ayling was known to have become a general practitioner in 1981, and this was thought to be affecting his ability to undertake his duties as a clinical assistant effectively, no consideration was apparently given by the hospital management to discussing the duality of his employment and its implications with the Kent FPC. Had this happened before 1987, when his contract with the Kent and Canterbury and the Thanet Hospitals was not renewed, a broader awareness of connections might have been made between the concerns about which hospital staff were aware and the complaint received by the FPC in 1991. This is equally true, if not more so, of the circumstances under which Dr Voysey terminated his appointment as a clinical assistant in colposcopy in 1988.

3.124   We heard from nursing and midwifery witnesses of an inability to get their voice heard by either their own nursing management or the consultant medical staff to which Ayling was accountable. Had their concerns reached the ears of the consultant medical staff in a form that was recognised, then connections might have been made between staff concerns and patient complaints which would have precipitated a wider investigation and a referral of possible professional misconduct to the GMC.

B) GP PRACTICE BEGINNING IN 1981

Introduction

3.125   Ayling became a general practitioner in 1981, and remained in general practice until 2000. This section of the report deals with the first period of Ayling's history in general practice from 1981 until 1991.

3.126   In 1981, whilst Ayling was still employed as a clinical assistant by the Kent and Canterbury and the Thanet Hospitals, he became the part-time partner of a GP in Cheriton High Street in Folkestone. In 1983 he became a full-time GP in that practice and also undertook sessions as a locum doctor in the local family planning service clinics. This aspect of his employment is covered in 'General Practice 1992–1998'.

3.127 Ayling was working as a single-handed GP with a part-time assistant (his former partner who had retired as a GP principal). Contact with his practice by other community nursing staff was apparently limited. In particular, we were told by Penny Jed, community midwife, that she *"had a lot of difficulty in accessing his pregnant patients..."*. Unlike the hospital nursing and midwifery staff, therefore, the Inquiry received little evidence about concerns from community nursing staff such as health visitors. Evidence from the community midwifery staff is discussed in 'General Practice 1992–1998'.

3.128 In 1985 the Kent Family Practitioner Committee (FPC) was made aware of a specific incident concerning Ayling's allegedly distressing conduct of an examination. In 1991 its successor, the Kent Family Health Services Authority (FHSA) was made aware of another incident which was, eventually, the subject of a criminal conviction in 2000.

3.129 However, as set out in the previous section, during this time there was a growing body of concern and complaint about Ayling in the hospital setting which led to the cessation of his employment in the Kent and Canterbury and Thanet Hospitals in 1987 and 1988 but which was not passed to the Kent FPC.

3.130 Amongst Ayling's colleagues in general practice, there was also an awareness of the distress caused to his patients by his questionable conduct of examinations. In particular, a number of patients transferred from Ayling's practice to a neighbouring practice, the White House Surgery. For historic reasons, this practice interviewed all patients requesting a transfer from Ayling's practice, and other local practices, and the partners conducting the interviews kept notes of each interview. The notes from 1985 until 2000 were summarised for the Inquiry and presented in their evidence. Because of the significance of this knowledge, this is explored in some detail in this section.

Concerns about Conduct of Consultations
3.131 During the period covered by the Inquiry's terms of reference, a number of common themes emerge from the evidence submitted to the Inquiry about the way in which Ayling undertook the examination of his patients and his approach to them. We list these below and detail some of the evidence we have received on the issue.

Conduct of intimate examinations
3.132 Patients were routinely asked to remove all their clothing for Ayling to undertake breast and vaginal examinations. They were not offered any covering whilst they were on the examination couch. We record here, that at the criminal trial, Ayling referred to the non-covering of patients as an attempt to reduce the risks of cross-infection. Patients were also often questioned in an inappropriate manner about their personal history; they told us:

"I underwent a smear test. He told me to take off all my clothes so that he could carry out the test. I asked him why this was necessary and he told me that he wanted to carry out a breast examination as well. I removed my clothes and Ayling carried out the smear test. I was never offered a chaperone during any of the tests that were carried out in Ayling's surgery."

"On this and every subsequent occasion that he undertook an examination, Ayling would ask to me to remove all of my clothes, so that I was completely naked. He would often sit in his chair, with his back to me, writing notes whilst I got undressed and on to the examination couch. There was never any cover, I do not recall there being a screen, and Ayling never offered me a female chaperone at any of these appointments."

"I told Ayling about the thrush and he said that he wanted to take a swab. He told me he wanted me to remove all my clothes below the waist. I did so as I had had smear tests before and I knew that this was the common procedure …Ayling then asked me whether I had ever had a breast examination. I told him I had not. He said "we'll do that while you are here". He told me to remove the rest of my clothes, including my bra. I sat on the couch and did so. I was very embarrassed at being completely naked in front of Ayling so I held my top tightly over my bottom half."

"I was asked by Ayling to remove my clothes from the waist down. Ayling then examined me whilst I was half naked. I felt humiliated. He did not offer me a chaperone. He did not offer to leave the room when I undressed. He did not offer to pull the screen across so that I could protect my dignity. He just stood there whilst I removed my lower garments."

"I did not argue and got undressed behind a screen. I felt very uncomfortable as there was nothing there to cover myself with, but I got on the bed and laid down, trying to cover myself with some of my clothes but he took them away."

"I remember I felt so vulnerable and embarrassed, that I grabbed my t-shirt or jumper so that I could use it to cover the top half of my body."

"I would not answer him as I was embarrassed by what he was saying, so he started drawing matchstick men and women in different sexual positions, asking me which I did and how often. I could not believe it. I was embarrassed and all I could say was "I don't know". I think he must have realised I was embarrassed so he stopped the conversation."

"He asked me at the end of one examination "Did you enjoy that?" To which I answered, "No, I don't enjoy being prodded about.""

Frequency and conduct of vaginal and breast examinations
3.133   Ayling conducted breast and vaginal examinations which were thought by patients not to be necessary in response to their reason for consulting him, and unduly prolonged.

"I did not have that many appointments with Ayling but when I did go to see him I always felt quite uncomfortable. He would always try and persuade me to have a breast examination. If I refused (which I did on a number of occasions) he would get 'shirty' and defensive with me and give me a long lecture about how he had discovered a number of cases of breast cancer and that my breasts should be checked."

"Ayling was very bullying towards me and insisted that I had the breast examination saying that he was my doctor and he knew best. He made it clear that if I didn't do as he asked I would not get the [morning after] pill. I started crying and got very upset."

"Ayling carried out a number of breast checks, smear tests and internal examinations. My notes clearly illustrate this. They were at least annually, which is shown in my notes, although I would suggest that they might even have [been] more often than this. It felt to me that every time I went to see Ayling he would try and carry out a breast examination or tell me that that I needed a smear test or internal. He never offered me a chaperone for any of the examinations. When he carried out a smear test Ayling would always also do an internal examination. He would say it was "just to check everything was in order.""

Consent to examination and treatment

3.134   Patients felt pressured into undergoing examination and treatment without being given adequate explanations. This concern echoes the experience of a hospital antenatal patient who was examined by Ayling in 1993 (see Hospital Practice 1984–1994).

"I was nervous and said I would be happy to go to a nurse at the clinic for a further test, but he insisted that he was an expert. He kept going on about it and in the end I agreed."

"I told him I did not want this but he put me under great pressure saying that I might have breast cancer and I reluctantly agreed."

"He then went on to tell me a story of a mother of two who was about my age who had died of cervical cancer as she had not had that treatment done. He implied that she died whilst waiting for a hospital appointment. Given everything that he had said I agreed to let him carry out the procedure."

"At no point prior to this examination did Ayling tell me that colposcopy would involve taking different samples. He had merely said the colposcopy would involve looking at the neck of my womb. I feel he did not prepare me for what to expect at all and this made the whole experience even worse."

"He told me he would need to examine my breathing and told me to remove all my clothes from the waist up. I felt very uncomfortable doing this and I asked why I needed to. He replied by asking if I was questioning his judgement. I was left with no choice but to agree with his request."

"I knew that it was perfectly possible to listen to a woman's chest without her having to remove her bra. However, I didn't feel that I had much choice. He was the doctor after all."

"He used my fear of getting cervical cancer as a way of keeping control over me and subjecting me to frequent examinations, which now appear to have been unnecessary."

Inappropriate contact with patients

3.135   Where patients either made a complaint or exercised their right to change GPs without explanation, they found that Ayling would seek them out and challenge their action – behaviour we also heard about in the hospital setting.

> "I recall that I went to Ayling's surgery and told the staff that I was changing doctors. Then to my consternation, when I had left the building, Ayling chased me down the road asking me why I was leaving the surgery. I felt extremely intimidated by this, and I made an excuse about moving away …"

> "Ayling then turned up at my parent's house … to discuss the letter. I told him that I had nothing left to say to him. He seemed angry…Ayling admitted responsibility and said he was sorry, but said that he had taken a second opinion and I was the only person ever to have reacted in this way [to antibiotics]."

Chaperones

3.136   Despite the apparent availability of a chaperone, which we discuss in more detail below, this was not routinely offered.

3.137   We understand that Ayling did not routinely [use] a chaperone but had a notice in his waiting room explaining that one could be made available if requested. We also understand that Ayling had been advised by the Local Medical Committee to put up a similar notice by the examination couch. However, we heard evidence that:

> "He did not offer me a female chaperone, and he insisted that this was fine, as his wife was just the other side of the door."

> "When I got to the surgery I asked the doctor for a nurse to be present, he started to get stroppy and told me I was too big to have a nurse present, but I insisted, in the end he went away and got the nurse."

> "I recall that when I was examined by Ayling there was no nurse present as a chaperone, nor was I offered the choice of having a chaperone present."

> "At no time was there a nurse present during these checks and I was never asked if I would like one to be present."

Entry into General Practice

3.138   On 9th December 1980 Ayling wrote to the Medical Practices Committee (MPC), applying for a place on the Medical List of General Practitioners. His intention was to enter a partnership with Dr Ribet, who was then the sole practitioner at 19 Cheriton Road in Folkestone. The application was supported by the FPC of the Kent Area Health Authority, which had consulted with the Kent Local Medical Committee (LMC). The FPC considered that Ayling's addition was suited to the needs of the practice and advised the MPC that he would be counted as half a principal, earning 50% of the basic practice allowance.

3.139   Although Dr Ribet's list size was then about the national average for a single-handed practice, the MPC acceded to the FPC's recommendation on the basis of the *"exceptional circumstances"*. However, they made it clear that Ayling's addition did not imply that the practice merited two principals.

3.140 On 1st February 1981, Ayling entered into partnership with Dr Ribet. At that time there was no requirement that would-be GPs undertook training for the role, organised by the Royal College of General Practitioners (RCGP). Such a training programme began in the late 1970s. It became mandatory for would-be GPs in February 1981, only a few months after Ayling had been accepted as a principal in Dr Ribet's practice. A brief summary of the position is given in Annex 5.

3.141 When Ayling entered general practice, he joined a service whose organisational arrangements had remained fundamentally unchanged since 1948. General practitioners were 'independent contractors' – that is, self-employed persons who have entered into a contract for services with another party. Such a contractor is not told how to do a job: "As an independent contractor a GP should not be told by a health authority or health board how to practice. Health authorities should seek to persuade and advise, not direct or control". Whilst general practices had developed services since 1948 (for example, from 1974 onwards GPs began to provide contraceptive services for their patients), the structure of the GP contract with the NHS remained the same. Each GP, whether in partnership or single-handed practice, had his or her own list of patients, held an individual contract with the FPC, was individually remunerated for the services provided to patients and employed their own support staff such as receptionists and nurses on such terms and conditions as they wished and for which they were reimbursed by the FPC.

3.142 In the first two years of practice as a GP, Ayling worked with Dr Ribet as a half principal. By December 1982, the reversal of their roles was under discussion with the FPC as part of arrangements designed to provide for Dr Ribet's eventual retirement. For Ayling to secure the partnership succession, it was necessary for him to have been a full-time principal for at least a year prior Dr Ribet's retirement. Ayling proposed to carry out 6½ sessions per week, plus associated visits, which would qualify him to be treated as a full-time principal, whilst Dr Ribet worked part-time.

3.143 In January 1983, the practice submitted an application for approval of this reversal, which was accepted. When Dr Ribet subsequently retired Ayling took over the practice. Dr Ribet continued to act as his assistant until the merger with Dr Hossain and partners in January 1999. Although Dr Ribet still undertook two half day sessions per week, from that time onwards we consider that Ayling was effectively operating as a sole practitioner. On 3rd December 1990 Ayling applied to join the Child Health Surveillance List, noting that he had attended an approved course in Paediatric Surveillance within the last 5 years and was currently providing Child Health Surveillance in line with the District Health Authority's agreed programme.

The Surgery at 19 Cheriton High Street
3.144 Details about Ayling's surgery were given during the course of his criminal trial:

3.145   The size of his list was some 2,000 patients and the surgery was modernised in about 1989.

3.146   The Senior Receptionist at the time when Ayling joined the practice would become his wife, Mrs Jeannette Ayling, in 1984. Another receptionist joined the surgery following its modernisation.

3.147   From the mid 1980s the surgery also took on as Practice Nurse, a woman who had previously worked at the surgery for three mornings a week.

3.148   When Ayling joined the practice in 1981, a midwife was already attached to it. However, wanting to undertake *"routine surveillance"* of his antenatal patients himself, Ayling did not find this arrangement satisfactory and replaced her with a community midwife who would see patients in their homes. Each midwife was accountable to her hospital and would have a number of patients from different practices – perhaps two or three within her workload.

3.149   In 1985, Mrs Ayling became the Practice Administrator and her hours increased. In 1990, she obtained a Practice Manager's Certificate and in 1995 an award for secondary assessors in NVQs.

Chaperones

3.150   The Inquiry was particularly interested in the access patients had to chaperones in Ayling's practice because a number of bodies suggested that chaperones were a key means of assuring patient safety; yet, despite this, the Inquiry heard a number of conflicting accounts of the role and responsibilities of a chaperone. We discuss this ambiguity in more detail later in our Report.

3.151   According to Ayling, when the surgery was modernised in the late 1980s a notice was placed between the two window louvres in the reception area, which stated:

> "Examination of Patients: If a patient needs to be examined and would like another person or the practice nurse to be present, would he/she kindly tell the receptionist."

3.152   Mrs Ayling's recollection was that the sign was put up in 1984, when Ayling became the principal in the practice, and that it stated:

> "Should you require a chaperone, please feel free to bring someone of your own choosing, or ask the nurse or receptionist."

3.153   She emphasised that many patients brought members of their family along and were encouraged to have them present; alternatively, chaperones were provided if requested.

3.154   In August 1998 Ayling was advised by the-then Secretary of the LMC, Dr Ashton, and the Medical Advisor of East Kent Health Authority (EKHA), Dr Snell, to put a further notice above the examination couch, advising women of their right to request a chaperone. Ayling gave evidence at trial that this was subsequently done. It was not Ayling's practice, as a matter of routine, to ask patients whether they wanted a chaperone, when he proposed to carry out an intimate examination. Ayling's evidence at trial was that, if a patient did request a chaperone, the practice nurse would be asked to perform that function if she was available. If she was not, then a member of the reception staff would be asked to come in and sit on the far side of the screen that was present in the room. Although he stated that this would be *"no problem"*, he continued:

> "Q: Would the receptionist be always available to do that on request?
>
> A: We would make the receptionist available. There would be no problem.
>
> Q: Was it practicable to provide a chaperone on every single occasion that you saw a female, even if it is limited to an intimate examination, even without a request?
>
> A: It was extremely difficult. It would completely interrupt the working of the surgery. The receptionist gets so busy, that they're running around. It is a thing which, if one has to, one makes allowances and one does it. Then it means that the rest of the surgery has to wait. So I would say it's very impractical."

The Evidence of Healthcare Staff

3.155   We received statements from two Health Visitors employed by the Health Authority at Ayling's surgery during the late 1980s and early 1990s. It was their responsibility to take over from the community midwives when babies reached ten days old.

3.156   The first of the Health Visitors, Margaret Woolley, was aware that Ayling would perform postnatal examinations on patients at the time of the baby's 6-week check. This would involve internal examinations and sometimes a smear test. She did not notice any distress on the part of patients but was aware that a number of mothers left the practice at approximately 6 weeks to 3 months.

3.157   The second Health Vistor, Gaynor Luckett, recalled only one concern about Ayling, from a patient who asked why he had come to visit her at home to ask why she had left his practice – an action which other patients have complained of in their evidence to the Inquiry. She had also heard rumours on the professional grapevine of concerns about Ayling's clinical decision-making; although she had not picked up any sense that these concerns related to his professional conduct.

The Concerns raised by Patient F in her letter written in March 1985

3.158   In March 1985, Patient F asked to be removed from Ayling's medical list as a result of an examination conducted by him. She had seen Ayling for the first time on 4th March 1985, having been a patient of Dr Ribet since 1968. She was asked to return a week later and on that occasion was examined by Ayling in a manner that left her extremely distressed. She therefore wrote to the FPC requesting the removal of her and her family from Ayling's list of patients. It appears from the documents in the Inquiry's possession that, unbeknown to her, Ayling also requested that she and her family were removed from his list.

3.159 Patient F explained to us that the only response she received was a letter from the FPC, explaining that Ayling had asked that they be removed from his list but 'back-dating' this removal to 3rd March. Whilst this now appears to have been a simple administrative error (as a similar letter sent to Ayling correctly gave a date of 3rd April), the patient explained to us that it spurred her to write a further letter to the FPC, which she supplied to us in draft. In that letter, Patient F explained why she was unhappy with Ayling's actions, describing how he had undertaken a painful gynaecological procedure without her consent during the course of his examination. She told us that although she did not expressly request an investigation, she was hoping that the FPC would *"be professional and instigate such an investigation into Ayling's treatment of [her]"*. Instead she received a pro forma letter from the FPCs stating that:

> "The Administrator acknowledges receipt of your communication of the 2nd April 1985, the contents of which have been noted."

3.160 Patient F subsequently visited the White House Surgery requesting that her family be added to the surgery's list. She was interviewed by Dr Pickering, who noted that she had been hurt by Ayling during an internal examination and that she had already written to the FPC.

Conclusion

3.161 In our view Patient F's letter to the FPC in 1985 amounted to a complaint about Ayling's practice and raised serious concerns about his approach to the examination of female patients. Although the only copy of the letter is in draft, and the FPC records supplied to us did not contain a copy of the letter sent, we accept that Patient F sent the letter described.

3.162 The most likely explanation for the lack of action on the part of the FPC was the failure of an administrative officer to identify that Patient F's letter amounted to a complaint. We heard evidence that the administrative staff dealing with transfer requests in the mid-1980s numbered about 80. They were dealing with some 200,000 patient transfers a year; roughly 4,000 each week.

3.163 In such circumstances, the failure to recognise Patient F's letter as a complaint is understandable. However, the effect of this failure was first, to miss a clear opportunity to investigate Ayling's gynaecological practice; and secondly, to lose valuable information about Ayling's conduct and performance which would have informed subsequent consideration of his practice by the FHSA in 1991 and 1993.

3.164 Whilst no concerns or complaints about Ayling were apparently made known to or received by the FPC between 1985 and 1991, patients who were unhappy and uneasy about having Ayling as their GP during this time were making their reasons for wishing to transfer from Ayling's practice known to GPs in a neighbouring practice, the White House practice. We explore the detail of this below.

The Police Complaint 1991

The Evidence of Mr Homeshaw and Dr Savege

3.165 David Homeshaw was the Chief Officer of the Kent FPC and later the FHSA from 1985 until 1992. Prior to that he had been Deputy Chief Officer of the FPC for a period of about five years. We found Mr Homeshaw to be a reticent witness, who was unwilling to contribute constructively to our investigation of complaints about Ayling's conduct and performance in the GP setting. Given the seniority of his former position within the Health Service, we found this surprising and unhelpful.

3.166 Mr Homeshaw's approach to us contrasted with that of Dr Peter Savege, the Medical Director of the Kent FPC and FHSA between May 1990 and 1994. When considering his part in the events of 1991 and 1993, Dr Savege was willing to reflect on his actions or lack of actions and to agree that, in certain respects, he was found wanting. His involvement in the Ayling story is considered further later in the Report.

3.167 On 9th January 1991, a young patient of Ayling made a detailed and immensely troubling complaint to the Kent Police about the way he had examined her at his Cheriton Road Surgery. Her Police statement ended with a comment that she had felt *"dirty and abused"*, as if she had been *"sexually abused and defiled"*.

3.168 Ayling was ultimately tried and convicted of indecent assault against the patient in 2000. However, in 1991 the Crown Prosecution Service took the decision not to prosecute. Instead, the matter was brought to the attention of the FHSA by a letter from the Kent Police dated 22nd May 1991, in which they described the patient's account in the following terms:

> "The allegation was that Dr Ayling had carried out an internal examination without any consent, that he had prolonged the examination unnecessarily and had made suggestive comments during it. It was also alleged that he had insisted she strip naked and had "fondled" her breasts, and pushed his leg against her naked thigh."

3.169 The letter concluded:

> "The details of this allegation are being forwarded to you, together with the statements and records of interview. It is felt that Dr Ayling's actions were insensitive to say the least and perhaps [he] should be advised as to his future conduct during similar examinations."

3.170 In response to the Police letter, Kay Heatherington, the local District Manager of the FHSA, wrote a memo to Dr Savege on 6th June 1991, asking him to undertake the *"advisor's role"* in relation to Ayling's future conduct. The memo, together with the letter from the Police, was copied to Mr Homeshaw.

The Response of the FHSA

3.171 Dr Savege told us that following receipt of Kay Heatherington's memo he went to see Mr Homeshaw to discuss the matter. He stated that during the course of their discussion it was agreed that Mr Homeshaw would go and speak to Ayling. In a supplemental statement he said that this strategy was also discussed with Chairman of the FHSA, Professor Peter Higgins, who agreed to liaise with Mr Homeshaw.

3.172 For his part, Professor Higgins had no recollection of a Police referral. Mr Homeshaw also told us that he now had no specific recollection of the matter. Nor could he remember any conversations about it with Dr Savege or Professor Higgins. On reviewing the letters from Kay Heatherington and Dr Savege for the purposes of the Inquiry, he was clear it was the role of the Medical Director to discuss clinical procedure with a another doctor and that he could not have properly performed such a clinical function.

3.173 In any event, Dr Savege wrote to Ayling on 11th June 1991 offering to discuss matters arising out of one particular complaint if Ayling thought it helpful to do so. He ended the letter by stating that his major concern surrounded the lack of a chaperone and expressing the hope that Ayling would *"already have addressed this omission from [his] previous procedure"*. Neither Dr Savege nor Mr Homeshaw subsequently met Ayling to discuss the matter.

Conclusion

3.174 Whatever discussions took place following receipt of the Police letter in May 1991, it is clear to us that the incident was not taken sufficiently seriously by the FHSA's senior management and that there was a significant failure on their part to ensure appropriate investigative or supervisory action. In particular we are critical of three aspects:

3.175 First, neither Mr Homeshaw nor Dr Savege took it upon themselves to visit Ayling to discuss the incident;

3.176 Secondly, Mr Homeshaw's actions were not those which might be expected of an experienced Chief Officer with knowledge of the family practitioners in his area, and particularly one with a newly appointed Medical Director: he did not apparently put in place any procedure or process to assure himself that remedial action had been taken.

3.177 Thirdly, no attempt was made to contact the patient herself to ascertain whether she needed support or wished to pursue a formal complaint against Ayling, either through the FHSA or the GMC. Although no criminal prosecution was to occur, these avenues remained open.

3.178 In our view these failings were exacerbated by the fact that no records were made of the discussions which took place about the incident within the FHSA itself. Once again, the consequence of this was the loss of significant information about Ayling's practice; information which would have been valuable when further serious concerns were raised in 1993. Again, this absence of documentation within the FHSA ensured that an opportunity to establish a written record of concerns of significance regarding Ayling's practice was missed and this clearly made any subsequent review of his history more incomplete.

Patient G

3.179   Another patient of Ayling's has told the Inquiry that at about the same time of the Police complaint in 1991 she spoke to her Health Visitor, Gaynor Luckett, on two occasions about the repeated examinations given to her by Ayling and the fact that he kept touching her all the time. According to the patient's evidence, Ms Luckett minimised her concerns, telling her not to be so silly and persuading her that she should return to Ayling's surgery.

3.180   The patient saw Ayling again in April 1991, when the records state *'Health Visitor made her come'*. She told us that shortly thereafter Ayling came to her home uninvited. He asked her, she claimed, in a threatening manner, whether she had been saying or suggesting that he had been behaving in an untoward manner towards her. After this abusive and violent episode, she decided that she would not be able to complain, but also that she would change doctors.

3.181   The Health Visitor concerned has told the Inquiry that she recollects a question from *'one'* of Ayling's patients (whom she does not name). The patient was concerned why Ayling had come to her at home to ask why she had left his GP practice. She cannot recollect the patient's reasons for wanting to change GPs. Nor can she remember her response, although she *'probably'* told her she was entitled to change her GP if she wanted to, but if she had any further concerns then she should contact the FHSA.

The White House Surgery

Introduction

3.182   The White House surgery was situated only a few hundred metres from Ayling's surgery in Cheriton Road. Despite this proximity there had been a difficult and uneasy relationship between the two practices since the 1960s when Dr Ribet had complained to the General Medical Council that the White House was "poaching" his patients. That incident was remembered by the more long-serving White House doctors, who argued that the consequences of this had an effect on their actions in the 1980s.

3.183   The Inquiry's reason for hearing evidence from four partners at this practice arose primarily from the fact that, from 1985 until Ayling's conviction in 2000, a succession of patients transferred from his practice to the White House surgery. During this time, partly as a result of the problems connected with Dr Ribet's complaint to the GMC and to protect themselves against any further accusations of canvassing, the surgery had designated a partner to interview transferring patients to discover the reasons for their wish to do so. It turned out that many female patients referred, in more or less explicit terms, to apparent misconduct by Ayling in the context of breast and vaginal examinations.

3.184   The Inquiry heard from four doctors at the White House:

    3.184.1   Dr Heffernan – who practised there from 1958 to 1992 and was the senior partner from 1985 until his retirement;

    3.184.2   Dr Pickering – who practised there from 1961 until his retirement in 1995;

3.184.3   Dr Jedrzejewski (known as Dr Jed) – who has practised there since 1984 and who became the senior partner on Dr Heffernan's retirement; and

3.184.4   Dr Anderson – who joined the Practice in 1993 and is still a principal there.

The Transfer Interviews

3.185   Over the period from 1985 onwards, the two partners designated to carry out these interviews were Dr Pickering, until his retirement in 1995, and then Dr Anderson. Dr Pickering told us in his statement that a central book was kept which logged the patients requesting transfer and his decision. However, in addition he kept his own personal notebooks where he made notes of these interviews. These were never shown to anyone, not even to his partners, and he retained them on his retirement. However, he supplied us with a transcript of his interview notes, omitting names, of all the patients who he interviewed who requested transfer from Ayling, from February 1984 to March 1995.

3.186   We deal later with Dr Pickering's reaction to these interviews. However, it is right at this point to give an idea of the number and type of incidents noted in the transcripts. Many of the issues raised related to matters outside the scope of this Inquiry and we concentrate only on those that should have given cause for concern. However it does seem that there were around 32 concerns raised by patients in the interviews between 1985 and 1995 that really needed more careful examination.

3.187   It is fair to say that the nature of these concerns varied and that some were more serious than others. The types of comment made by patients included:

- Excessively painful vaginal examinations;
- Repeated smear tests;
- Being asked to strip completely naked during examinations
- Repeated breast examinations unrelated to any medical complaint; and
- Intrusive questioning and a crude or sexual manner.

3.188   Once Dr Anderson took over the transfer interviews in 1995, he kept a central register of patients requesting transfer and also kept a record of his interviews in his personal diaries in which he also recorded all on-call visits. He told us of twelve patients who had expressed concern about Ayling's behaviour during the period from 1995 to 1998 involving frequent breast and vaginal examinations and inappropriate questioning. Samples of these entries are as follows:

- 'Pregnant? 3/12 No scan. He wanted to physically examine her – to confirm pregnancy. She declined as "unnecessary". He suggested she leave his list'
- 'Alleges frequent breast and below examinations which they feel inappropriate'
- 'Every time I want a pill it is an internal'

- 'Alleges frequent and inappropriate breast examinations. Inappropriate questioning re sexual history'
- 'Alleges too many personal examinations. Touching, inappropriate remarks. "How did you enjoy that after PV"'
- 'Alleges inappropriate breast examination. Colposcopy without chaperone. Auscultation – bra off!'

3.189   We now comment on each of the four doctors' evidence.

Dr Pickering and Dr Anderson

3.190   Dr Pickering had the prime knowledge of the transfer requests from Ayling's practice for ten years from 1985. We have already referred to the 32 interviews during this period which, to a greater or lesser degree, should have raised concerns about Ayling's conduct. Dr Pickering was taken through many of these in detail while giving evidence and on a number of occasions he accepted that what had happened was wrong. Indeed, talking about the period at the end of 1986 he said:

> "I certainly deplored all this. I thought it was awful. It made me quite ashamed for someone to be in the same profession, working in this kind of way."

3.191   He was asked to explain how it was some years after the first report of conduct which might give rise to concern before he took any action at all. He offered a number of explanations.

3.192   At first he saw the issues as individual ones and felt that, even if they amounted to deplorable action on behalf of Ayling none of them on its own warranted action.

3.193   It was then put to him that by the end of 1986 he had six separate examples of similar poor or highly questionable clinical practice. Although he felt that the number of relevant complaints was four at this stage he hoped that:

> "it would put itself right because we all knew that this was the kind of thing that one couldn't and didn't do as a Doctor and that any man of reasonable intelligence should realise that this was not on and perhaps it would stop, hopefully."

3.194   He seemed to distinguish between those that were examples of embarrassment and a dislike of Ayling's crude manner from those that were of a sexualised nature or possibly even gave evidence of assault. Even taking the second of these categories, he accepted that there had been four instances of significant concern that needed resolution.

3.195   He felt that there would be little value in raising the issue formally with bodies such as the LMC or the FPC on the basis of such relatively little evidence, nor was it any use asking them whether they knew anything about Ayling. It did not occur to him to ask the patients themselves in the light of the fact that he knew of a number instances they had raised, whether they would wish to pursue the matter any further.

3.196   He said that the practice had no contact with Ayling at all and they certainly were not friends in any way.

3.197   Over and above this Dr Pickering felt strongly that to make a complaint against a fellow practitioner was a very serious step to take. It had been drilled into him from the date of qualification *"you must never denigrate a fellow practitioner, a colleague"*. He said that his Hippocratic Oath said the same thing. He must never run the risk of defaming a colleague's character; particularly where there was a risk of retaliation by counter-allegations of clinical or emotional incompetence.

3.198   By 1987 the accumulated number of concerns raised by patients in the transfer interviews with Dr Pickering had given him a sense of "vague unease" and having discussed matters with his partners, he decided to speak to Dr Donald Montgomery, who was then one of the most senior GPs in the Folkestone area. His purpose was to encourage Dr Montgomery to speak with Ayling and ask him to mend his practice before a public scandal unfolded within the town. Dr Montgomery assured him that he would speak to Ayling and telephoned him sometime later to say that he had done so but that Ayling had denied any inappropriate behaviour.

3.199   Despite this apparent failure of Dr Montgomery's approach, Dr Pickering persisted somewhat naively in hoping that Ayling's behaviour would alter. However, the year 1988 brought five further examples of questionable action – two of which clearly related to allegations of inappropriate sexualised behaviour. One of the patients alleged that Ayling had leaned against her with a hard penis while she was naked during an examination. It was clear from his evidence that Dr Pickering did not consider himself under a professional duty to refer these and other instances of serious misconduct to the GMC, despite their guidance (discussed later in our Report) that he should do so. His response to this criticism was forceful:

> "There are occasions when I have to override this advice from the GMC. This is overridden by my fear of retaliation, of being accused of defamation of character. So serious might the consequences be to me, personally, that I might have to leave the town. I couldn't risk my good reputation in the town by making a complaint unless it was of a more serious nature".

3.200   Dr Pickering's other concern about going to the GMC was patient confidentiality. However, it did not occur to him either to discuss that matter on a confidential basis with any of the relevant responsible bodies or to ask the patients whether they would allow him to do so. According to his evidence, what he did do was tell patients that they could complain to the FPC. He even went so far as to give them the address, which was on their medical card. In this way he felt, *"I made it as easy as I could at the time"*. Little consideration appears to have been given to the potential embarrassment a patient might have suffered in making such a complaint without his support.

3.201   In 1989 Dr Pickering had a second conversation with Dr Montgomery and told him that the problem with Ayling was continuing. Dr Montgomery himself did not recollect such a conversation. But in any event, given the volume and seriousness of information Dr Pickering had by this stage received, it should have been clear that further informal advice would be wholly ineffective and that more radical action was necessary.

3.202 It was not until late 1993 that Dr Pickering decided to approach the Kent LMC, after further discussions with his partners. He told the Inquiry that he went to see Dr Robinson, the Secretary of the LMC (now deceased), on 12th November 1993. He said that the interview lasted 30-40 minutes and that *"I told him everything I knew"*. He took his notebooks with him and read from them. Dr Robinson certainly listened but Dr Pickering did not come away with a clear impression of what he intended to do. His recollection was that Dr Robinson did not really take it as seriously as he thought he should. He felt this because he had to give Dr Robinson a whole number of incidents before he could convince him that this was a serious matter. Although he did not read out all of the incidents to Dr Robinson, he felt that he read out those that had a sexual connotation, i.e. amounted to assaults. It was agreed Dr Robinson would consult further and report back on what action had been taken.

3.203 A Local Medical Committee was (and remains) the body recognised by successive NHS Acts as the professional organisation representing GPs to the FPC and its successors. As well as representing their views, LMCs provide advice to local practitioners on issues relating to general practice such as fees and remuneration, partnership disputes or occupational health matters.

3.204 About three to four months after the interview (which Dr Pickering felt was a long time), Dr Robinson telephoned to say that there was no need for the LMC to do anything as the William Harvey Hospital, which employed Ayling as a part-time clinical assistant, had received complaints of a similar nature and was taking action. (These incidents are discussed in 'Hospital Practice 1984–1994'). Dr Pickering said he remembered this telephone call rather clearly and his impression was that they had not been thorough. He thought that the LMC were taking the easy way out and ducking out of some responsibility, putting it onto the hospital. In fact he remembers that Dr Robinson used the words *"Good news"* as a reference to the fact that the hospital was taking action and the LMC need do nothing.

3.205 Although Dr Pickering's reaction at the time was one of disappointment, he did not feel that he had any obligation to take further action. He regarded the LMC as a body appointed to look after GPs and to see to these things. However, he accepted at the Inquiry that he should have taken things further. In the first place he should have contacted the LMC to ask why they had done no more. What did not occur to him, was to question how any action taken by the hospital would affect Ayling's practice as a GP. He thought that if, for example Ayling had been *"convicted of indecent assault in the hospital"* he would have been taken off the Medical Register. However, he did not know what was happening, nor did he make his record of the transfer requests available to anyone. What he did do was to tell his partners in 1994 that matters had not been resolved and that the situation was continuing.

3.206 On his retirement in 1995, there was no formal hand-over to Dr Anderson of the job of interviewing patients who wished to transfer from Ayling's surgery. Dr Pickering retained his notebooks on the basis that, once the patient had joined the practice, the reasons for doing so were historic and he was given this information in confidence. He considered that Dr Anderson would have known, like the other partners, of his concerns and did not need the notebooks in order to carry out that function. It did not occur to him that the failure to give Dr Anderson the notebooks resulted in the loss of the extensive body of knowledge, information and evidence that he had accumulated. The result was that, when Dr Anderson started to receive disturbing information from potential patients about Ayling's behaviour and conduct he virtually had to consider this afresh without being able to link it to similar information from previous years.

Dr Anderson

3.207 Although Dr Anderson was not given access to the notes that Dr Pickering had made at the transfer interviews, he did have a conversation with Dr Pickering in which concerns were raised about Ayling performing too many intimate examinations. Dr Anderson was also aware of the earlier complaint of patient poaching made against the White House surgery. He asked the other partners at the outset what criteria they wished him to use when reporting to them any issues that were raised by patient transfer interviews. He was told that he should use his own judgment.

3.208 Dr Anderson said that there were no regular partnership meetings until 1995, when a pattern of business meetings was established each Monday lunchtime. However, before then, there were quick and informal discussions over lunch; although not all the partners would always be present. It was during these discussions that the subject of Dr Pickering's approach to the LMC was raised and Dr Anderson was aware that Dr Pickering was not entirely happy with the result of his visit to the LMC. However, it was felt that the matter was now out of their hands, although Dr Anderson accepted that it was difficult to see how any action taken by the hospital would have influenced Ayling within his general practice.

3.209 Dr Anderson accepted that, with hindsight, even the first two incidents reported to him in 1995 should have prompted action. By the end of 1996 he had come to the conclusion that there was *"sexual deviation"*. He distinguished this from actual sexual assault, which he did not suspect until some time later. When asked why he had not offered patients more help, perhaps to encourage them to complain and to assist them in doing so, he said that his concern was that, given the issues at stake, it would be difficult for the patient when the complaint reached the Health Authority. At this point, the patient was effectively on her own. Dr Anderson commented that this judgment on his part did reflect the culture of the time. It frequently was down to the patients to complain and indeed was considered quite bold for a doctor to say to a patient as he did *"You should complain. I think you've got a case"*.

3.210 Furthermore, Dr Anderson also identified the additional difficulty for some patients, that the distressing and embarrassing subject of the complaint itself made it distasteful for some to even discuss. Nevertheless, by 1998 Dr Anderson had become sufficiently concerned to telephone his Medical Defence Organisation (MDO) to seek advice as to how to proceed. He was asked if anybody had approached either the LMC or Ayling himself. He said that he thought they had. He was told that, unless a patient came forward to complain, there was little he could do.

3.211   He regarded the advice from his MDO as an impediment to dealing with Ayling and he spoke to a local GP, Dr Maitra, who mentioned that one of his patients had formally complained to the Health Authority. Dr Maitra had suggested that it was therefore not necessary to do anything further, but Dr Anderson was still receiving deeply troubling information from patients wishing to transfer from Ayling's practice and decided that he should approach the Medical Adviser to the East Kent Health Authority (EKHA) himself. As discussed elsewhere in our report, he subsequently spoke to Dr Snell, the EKHA's Medical Adviser, on 5th November 1998, and thereafter became involved in the ongoing Police investigation.

Conclusion – Drs Pickering and Anderson

3.212   We recognise that Dr Anderson's lack of access to the information contained in Dr Pickering's notebooks meant that he was unable to place the information he was accumulating from the transfer interviews into the context of a lengthy history of similar information from previous patients wishing to transfer from Ayling's practice. Nevertheless, by the end of 1996 he was in possession of enough worrying information to warrant a formal expression of concern to the appropriate authorities. We appreciate his recognition that he should have acted at this stage.

3.213   On the other hand, it seems to us that Dr Pickering's continued assertion that the possible damage to his reputation and the interests of his family outweighed any consideration of the harm that might come to patients' emotional wellbeing was at worst to verge on the culpable and at best to rely on a selective interpretation of GMC guidance. In the 10 years of his increasing awareness and knowledge of what patients were reporting to him about Ayling, Dr Pickering's response was to raise this twice with colleagues on an informal basis. The lack of insight he showed to the Inquiry into the consequences of his taking no other action was disturbing, particularly in light of his expressed views of Ayling's behaviour.

Dr Heffernan and Dr Jedrzejewski ('Dr Jed')

3.214   Dr Heffernan and Dr Jed were the senior partners at the White House Surgery during most of the period under investigation: Dr Heffernan until his retirement in 1992 and Dr Jed from 1996 onwards. Dr Heffernan's description of a senior partner was that he was *"first on the list"*. He held the position because he had been the longest at the surgery and thought that the other partners regarded themselves very much as equals. He had no extra powers but did have the responsibility for dealing with the practice's finance and solving occasional staff problems. During his time there were very few formal partnership meetings, two a year at the most. There was an informal system which meant that, in the late morning, there was often an opportunity for two or three partners to have an informal chat over coffee in the common room.

3.215 Dr Jed went from being the junior partner in 1984 to becoming senior partner in 1996. He agreed with the evidence that communication between partners in the earlier years was informal and unstructured. He told us that there was a brief period during the 1990s when they started having monthly evening practice meetings and that the current practice is to hold a formal meeting every Monday lunchtime. He confirmed the reasons for holding interviews with patients wishing to transfer from Ayling's practice, although he accepted that if these picked up evidence of deviant behaviour this should have been considered and addressed.

3.216 Dr Jed's recollection of the approach in 1993 to the LMC was that Dr Pickering told the partners that the same issues were still there and, in addition, there was the difficulty over the lack of a chaperone. He did not pick up any hint of sexualised behaviour. He felt that the LMC was the right body to approach because the FPC and the newly constituted FHSA were regarded as the *"pay and rations"* bodies. The practice did not have dealings with the Medical Director of the FHSA. Asked how the response from the LMC that the hospital were taking action could affect Ayling's practice as a GP, Dr Jed said that they thought that the LMC would somehow be responsible for taking wider action or for ensuring that that action was taken. He regretted, in hindsight, the fact that none of the partners had asked the LMC what was happening, but said they found it inconceivable that the LMC would have the information about the hospital taking action against Ayling and not inform the FHSA about it.

3.217 An agreed role for senior partners in dealing with issues of concern from patients was never established. However it is quite clear to us that the person occupying that position had some responsibility to ensure that the concerns that Drs Pickering and Anderson were picking up were acted upon. Dr Heffernan's tenure coincided with the earlier period when concerns were first emerging, and with the referral to Dr Montgomery. By the time Dr Jed became senior partner in 1996, the concerns were mounting and the approach to the LMC had occurred with no action on the part of that body.

Conclusion – Drs Heffernan and 'Jed'
3.218 We consider that Dr Heffernan, who was very open in the way he gave evidence, was simply lackadaisical, taking a very relaxed view of the role of a senior partner. This approach, he now accepted, made him look somewhat foolish. Dr Jed was in a different position given the unsatisfactory outcome of the action, albeit limited, which Dr Pickering had taken and of which the other partners were apparently aware. We believe that at the very least he should have enquired of Dr Anderson what was happening. Nor do we accept that he could have been unaware that the persistent concerns identified by Dr Pickering and Dr Anderson related to allegations of sexualised behaviour and not simply poor practice by Ayling.

Conclusion – The White House Surgery
3.219 We have commented on the individuals who gave evidence but it has to be said that the failure of the practice as a whole to report the litany of complaints to any relevant bodies was a major factor in Ayling being able to continue practising over such a long period. In particular, it was the

preference for informal approaches to colleagues rather than taking the step of reporting to a relevant body such as the FHSA or GMC that led to such a lack of action.

3.220 During the course of our hearings, much time was spent identifying the professional duties of doctors from the mid 1980s onwards to report concerns about other practitioners' conduct. Particular reference was made to the GMC's publication of its 1985 Annual Report and the guidance contained in 1987 edition of 'Fitness to Practise'. Nevertheless, as the evidence of the White House partners illustrated, if such guidance was even known, at the time it was considered secondary to practitioners' self-interest, misguided views of confidentiality and a cultural reticence to inform on professional colleagues.

C) HOSPITAL PRACTICE – 1984 TO 1994

William Harvey Hospital

Introduction

3.221 In this section the concerns generated during Ayling's employment as clinical assistant in colposcopy at the William Harvey Hospital (WHH) are set out and the response to these discussed.

3.222 During this period, Ayling was employed in full time general practice and, until 1987, as a clinical assistant in the Kent and Canterbury and Thanet Hospitals. For a year, from 1987 until 1988, he was also employed as a clinical assistant to undertake a colposcopy clinic at Thanet Hospital.

3.223 This concurrent employment was apparently unknown to the William Harvey Hospital. Neither the reasons for the cessation of his employment in 1987 and 1988, nor any detail of the concerns and complaints about Ayling's manner and behaviour, particularly amongst the nursing and midwifery staff in the Kent and Canterbury and Thanet Hospitals, were known to the William Harvey Hospital.

Ayling's Appointment as a Clinical Assistant

3.224 In late 1983 South East Kent Health Authority invited all general practitioners in the area to apply for the post of Clinical Assistant in Obstetrics & Gynaecology at the William Harvey Hospital in Ashford. Ayling applied for the post, stating that he had experience in colposcopy and was anxious to obtain a hospital appointment in the area. Although initially unsuccessful, he was subsequently appointed to the position and on 29th March 1984 he commenced work as Rodney Ledward's Clinical Assistant. The advertisement read: "Applications for the above post [i.e. Clinical Assistant in Obstetrics & Gynaecology] are invited from General Practitioners with an interest in colposcopy. The appointment is for one session a fortnight and involves attendance at the recently established colposcopy clinic at the William Harvey Hospital (with Mr R.S. Ledward)".

3.225 In 1984, colposcopy was a relatively new procedure. Mr Ledward 'inherited' the clinic from Mr Pool on his retirement. The clinic was run as part of a gynaecology outpatient clinic. Mr Pool was replaced by

Mr Stewart, whose main specialist interest was colposcopy and who introduced one or two dedicated colposcopy sessions per week. As in north east Kent, there were four consultants in obstetrics and gynaecology (Mr Davies, Mr Ledward, Mr Stewart and Mr Ursell) covering between them acute services at the William Harvey and Buckland Hospitals, and non-acute services at the Royal Victoria Hospital in Folkestone and the Queen Victoria Hospital in Deal as well as a clinic in Romney. Ayling was required to undertake one session per fortnight, commencing on 29th March 1984. However, according to Ayling's evidence during his criminal trial he was occasionally asked to cover for another GP and undertake maternity work at the Royal Victoria Hospital in Folkestone. This took place once every two or three months. It is also apparent that he undertook a number of sessions in the Colposcopy Clinic at the Buckland Hospital in 1992.

3.226 Ayling's appointment was subject to renewal every two years. On 27th March 1986, it was renewed for a further year. Mr Ledward warned Ayling that he intended to advertise the post so as to give other GPs in the area an opportunity to apply for it – but Ayling would be encouraged to reapply for the post. However, it is not apparent that this re-advertising process ever took place, as new consultant posts started to be discussed instead. Rather, the post continued to be renewed for periods of two years up until 1994.

3.227 The Inquiry was told that there were differences of opinion between the consultant staff, with Mr Stewart and Mr Ledward holding opposing views and thus agreement on changes in the overall policy and direction for the obstetric and gynaecology services was extremely difficult to achieve However, in the 1990s, the colposcopy service was restructured, despite opposition from Mr Ledward, Mr Davies told the Inquiry: "We increased the number of staff within the directorate and gradually parted company with the GP clinical assistants, replacing them with career obstetricians and gynaecologists. As far as the colposcopy clinic was concerned, we had appointed a staff grade doctor, Mr Kumi, who was a colposcopist."

3.228 For the period of Ayling's employment as a clinical assistant his supervising consultant was Mr Ledward but it would appear that the same issues of lack of supervision and isolated practice that we identified in his employment at Thanet and KCH were present in this period of his employment. The internal disagreements within the Directorate of Obstetrics and Gynaecology and the approach of Rodney Ledward to his own professional and contractual responsibilities (which have been the subject of a separate Inquiry led by Jean Ritchie, QC) may also have been contributing factors.

Concerns about Ayling's Practice
3.229 In this section we detail the evidence that has been presented to the Inquiry. Our intention in setting it out as below is to enable us to make a judgement on the actions taken when significant concerns were raised. We do not attempt to verify or quantify those concerns other than to acknowledge the evidence we received that they occurred.

3.230 We received evidence from four nurses who worked with Ayling in the Colposcopy Clinic at the WHH. In some respects their evidence as to Ayling's general behaviour echoes that of the midwives from Thanet and the Kent and Canterbury Hospital(KCH):

3.231 One nurse reported on some occasions she was forced to intervene to stop Ayling when it was clear that the patient had had enough. She considered that Ayling was cruel and deliberately brutalised women.

3.232 Ayling was said to make detailed diagrams of the patients while the colposcope was still in position. Other practitioners would complete such drawings later, thereby avoiding prolonging the discomfort and embarrassment of the procedure.

3.233 Ayling would refer his own GP patients to himself. This was not considered good practice, as patients would not have the benefit of a second clinical opinion. However, it is not clear whether Ayling's motivation for this was sexual or whether he was excessively possessive of his patients.

3.234 Two of the nurses who gave evidence stated that they expressed their concerns about Ayling to their managers but that nothing was done about it. Ayling's conduct was also reported to the Senior Nursing Officer, Mrs Gower, who is now deceased. She was said to have attempted to observe Ayling in the Clinic on one occasion but was called away by her bleeper. There is no evidence that any attempt was made to repeat the observation or to investigate matters with any degree of thoroughness.

3.235 As a result of the lack of response to the concerns about Ayling, two of the nurses eventually sought employment elsewhere in the hospital. That caring members of the nursing staff were driven to resignation is a serious indictment of those charged with the responsibility for Ayling's employment; namely the hospital's management and the consultant accountable for his work, Mr Ledward.

3.236 This seems to us to be yet another example of a missed opportunity. There was clear evidence that Ayling's conduct was at best unsatisfactory and yet nothing was done either at the time or for future reference to bring it to an end. The area of work could not be said to be mainstream which may have compounded the lack of attention given to putting the matter right.

Complaints

Introduction

3.237 We received evidence that four specific complaints were made about Ayling during his employment as a clinical assistant in the South East Kent Hospitals. Before setting out those concerns it is necessary to provide brief summaries of the positions of three of the witnesses involved in those complaints.

3.238 The first, Mr Mark Addision, was the Unit General Manager of the Hospitals Unit of the South East Kent Health Authority from April 1991 until April 1994, when he became Chief Executive of the newly formed South Kent Hospitals NHS Trust.

3.239   The second, Dr Noel Padley, was a Consultant in Histopathology and Morbid Anatomy at the Royal Victoria Hospital. From May 1994 he was the Medical Director of the South Kent Hospitals NHS Trust, prior to which he had been a Consultant representative on a number of committees, including the Unit Management Team.

3.240   The third, Mrs Merle Darling, was the Director of Nursing Services and Quality Assurance at the South East Kent Health Authority. One of her duties in this post was to take primary responsibility for addressing issues, concerns and complaints raised by patients and staff.

Complaint by a student midwife – 1992

3.241   On 21st April 1992, a student midwife in the Colposcopy Clinic at the WHH made a complaint about Ayling's conduct in the course of a clinic which, if upheld, may have amounted to an indecent assault. In the course of her complaint, made that same day, she said that Ayling had first invited her to sit on his knee and then *"grabbed her by the waist and then the buttocks"* to move her closer to him and to the teaching microscope, through which he had been visualising a patient's cervix. She stated that the episode had been witnessed by Nurse McDonald, who saw Ayling *"groping"* the student's buttocks. Nurse McDonald gave a statement during the Police investigation in 1999 and one to the Inquiry. In these, she confirmed the allegation of indecent and unnecessary touching, and also stated that she thought she had also given a statement to the hospital authorities at the time. The incident was brought to the attention of Merle Darling, who interviewed the student concerned. The written account of the incident followed at Ms Darling's request. Ms Darling told the Inquiry that she had kept Mr Addison fully informed *"because of the sexual element of the complaint"* and that *"he thought it better that he follow it through with Dr Padley"*. Mr Addison agreed that he was asked to follow it through *"though not so much with Dr Padley but with Ayling"*. He did not, at any time, speak with the student herself.

3.242   Ms Darling agreed that Mr Addison would take up the matter directly with Ayling. However, no meeting took place until 16th June 1992 – by which time Ayling claimed that he could no longer remember the encounter. As Mr Addison's letter to him on 17th June 1992 indicates, the whole incident was put down to the student's misinterpretation of unnecessary physical contact by Ayling.

3.243   The unsatisfactory nature of the investigation into the complaint and Mr Addison's involvement was compounded by the fact that neither he nor Ms Darling made expeditious arrangements to see the student herself. This appears to be the result of mutual misunderstanding on their part, but the upshot was that she was not seen until 30th October 1992, over six months after the original complaint.

3.244   Although it was suggested to the Inquiry that Nurse McDonald did make a statement to the health authorities at the time, we have been unable to trace a copy of it. It could have been important contemporaneous corroboration for the student's allegation that Ayling's behaviour was indecent. It might also have revealed that, according to Nurse McDonald's statements, Ayling had telephoned her after the incident, saying: *"Who's been a naughty girl telling tales?"* Such information was lost by the perfunctory and inadequate nature of Mr Addison and Ms Darling's investigation.

Patient H

3.245   On 15th December 1992, Patient H was seen by Ayling in Mr Ledward's Colposcopy Clinic held at the Buckland Hospital. She told the Inquiry that during this consultation she was inappropriately touched by Ayling and that he had been flirtatious with her, making wholly inappropriate sexually explicit remarks. Corroboration for this may be found in Ayling's own contemporaneous notes of the incident, which he made in Patient H's medical records and which are unusually defensive:

> "Suddenly quite flushed at the end of an uncomplicated procedure and a little tearful. She said she found the whole thing upsetting and yet the only significant occurrence was that she appeared faint at one point … Nurse commented that (the presence of the patient's) two year old boy could be significant. At no time was any remark, suggestion or manner of handling the patient in any way untoward."

3.246   Patient H told us that she went back to the Buckland Hospital personally a few days later, to make a complaint about Ayling. Her comments were noted in manuscript by a member of staff and she was then asked to read through and sign the document. Despite the seriousness of her experience Patient H received no reassurance from the hospital authorities and no feedback about her complaint – a matter which Mr Addison acknowledged in his evidence was extremely regrettable.

3.247   This was a notable lapse in relation to the established procedures. Had the procedures been followed properly, the picture that was emerging of Ayling's behaviour would have been much clearer at an earlier stage. As it was, it was a poor response to a legitimate concern.

3.248   Copies of Patient H's original complaint have since been lost. However, reference to her *"verbal complaint"* is made in a letter from Mr Addison to Ayling dated 18th March 1993, in which he was endeavouring to initiate a meeting. According to Mr Addison's diary he subsequently met Ayling on 13th April 1993 – although there are no records of their conversation and no evidence as to the outcome.

Anonymous Complaint 1992/3

3.249   From the evidence we received, it appears that a further complaint was made about Ayling during the course of 1992 or 1993. This complaint appears to differ in several significant respects from that made by Patient H and, having considered the issue carefully, the Inquiry concludes that it is likely that the complaint was made by a different patient of Ayling, whose identity remains unknown. However at this distance from the actual event, it cannot be said with certainty to be so. What this clearly demonstrates is the importance of a contemporary note being properly made and filed, as **a matter of record**. Although a picture can be developed later to show events that took place, nothing fully can replace a complete and comprehensive narrative properly recorded at the time. Again another missed opportunity where poor record keeping had a significant effect on future events.

3.250 Dr Padley told us that the complainant had contacted Mr Addison directly by telephone on only one occasion. The substance of her complaint was that she had felt Ayling's erect penis against her thigh as he leaned over to examine her in the Colposcopy Clinic in one of the South East Kent hospitals. Despite the seriousness of her allegation, the patient had insisted on remaining anonymous and had resisted the offer of anyone going to see her.

3.251 For his part, Mr Addison was unable to remember the patient's complaint or his subsequent conversations about it with Dr Padley. He was also unable to explain why no note of the complaint was made or indeed why there was no documentation relating to the incident or his and Dr Padley's discussions.

3.252 Nevertheless, it is clear Ayling knew about such a complaint since he wrote to Mr Addison on 6th September 1993 referring to *"the lady in the colposcopy clinic"* and offering to clarify the matter. He denied that anything untoward had happened. His explanation for the incident was that:

> "the lady was in a very unhappy frame of mind at the outset through having been called to the colposcopy clinic in the first place. From that moment on the wrong interpretation was placed on everything that was said. However, I trust, you will have pointed out to the lady that what she felt against her leg could not possibly have had any sexual connotation whatsoever."

Patient I

3.253 In April 1993 a fourth complaint was made about Ayling by Patient I, a patient of his in the Antenatal Clinic of the Royal Victoria Hospital. In her letter to Merle Darling on 8th June 1993 Patient I stated that Ayling had made inappropriate sexual comments, had pressurised her into an inappropriate internal examination and had afterwards attempted to comfort her by pressing her cheek against his as if she were a child. On any ordinary reading of the letter, the experience she described amounted to a traumatic and abusive episode. It later led to one of the convictions at Ayling's criminal trial. Dr Padley said that he interpreted the incident as:

> "something worse than sexual abuse… if that's possible…her very basic rights as an individual had been abused here and it had [affected] her very deeply… He had succeeded in…abusing her in a very fundamental way because he had taken advantage of [her] powerless position."

3.254 Merle Darling subsequently met Patient I to discuss her experiences. Mr Addison also sent her a letter on 6th July 1993, apologising unreservedly for her humiliation and distress and assuring her that:

"It has now been established that Dr Ayling will not be conducting these clinics in future. If for some unforeseen reason he has to be present, one of the midwives will chaperone the patient, instead of a Nursing Auxiliary who has undertake this role until now."

3.255   Notwithstanding this assurance, it appears that Ayling continued to work in the WHH Antenatal Clinic on at least four further occasions following her complaint – clinics which Dr Padley acknowledged he should not have been doing.

3.256   Further, despite the seriousness of the issues raised by Patient I, it does not appear that either Merle Darling or Mr Addison raised the matter with Ayling directly or met with him to discuss her complaint. This is all the more surprising since Ayling appears to refer to it directly in his letter to Mr Addison on 6th September 1993, stating that he had heard from Mr Ledward that a patient of his in the Antenatal Clinic had complained, and complaining that a response had been sent without consulting him.

3.257   Mr Addison told the Inquiry that he had not seen Ayling about the matter and had assumed that was being done by Merle Darling; a failure of communication akin to that which had occurred in 1992. However, despite the inadequacy of his investigation, it appears that Mr Addison did speak to Mr Ledward and compelled him to ensure that Ayling no longer conducted Antenatal Clinics. This was no small achievement, given Mr Ledward's authority as a senior Consultant in the Hospital and his consistent support for Ayling. As Mr Addison himself acknowledged in his evidence: *"The fact that Ledward was Dr Ayling's boss was part of the problem throughout"*.

3.258   On 15th September 1993 Mr Addison wrote to Ayling in these terms:

"You will know that clinical assistantships are the subject of reasonably frequent turnover so that the mutual learning process which takes place between hospital and general practitioner clinicians can be more widely shared. For these reasons Mr Ledward and myself think it is in everyone's interests therefore that your own tenure of post ceases once this financial year is over. I should be glad therefore if you would accept this letter as notice of our intention to terminate your clinical assistant appointment with us.

"No doubt there will be plenty of opportunity before you complete your duties to thank you for the contribution you have made to the hospital gynaecological services in South East Kent."

3.259   Ayling's response to the letter was to seek advice from the Medical Defence Union (MDU), who then wrote to Mr Addison seeking an explanation for the non-renewal of his contract. Mr Addison replied to the MDU on 12th April 1994 stating that:

"The situation is not one of dismissal and Dr Ayling has not been the subject of any disciplinary proceedings or investigation. His employment has been on the basis of a Clinical Assistant appointment for a fixed term period and that period has come to an end…"

3.260 When questioned by the Inquiry as to the apparent disparity between these anodyne assurances and the specific complaints of misconduct that had led to the cessation of Ayling's employment, Mr Addison described the letter as strictly factual. He took the view that they had not had the information necessary to dismiss Ayling and had used the expiry of his contract as an excuse to end his employment permanently; the same mechanism adopted by Dr Voysey in 1988. Both were examples of how the expedient use of a rolling contract became a mechanism to disguise the lack of action in addressing the real problems that they had found.

Contact with the Family Health Services Authority

3.261 At some point during the latter half of 1993, Mr Addison had asked Dr Padley to discuss Ayling with the Medical Director of the Kent FHSA. Dr Padley subsequently identified Dr Peter Savege and telephoned him.

3.262 According to Dr Padley's evidence, during the course of their conversation Dr Savege immediately recognised Ayling's name and mentioned that there had been a Police referral about him in 1991. Dr Padley then discussed the three complaints that he was aware of; namely those of the student midwife, the anonymous patient and Patient I. Dr Savege's response was to assure Dr Padley that the matter would be dealt with when he met Ayling formally as part of a process that he had agreed with the Chief Executive of the FHSA, Mr Homeshaw.

3.263 Dr Padley and Dr Savege also discussed the possibility of a referral to the GMC, which the former felt should be made by the FHSA on the basis that Ayling worked primarily in General Practice. According to Dr Padley, it was agreed that Dr Savege would make such a referral if there was sufficient evidence available. However, in the event no such referral was made by either the FHSA or by the management of the South East Kent hospitals – and although Ayling's hospital career came to an end, his work as a GP continued without interruption.

3.264 Dr Padley was critical of the way in which matters had been resolved in 1993. He said that it did not seem to him that the outcome had addressed the problems and that *"if this was the best the system could do, then it didn't fulfil what it should [have been] doing and was …unsatisfactory"*. He maintained, however, that the reason why the William Harvey Hospital had not done more when it understood that Dr Savege was not pursuing the matter, was that it had done what it could within the systems then available to it.

3.265 Mr Addison candidly accepted that if there had been some form of wider investigation undertaken in 1993, for example of the nurses in the Colposcopy and Antenatal Clinics, then it was likely that more evidence would have emerged. He agreed that such evidence may well have strengthened the complaints and that there might have been a more forceful referral to make to the FHSA and the GMC.

Patient J

3.266 In addition to the events above, it is worth noting that corroboration for the contemporaneous concerns about Ayling's behaviour being sexualised is provided in a written complaint to the Senior Nursing Officer of the Royal Victoria Hospital, Ms Kennett, on 2nd March 1994. In her letter, the patient (who did not give evidence to the Inquiry) complained that a midwife had commented to her that Ayling was *"known for his internals, fiddling about and touching breasts"*. She considered that such comments, concerning another member of staff, should not have been made to her. Taken together, therefore, proper consideration of these issues should have meant that there were already sufficient grounds established that should have led to a wider investigation in to what Ayling was doing.

3.267   Mr Addison replied to the patient on 31st March 1994, apologising for the unnecessary distress she had suffered. He said that whilst the midwife concerned could not remember her exact words, she felt that she had spoken only to warn her that the Doctor would most likely carry out an examination of her breasts and possibly an internal examination. The midwife had been *"suitably disciplined"*.

3.268   In our view it is unfortunate that Mr Addison's attention focussed on the indelicacy of the midwife's comment and not on its substance, namely the fact that there was a general view amongst some of the staff that Ayling's conduct could be sexualised and inappropriate. There is no evidence that the patient's letter, or the other more direct complaints, prompted a wider investigation of Ayling's practices or that the midwife's comments were linked with the other four complaints made during the course of 1992–93. It is worth just noting however that this happened about the time that Ayling ceased working at the Hospital. That may account for why the complaint was not regarded as "live" or ongoing.

Conclusion

3.269   We find it surprising that each complaint was treated only as an individual and separate complaint. Four complaints within two years from within the same organisation with a common denominator of the same named practitioner's questionable behaviour and practice should have been identified as a pattern of activity that raised concern. We do not understand why no connection was made which might have prompted more positive action than the non-renewal of Ayling's contract. In fact we also know that a fifth complaint of a similar nature was made after the non-renewal; as he had already left, that complaint was not pursued.

D) GENERAL PRACTICE – 1992 TO 1998

Introduction

3.270   In this section we deal with the awareness amongst the community midwives of concerns about Ayling and concerns arising from other aspects of Ayling's work whilst he was in general practice, in particular his employment as a locum doctor in the family planning clinics run by the SE Kent District Health Authority (SEKDHA) and his participation in the local GP deputising co-operative, SEADOC.

3.271 By 1992, Ayling's employment in the Kent and Canterbury and the Thanet Hospitals had ended, although he was still employed by the William Harvey Hospital as a clinical assistant in colposcopy.

3.272 The first "joined-up" examination of concerns about Ayling in the various settings in which he worked was made in 1993, when the FHSA's Medical Director was made aware of concerns about Ayling by both the Director of Public Health for the SE Kent DHA in respect of her responsibilities for the family planning clinics, and the Medical Director of the William Harvey Hospital in respect of Ayling's employment as a clinical assistant. We have paid particular attention to the process and outcome of the events of 1993, not only because it was the first time information from different health care sectors about Ayling was shared with the FHSA but also because this was only two years after the Police referral to the FHSA in 1991.

3.273 We decided that it would be appropriate in this section to deal with the concerns about Ayling amongst the community midwives. This is because from 1992 until 1998 one midwife in particular was attached to Ayling's practice and is named by a number of patients as the recipient of their anxieties about the manner in which Ayling conducted himself as their GP.

3.274 In this section we also deal with the concerns generated by Ayling at SEADOC and how these were handled. The majority of complaints were about his tardiness or failure to visit but those that raised concerns about his motivation for undertaking intimate examinations were handled in a way which echoes the response of Ayling's colleagues in the White House surgery.

The Family Planning Service in South East Kent

3.275 Until 1974 family planning clinics in South East Kent were provided by the independent Family Planning Association. From that date they were integrated into the NHS, and were provided as part of the range of community health services managed by the Community and Priority Health Services Unit of the SE Kent District Health Authority until 1993 when they became part of the Canterbury and Thanet Community Healthcare NHS Trust. Dr Ann Farebrother was Director of Public Health for the South East Kent District Health Authority from May 1990 until March 1994. She was responsible for the management of doctors working in the district's Family Planning Clinics although she told the Inquiry:

> "It was an odd situation because I wasn't working for the same organisation as the family planning doctors were, but the idea was that it had to be a doctor and preferably a doctor who knew something about family planning, and that was why I volunteered to do that. But it was an odd situation and it was not very formally constituted, I do not feel."

3.276 General practitioners working in the clinics were accountable to the Family Planning Service in relation to the work they undertook within the clinics. The service was led by a consultant in genito-urinary medicine, Dr Sarkhel who told the Inquiry he became 'titular head' of the Family Planning Services in 1984. This involved being responsible for the medical administration of family planning clinics, ensuring that clinics were adequately staffed by trained doctors and nurses. He believed that disciplinary and employment issues in relation to those staff were the responsibility of the Director of Public Health. The Family Planning Service had a number of policies, including a rule that male doctors should have a nurse chaperone when they were carrying out intimate examinations. It is unclear whether this had been in a written form until Dr Sarkhel confirmed this in writing to staff in the early 1990s.

3.277   Doctors were employed on a sessional basis to work in family planning clinics and additionally, a number of GPs were employed on a locum basis to cover for absence. To be eligible for inclusion on the locum list, GPs had to be trained in family planning techniques and to hold the Family Planning Association Certificate. One of the locum doctors was Ayling, who had the relevant certification.

3.278   The Inquiry was unable to establish a complete picture of the clinics at which Ayling worked as a locum, but witnesses mentioned clinics at Vicarage Lane, Ashford; the Dover Health Centre and the Baker Road Clinic, Cheriton, Folkestone.

Concerns in the Family Planning Clinics
3.279   Although it had been Dr Farebrother's practice to record complaints about doctors in their personnel files, no written material of relevance has been found for the Inquiry. Instead, information about complaints relating to Ayling derived from the memories of individuals, notably Val Dodds, a Family Planning Nurse at the Baker Road Clinic in Cheriton, and Dr Farebrother herself.

3.280   The Inquiry heard from a nurse who worked at the clinic at Vicarage Lane, Susan Hanna. She told the Inquiry that the clinic's chaperone policy was, and continued to be, that a male doctor should be accompanied when examining a female client. She remembered Ayling working as a locum at the clinic, probably in about 1992. She found him professional and friendly, until her view changed as the result of an incident which she remembered taking place. She said this concerned a young female patient who needed a cervical smear. She had passed the notes to Ayling to perform the smear but had waited in attendance so as to be present as a chaperone. When she was not called in, she entered without an invitation. She recalled that the patient was naked, without the blanket usually provided, and distressed. The smear had been performed already.

3.281   The nurse spoke first to the senior nurse at the clinic, who agreed that the patient should be given an opportunity to make a formal complaint. As a result, she spoke to the patient again, when the consultation with Ayling was over, and explained that she should not have had a smear without a chaperone, or been left naked. The patient told her that Ayling had given her a full physical examination. She was offered the opportunity to make a formal complaint, with the nurse's support. The patient, however, did not want to press such a complaint, at least immediately – she wanted to go home. Despite the reassurances from the staff, she never came back to complain, or made further contact with the clinic.

3.282   The witness told the Inquiry that she also spoke to Ayling about the incident, together with the senior nurse, Vanessa Lowe. Ayling suggested that he had not been able to find a chaperone, and denied that anything untoward had happened. The full examination reflected his care for his patients.

3.283   Although the Inquiry was told that a written record or complaint about the incident was made by the nurse to her superior, Sue Sullivan, the witness did not have a copy and no action that she knew of appeared to have followed. However, she herself was off work during a large part of the remainder of the year, and she remembered that Ayling stopped working as a locum in the clinics shortly thereafter.

3.284   Vanessa Lowe too gave a statement to the Inquiry. She stressed the very limited number of locum sessions carried out by Ayling at Vicarage Lane, from about 1991 onwards. She noted that his practice differed from the other doctors that she worked with, insofar as he would carry out breast and vaginal examinations when prescribing the contraceptive pill for the first time. Clients did not generally like these examinations, although they recovered quickly and generally took the view that it was good to have had them in the context of their general health. She spoke to Ayling about the matter, but he defended his right to make the examinations that he considered were necessary. He was the one responsible for prescribing. He also invoked his status as a gynaecologist. She had also noted that it was not his practice to use chaperones. She confirmed Ms Hanna's account of the practice on chaperones at the clinic, although she added that this was not a written policy at the time. In addition, she too remembered the incident described by Ms Hanna, although she added that the reason given by Ayling for the need to conduct a full examination had been that the patient wanted to go on the pill. She said that they had spoken to Dr Sarkhel, the consultant for the family planning clinics, shortly afterwards, and that as a result Dr Sarkhel produced a written policy specifically stating the need for male doctors to be accompanied by a chaperone.

3.285   Mrs Lowe noted that many patients would not have known whether to complain, as they would not have known whether anything untoward had happened. Furthermore, particularly if very young, they might have been embarrassed to admit that they were attending a family planning clinic. There were no notices in the clinic stating clearly to whom complaints should be addressed.

3.286   Susan Sullivan also gave evidence to the Inquiry. She remembered that Vanessa Lowe had passed on concerns to her. The concerns were similar to those expressed to us by Sue Hanna, although they appear to have related to a separate incident. She did not remember the incident recalled by Ms Hanna, but did acknowledge that Mrs Lowe had spoken to her to express her concern that Ayling was not a person who she wished to work with. Mrs Lowe had told Ms Sullivan that this stemmed from an incident in which Ayling had carried out an unchaperoned vaginal examination on a young person visiting the Young Persons' Clinic for the first time. He had immediately been told by Ms Lowe of the need for a chaperone, and that – in order to encourage young people to attend such clinics – a policy decision had been taken that these examinations should not be performed at the first visit as a matter of routine, as they were very unpopular. However, according to her, once she had 'turned her back', Ayling proceeded to carry out exactly the same examination on the other young girl who had attended with her friend.

3.287   Ms Sullivan did not raise the matter further with Ayling, as she was not his line manager. Her evidence to the Inquiry suggested that she would have anticipated that he would have defended his right to make his own clinical decisions about a patient's needs. However, she spoke to Ann Farebrother about these issues. She did not see any need to document or address the matter more formally as the patients themselves were not complaining.

3.288   In her evidence to the Inquiry, Val Dodds told us that over a period of time a number of Ayling's GP patients came to the Baker Road Clinic and raised concerns with the nurses about his performance of breast and vaginal examinations which they felt were unnecessary or excessively frequent. Some patients said that they had been asked to remove all their clothes when this was not clinically justified by their complaint. The patients did not explicitly state that Ayling's conduct or motivation was sexual. However, they felt that these examinations were inappropriate and were embarrassed and upset by Ayling's practice.

3.289   Val Dodds' response to these concerns was threefold. First, she advised patients to attend the Clinic for matters of family planning and sexual health and to change GPs if necessary. Secondly, she encouraged them to make written complaints about Ayling – although there is no evidence that any patients ever in fact did so. Finally, she spoke to her managers and to a medical officer of the SEKDHA, Dr Patricia Wheatley. The response she received was that nothing could be done about the concerns unless they were put in writing by a patient.

3.290   Val Dodds also told us that at some point during the 1990s she and Dr Farebrother were members of an interview panel considering applications for a medical vacancy in a Young Persons' Family Planning Clinic. Following Ayling's interview, she recollects questioning whether it was appropriate to employ Ayling given the concerns about him. Dr Farebrother is said to have commented that such information should not be considered in the context of Ayling's application. However, SEKDHA's Personnel Officer took a different view and Ayling was not appointed to the post.

3.291   Dr Farebrother herself could not recall any such discussion taking place during the course of such an appointment process, and no records of an application for such a post by Ayling were received by us. However, she did remember speaking to Val Dodds on a different occasion at the beginning of 1993 about concerns in relation to Ayling's performance of intimate examinations. According to Dr Farebrother's written statement, she had been telephoned by Val Dodds, who told her:

> "about a number of concerns that she had received from nurses concerning Dr Ayling's practice. I cannot remember if these related to one specific clinic … or whether there was more than one … probably

the latter. The concerns were to do with Dr Ayling working as a Family Planning doctor (as opposed to his practice as a GP) and these concerns were similar to other concerns that have since been raised, such as over familiarity, unnecessary pelvic examinations and being overtly sexual. This last point was raised in connection with making the patient feel uncomfortable. From what I could gather, there were sexual connotations in what he was doing and saying."

3.292 In her oral evidence to the Inquiry Dr Farebrother appeared less certain that there was a sexual element to the concerns she received. She repeatedly referred to the apparent ambiguities of the information she had been given and her contemporaneous understanding of Ayling's behaviour – characterising his conduct as short of indecent assault and insufficiently serious to warrant referral to the GMC or the Police. The impression created by this contrast was that Dr Farebrother had come to regret the strength of her written statement and was seeking to dilute the assertions she had earlier made.

3.293 In the event, Dr Farebrother took what she herself described as *"the easy way out"* in taking Ayling's name off the list of locums and decreeing that he was not to be asked to do family planning clinics again. Embarrassed by the prospect of raising the issues directly with Ayling, she did not communicate her decision to him or discuss any of these concerns with him. However, she did take the proactive step of speaking to Dr Peter Savege, the Medical Director of Kent FHSA. In her statement she recollected telling him that Val Dodds' information emanated from three sources, namely the family planning clinics, the colposcopy clinics and Ayling's general practice patients; although in her oral evidence she told the Inquiry that she mentioned only two allegations and Dr Savege himself remembered only one complaint.

3.294 During their conversation, Dr Farebrother agreed with Dr Savege's suggestion that Ayling should receive counselling about his practice in conducting examinations. She subsequently heard from Dr Savege that he had visited Ayling himself. She gained the impression that Dr Savege had warned Ayling that his approach to intimate examinations was unacceptable and that he should reconsider the manner in which he conducted them. However, she also formed the view that it was felt the patients themselves were making too much of Ayling's behaviour and that the situation was not especially serious. She therefore took no further steps to pursue the matter.

3.295 Dr Farebrother acknowledged that she had not made any investigations herself at the family planning clinics because it *"never entered [her] head that this might be a criminal situation"*. She accepted that with hindsight she should have returned to the nurses or the patients themselves for further information, although she was aware that the patients did not wish to make formal complaints. She also accepted that she should have sought advice from the GMC.

Conclusion

3.296   We consider Dr Farebrother's lack of investigation and acceptance of Dr Savege's assurances about Ayling unfortunate. We are also critical of the decision to choose an expedient and partial solution to the problem created by Ayling, by removing his name from the list of practitioners used by the Family Planning Service. Her actions are illustrative of the then professional preference for informal discussion with a medical colleague rather than instigating a formal process of investigation and evidence gathering.

Dr Maitra and Dr Sarkhel

3.297   Dr Maitra was a principal in the Guildhall Street surgery, Folkestone, from 1989 to 1990. Thereafter he became a single-handed general practitioner. Between 1990 and 1998, he worked part-time in the Baker Road Family Planning Clinic and also at the Young Persons Family Planning Clinic. During the course of his family planning clinic work, Dr Maitra received several complaints about Ayling. In his written statement, he said:

> "Many of the complaints were non-specific and referred to [Ayling's] manner as well as to unprofessional conduct and would not have caused me concern in isolation. However, due to the number of complaints and their consistency, I advised patients to complain to the FPC/FHSA or, if they were alleging sexual assault, to complain to the Police … if I had received a complaint in writing I would have taken the matter to the FPC/FHSA and also to Dr Sarkhel, Consultant at the Family Planning Clinic. I needed the consent of the patient in order to act but I never received any written complaints from Dr Ayling's patients nor heard of any results of a patient lodging a complaint. As the patients were seen on a one-off basis, I was in no position to follow up my advice. I suspect that the patients were embarrassed and therefore unwilling to take the matter further. I could do nothing without the written consent of the patient."

3.298   Dr Maitra repeatedly stated that had not contacted the GMC or sought the advice of his medical defence organisation because, as he understood the position, he needed the consent of the patients concerned – which they had declined to give. Without such consent he would not have had the evidence to support his allegations and would have been *"harassed until and unless [he] proved that the complaint was made"*. Instead, he took his information to Dr Sarkhel.

3.299   Dr Maitra told the Inquiry that he spoke to Dr Sarkhel in about 1985, telling him that Ayling was *"examining without a chaperone and other things"*. According to Dr Maitra, he was told to *"get something in writing"* so that Dr Sarkhel could *"proceed forward"*. The upshot was that Dr Sarkhel issued a general letter to all those working within the family planning clinics, requiring them to use a chaperone when examining a patient. No steps appear to have been taken to investigate the matter further or to confront Ayling directly with allegations.

3.300   Dr Sarkhel gave evidence that he had become aware of concerns about Ayling from his nursing staff, who had worked with Ayling in family planning clinics and in the hospital setting. The concerns relating to patients' unhappiness with Ayling's performance of unnecessary internal examinations while they were completely naked. Having received this information, Dr Sarkhel chose not to shortlist Ayling for a clinical assistant post. He did not give Ayling the real reason for this; rather he told him that he wanted to appoint a female doctor to the position.

3.301 Dr Sarkhel also stated that he received concerns about Ayling's examinations from Val Dodds and another nurse; specifically, it was said that Ayling did not use a chaperone. He acknowledged that his response to this had simply been to write a general letter to all the doctors about the need to use a chaperone. No reference was made to specific concerns about Ayling; nor did Dr Sarkhel initiate a formal investigation into his practice.

3.302 It is clear that there were persistent misgivings about Ayling's practice within the Family Planning Service over a period of several years. This was coupled with a strong reluctance among the senior clinicians and management to investigate his conduct or do any more than minimise his exposure to female patients by ensuring that he was not employed within the local clinics.

Conclusion

3.303 The manner in which concerns about Ayling's behaviour and conduct during the sessions he undertook for the Family Planning Service were handled exemplifies the way in which other health organisations also responded to concerns, in particular the expediency of removing Ayling from the list of approved locums for family planning clinics as a perceived solution to the concerns he had generated.

3.304 No contemporaneous documentation was made of patients' or staff concerns and thus no record was created which would have identified and evidenced a consistent pattern of unacceptable behaviour. When complaints were made, no formal action was taken. There was an over-reliance on informal mechanisms to raise anxieties with managers and no thought of reporting such concerns in line with wider professional responsibilities.

3.305 Where remedial action was taken it was generalised to an extent that nullified the force of its application to Ayling.

3.306 Finally a complaint in writing was seen, wrongly, as a prerequisite for formal action and there was no readiness to take on an advocacy role for the patient in complaints of an intimate and sensitive nature.

Ayling's General Practice

The FHSA – 1993

3.307 On 29th October 1993, Dr Savege received a telephone call from Dr Noel Padley, the Medical Director at the William Harvey Hospital, informing him of three serious complaints about Ayling arising in the hospital setting. Two of these were from patients alleging impropriety in the context of intimate examinations. The other was from a student midwife alleging inappropriate physical contact by Ayling during the course of a hospital clinic. Each allegation is discussed more fully elsewhere in our Report.

3.308   By this stage it appears that Dr Savege had already spoken to Dr Farebrother and was aware of the additional concerns arising from the Family Planning Service. He was also aware of the 1991 Police referral following an allegation of indecent assault by one of Ayling's GP patients. Although Dr Savege himself told us that he had not remembered the 1991 referral in 1993, Dr Padley recalls the incident being mentioned and Mr Addison (who had spoken to Dr Padley) made a file note to that effect on 1st November 1993.

3.309   As set out elsewhere in our Report it appears there was a complete failure of understanding between Dr Padley and Dr Savege as to whose responsibility it was to refer Ayling's alleged conduct to the GMC. As a result, no such referral was made. Rather, Dr Savege's response to the information he had been given by Dr Farebrother and Dr Padley was to write to Ayling on 3rd November 1993 in these terms:

> "In recent days I have had several representations from different quarters regarding your technique in gynaecological examination.

> "It appears unlikely that any of those known to me will pursue an official complaint to the GMC, the FHSA or the Police. However, clearly you and I, from our different viewpoints, have to examine professional and patient issues.

> "I believe a conversation between us should take place at our earliest mutual convenience. Therefore, I will ask my secretary to make arrangements with you."

3.310   The letter is remarkable for a number of reasons. First, it suggests, in clear terms, that the *"representations"* were related to multiple incidents rather than being confined to two patient complaints, as Dr Savege would have us believe. Secondly it suggests, by the reference to the Police that the complaints were of a kind that could have led to criminal charges for indecent assault. Thirdly, it suggests that the complaints may have amounted to serious professional misconduct, by the reference to the GMC and the FHSA. Finally, it seeks to give inappropriate reassurance to Ayling that, so far as Dr Savege was aware, no official complaint would follow.

3.311   The meeting with Ayling took place at Dr Savege's office on 5th November 1993. Dr Savege recalled that it began with Ayling asking who the complainants were. Dr Savege told him that he did not have any names or information to show him. However, he asked him to describe a notional examination from start to finish. It seemed to Dr Savege that Ayling's description was plausible; Ayling understood the need to have a chaperone and undertook to perform no further examinations without one. He also said that he would make efforts to explain *"step by step"* to the patients what he was asking them to let him do.

3.312   When the allegation of the erect penis rubbing against the thigh (which had been reported by Dr Padley) was put to him by Dr Savege, Ayling produced a bunch of keys from his pocket, which could have rubbed against a thigh. Dr Savege accepted this explanation. He told the Inquiry that he was fooled by Ayling and that *"naively, it did not occur to [him] that he might have rehearsed that story elsewhere.... So [he] took it at face value"*. Indeed on 16th June 1992, Ayling had given an identical excuse to Mr Addison during a similar discussion of concerns about his behaviour.

3.313 The upshot of the meeting between Dr Savege and Ayling is best summarised by the letter that was written to Dr Padley by Dr Savege on 8th November 1993. The letter was copied to Ayling and stated as follows:

"Further to our recent conversation regarding technique in gynaecological examinations, I have had a full and frank discussion with Dr Ayling on 5th November 1993. My view is that a chaperone should always be available, that a consistent routine should be followed thoroughly and that every effort should be made to put each individual patient at their ease. Dr Ayling was very grateful that you and I had brought our concerns to his attention and convinced me that he entirely subscribed to the above thoughts. He also agreed that it might be sensible to remove the massive bunch of keys from his trouser pocket.

"It would be very helpful, if you should have any further concerns, for me to receive full documentation so that I can be of assistance"

3.314 The last sentence of the letter is consistent with the account given to us by Dr Savege, namely that he did not have any documents relating to the complaints raised at the William Harvey Hospital. It is difficult to fathom why there were so few written records relating to the concerns and complaints about Ayling and no sharing of the documentary material across the two health bodies.

Conclusions about the Events of 1993

3.315 There can be no question but that the combination of complaints circulating amongst the various health organisations, in the autumn of 1993, represented a major challenge to the individuals concerned. Their reactions to the complaints themselves demonstrates an unwillingness to acknowledge that a fellow doctor could be an abuser. Thus, even a noticeable consistency in the complaints reported did not raise suspicions of sexually driven motivation. The complaints were not treated in a systematic or professional way. The various health organisations did not join together to share information, to link investigations and to take the action that would have been appropriate. Police involvement was plainly justified. So, too, was a referral to the GMC.

3.316 Dr Savege fully accepted that his actions, following the referrals from Drs Padley and Farebrother, left a great deal to be desired. In particular, he conceded that he should have done a great deal more to equip himself with information before he went to see Ayling. He said that it had not occurred to him that there was material at the William Harvey Hospital to which he should have sought access. He did not seek to disassociate himself from responsibility for his actions and said that he had been naïve enough to believe that he had been given the salient features and that there was no other information available.

3.317 In relation to the referral made by Dr Farebrother, Dr Savege agreed that he should have quizzed her about her sources and suggested that the matters raised were serious enough to warrant an investigation. He went on to say that all three of the doctors involved *"could have pursued the search for information much more vigorously"* than any of them had. It seems to us that that must be right. If there had been a properly co-ordinated investigation of the complaints emanating from the various quarters in late 1993, and this had been coupled with the information given by the patient who complained to the Police in 1991, the probability must be that Ayling would have faced a GMC referral, at the very least. Yet another lost opportunity to bring Ayling's activities under closer scrutiny.

The Community Midwives

3.318 A number of community nursing staff, such as health visitors and midwives, were employed elsewhere in the NHS in east Kent but were 'attached' to Ayling's practice to provide services to his patients, Some former patients made statements to the Inquiry that they had told these staff of concerns about Ayling and his clinical practice and behaviour. No contemporaneous record of these concerns was made available to the Inquiry and none of these apparently went as far as a specific complaint. We recognise that the extent to which such staff might have been troubled about what they may have heard would have depended on both what they may have been told, the way in which patients described their concerns (we return to this theme later in our Report) and whether such staff had any prior concerns. However, one community midwife in particular, Penny Jedrzjewski, was named by several patients as the recipient of their expressed anxieties about mistreatment by Ayling.

3.319 Penny Jedrzejewski, known to her patients as Penny Jed, worked part-time as Ayling's community midwife from the end of 1992 until December 1998, when Ayling's surgery merged with the Guildhall Street practice. From October 1985 she also worked as a flexi-bank midwife at the William Harvey Hospital and at the Antenatal Clinic of the Royal Victoria Hospital in Folkestone.

3.320 Six of Ayling's patients have provided evidence to the Inquiry that they expressed concerns to Mrs Jed about Ayling's treatment between 1993 and 1997. Patient I gave evidence to us that she went to see Mrs Jed immediately after an examination by Ayling at the Royal Victoria Hospital on 16th April 1993. (Details of her experience and her subsequent letter of complaint are contained elsewhere in the Report.) She describes telling Mrs Jed that she had been pressurised by Ayling into undergoing an internal examination and that he had touched her breasts inappropriately, having coerced her into a breast examination. In her view she made it clear to Mrs Jed that Ayling had behaved indecently towards her during the consultation.

3.321 For her part, Mrs Jed remembers that Patient I was distressed and had felt *"violated and coerced into a vaginal examination"*, but insisted that there was no suggestion of sexual misconduct on Ayling's part. She disagreed that Patient I had conveyed her personal revulsion for Ayling although in Patient I's letter of complaint to the Hospital (which Mrs Jed had not seen) she had described him as a *"disgrace to his profession ... slimy and deceitful"*.

3.322 Mrs Jed's own experience of Ayling was that he was an old-fashioned practitioner who caused her a number of difficulties in the way that he managed his pregnant patients. Ayling had made it clear from the outset of their professional relationship that, in his view, he was an expert who did not need the assistance of a midwife. He treated Mrs Jed as if she were a *"domestic nurse"* and did his best to make it awkward for her to gain access to the patients. Often the referrals to her would be late and it was her impression that the decision not to involve her more was deliberate on his part. At the time, Mrs Jed discussed matters with her line managers but it was felt there was no system in place for dealing with the problem.

3.323 Mrs Jed said that some women would tell her that they did not like Ayling and would change to another GP, but they did not tell her the reason for the change. However, this did not happen very often. She was not sure how she came to know of changes but it could have been from discussions within the small team of Community Midwives in Folkestone. She had not asked the women why it was that they were seeking to change. In similar vein, Mrs Jed told us that patients would say that they felt uncomfortable with Ayling or did not like him. However, she did not consider it appropriate to explore this further with them at the time.

3.324 Mrs Jed was clear in her evidence that prior to 1997 she heard nothing from either her patients or her professional colleagues that could have led her to believe that there were sexual connotations to Ayling's conduct. She repeatedly stated that if there had been such concerns or complaints, she would have documented them in the patients' medical records or their hand-held notes, pointing out that she had indeed done precisely that in the case of the complaint that all agreed she had received from Patient I. In this respect, in relation to concerns of inappropriate sexual interest, Mrs Jed's recollection differs from that of other community midwives in Folkestone at the time. Ann Alexander, a community midwife based at Buckland Hospital told us that Ayling had a reputation for being *"a bit lecherous"* and that he would carry out breast and vaginal examinations in the Antenatal Clinic. Janet Rodway, a community midwife in Shepway from 1980 onwards heard talk that Ayling was carrying out unnecessary or inappropriate examinations, although she commented that the talk within the midwifery community was the level of *"hearsay and undertones rather than specific examples"*.

3.325 Ann Heseltine, a Supervisor of Midwives and the line manager of the community midwives in Folkstone from 1989 to 1995 told us that either Mrs Jed or another midwife, Peggy Lynch, had shared concerns about Ayling with her. The concerns included inappropriate breast examinations, asking patients to strip completely naked for examinations and failing to provide blankets for patients to cover themselves. Mrs Jed agreed that she had spoken Ann Heseltine about a number of worries about Ayling's outmoded practices, including his performance of breast and vaginal examinations when those were not clinically indicated. But she steadfastly denied having discussed issues of sexualised behaviour. Dottie

Watkins, Mrs Jed's line manager for much of the relevant period, told us that it was well known in the antenatal clinics in the 1980s that *"Ayling would get patients to undress and put on a hospital gown while he conducted the booking examination which included a breast and vaginal examination, early in pregnancy"*. Ms Watkins also recollected Mrs Jed telling her that patients would mention Ayling's practice of vaginal examinations in the early stages of pregnancy and that she would advise them that he was old-fashioned and that they did not have to agree to an examination if they did not want to.

3.326 Mrs Jed claimed none of this information about Ayling was shared with her even when, at a later stage, she raised with Ms Watkins concerns about his practice in the community. She agreed that it was possible she had told patients, who had had vaginal examinations in the early weeks of pregnancy, that Ayling's practice was very old-fashioned. However, she did not recall ever having a conversation with patients about their dislike of Ayling's vaginal examinations and could not account for Ms Watkins' evidence in this respect.

3.327 Mrs Jed told us that she first became aware of the sexualised aspect of Ayling's practice in 1997 when a patient spoke to her about a vaginal examination during which she had felt Ayling's erect penis against her thigh. The patient told her explicitly that she did not want the matter to be reported and that if Mrs Jed said anything, she would deny it (a request for anonymity which echoes those of the two patients who had spoken about similar incidents to Dr Voysey in 1988 and Mr Addison in 1992 or 1993). Mrs Jed said that she had believed the patient, told her that she should report the matter and that she would do everything she could to support her.

3.328 Mrs Jed told us that she had discussed the matter with Dottie Watkins, and they had decided to seek advice from the Royal College of Midwives. She had then telephoned the College and had been told that without the support of the patient there was nothing that she could do. It was suggested to Mrs Jed that she might have taken the matter, for example, to the Medical Director of the East Kent Health Authority. Her reaction was that she had sought the advice of her Head of Midwifery and that, then, she had not been aware of the structure. She had *"no insight, no knowledge"* as to whom she could have approached about the issue.

Community midwives – conclusion

3.329 We find it difficult to accept that a midwife as experienced as Penny Jed was unable to recognise the concerns that her patients were expressing, and that she did not make a connection between these and the general awareness amongst her colleagues, the other community midwives, of the anxieties generated by Ayling's conduct.

3.330 We recognise that Penny Jed was the only community midwife to be the recipient of a specific complaint about Ayling. However we believe that there was a degree of anxiety about Ayling's conduct of intimate examinations amongst the community midwives for which there appears to have been no channel of communication to those who might have been able to take direct action. We have called this "soft intelligence" and explore this further in later Chapters.

SEADOC

3.331 In 1992, GPs in Kent and Sussex set up a co-operative deputising service, and The Association of South East Kent and East Sussex Doctors on Call Ltd was established in August 1992. The name 'SEADOC' was adopted in 1994. It was, and remains, a non-profit making company providing out-of-hours service cover for its own members. Brief details of the history and organisation of GP deputising co-operatives are set out in Annex 6.

3.332 The administration of SEADOC is controlled by an Executive Management Group comprising the Medical Managers/Directors, an Office Manager and the Directors of Operations and Finance. There are six Medical Managers who are GPs drawn from each of the three areas covered by SEADOC, including two GPs from the Kent area. As a GP practising in the relevant area, Ayling joined SEADOC on its establishment in 1992.

3.333 We heard evidence from three representatives of SEADOC: Dr Bayles was Medical Manager for Complaints and Discipline from 1996; Dr de Caestecker was a Medical Manager from 1996 to 1999 and Complaints Manager from 1997 to 1999; and Dr Calver was a Trustee of SEADOC from 1996 to 1999.

Complaints Procedures

3.334 Patients who were seen by a deputising doctor and were dissatisfied could make a complaint in two ways. They could complain via their own practice's complaints system, or they could complain directly to SEADOC. Prior to 1994, SEADOC did not have a formal complaints procedure, although in practice complaints were directed to and dealt with by the Complaints Manager. In November 1994, the SEADOC membership approved a formal procedure which made it easier for patients to know how to complain as the envelope containing the call slip that was handed to a patient after a visit contained a printed message: "If you have any comments on the service which has been provided for you please contact SEADOC by writing to…" and then the name and address of the Complaints Manager was provided. In common with other NHS complaints procedures of the time, it was expected that complaints be put in writing.

3.335 However, complaints received by telephone were logged on an action sheet and then passed to the Complaints Manager. All complaints were acknowledged and a copy sent to the doctor concerned and to the patient's own GP. The relevant Medical Manager would investigate the complaint and aimed to respond within fourteen working days. The outcome of the complaint and the action taken was recorded. An analysis of both complaints and positive comments was prepared on a six monthly basis.

3.336 If a patient was not satisfied with the outcome they were informed that they could take the matter further either to the FHSA, PCG or PCT or to the East Kent Health Authority. Equally, following investigations and a meeting with the doctor concerned, SEADOC itself had the power to issue a warning to the doctor, to suspend him from the co-operative and to recommend his resignation, if the co-operative's officers decided that the complaint justified such disciplinary action.

3.337 As the Inquiry was told: "SEADOC ultimately dealt with disciplinary and conduct issues internally." This was a very powerful way of dealing with the Doctor's performance as he would be subject to the scrutiny of his fellow colleagues.

3.338 There seems to have been no procedure for keeping a record of complaints about a particular doctor. Although a file was held on each doctor who had a complaint made against them since the formation of SEADOC, these files were not fully formed and completed until about 1998 or 1999. If a new complaint came in about a particular practitioner, it was not routine to go back into the complaints system and see if there had been previous complaints about that practitioner. It was therefore impossible to see if there were any emerging patterns of concern or complaint.

Complaints about Ayling

3.339 Between 1993 and 2000 there were some ten recorded complaints made by or on behalf of patients about Ayling, to SEADOC. Over half of these related either to an alleged failure to visit or the length of time before doing so. Some took issue with Ayling's manner and at least one queried the clinical management of a case. However, none of these recorded complaints raised issues of sexual impropriety. In 1996, two doctors raised expressions of concern about inappropriate examinations. These are discussed below, but concerned patients who did not wish to complain formally. A further call was received from a patient who had been seen by Ayling in 1996, and who rang back questioning whether it had been appropriate to carry out an internal examination whilst bleeding in pregnancy. This was not perceived by SEADOC to be a complaint and was not treated as such so the patient received clinical advice and reassurance from another SEADOC doctor. One witness gave evidence to the Inquiry about an examination conducted by Ayling in July 1998, and told the Inquiry that she had rung SEADOC to complain. However, she had not heard anything further from them. For their part, SEADOC had no record of such a call, despite the fact that the procedure for recording complaints had been formalised by that time.

3.340 In relation to the complaints that were undoubtedly received by SEADOC, Dr Colledge comments that they were, "in essence, to do with his insensitive manner. I endeavoured to counsel him about this but was merely met with hostility. He was not a person who had insight, nor did he readily apologise for his errors or omissions."

3.341 Dr Bayles told us that the average number of complaints per doctor per annum was 0.175. The average number of complaints against Ayling per annum was 2.3. It must be said that he was working 30% more shifts per annum than most doctors in SEADOC, but this does not seem to us to account for the large discrepancy in the number of complaints relating to Ayling compared with the average. Dr Bayles explained that, until the mid to late 1990s SEADOC was very much on a learning curve and there were no formal systems in place (as indeed was the case with GP practices until the mid 1990s) for monitoring the frequency of complaints. This did not occur until SEADOC introduced its own clinical governance systems.

Inappropriate Examinations

3.342 Dr de Caestecker told us of two informal concerns raised about Ayling's manner of conducting intimate examinations that he remembered being made during the summer of 1996. The first complaint was relayed to him by Dr Colledge, who was also a Medical Manager for SEADOC at that time. Drs Colledge and de Caestecker recalled that Dr Colledge received an oral complaint from Dr Moffat, a GP in Ashford, which related to a female patient of his who claimed that Ayling had examined her in an unprofessional manner while he was working for SEADOC. Dr Colledge remembered that, when Dr Moffat was asked to invite the patient to make a written complaint giving further details, she declined to do so. Nevertheless, both Dr Colledge and Dr de Caestecker felt the information should be shared with a senior colleague in Folkestone and it was decided that Dr de Caestecker should speak to Dr Gary Calver who was then the Chairman of the South East Kent GP division.

3.343 It should be added that Dr Moffat did not recollect this incident. He remembered passing to SEADOC a complaint that Ayling had nearly dropped a baby he was examining (a complaint which is clearly documented), but he did not remember discussing any more informal concerns about unprofessional examinations. Given, however, the evidence of his colleagues, Drs Colledge and de Caestecker, he did not feel able to rule out the 'possibility' that he had indeed come to hear of such concerns and reported them to SEADOC. Further, the Inquiry did receive evidence from a patient in the practice who had been examined by Ayling when deputising for SEADOC in mid-1996. The patient, who was pregnant at the time, complained to her midwife about the manner of the examination when seen by her a month later. She was advised to raise the matter with Dr Moffat. Although the patient concerned is clear that she never did so, and Dr Moffat does not remember her case, it seems to us that it may have been this incident which reached Dr Moffat and was then reported to SEADOC.

3.344 At about the same time a patient of his informed Dr de Caestecker that Ayling had examined her in an unprofessional manner. This complaint arose from the fact that, after Dr de Caestecker had undertaken an internal gynaecological examination; the patient stated that she was pleased to note that he used latex gloves while doing so. She said that Ayling had not used gloves while undertaking a similar examination. Dr de Caestecker discussed what he had heard with his partner, Dr Robertson-Ritchie. They agreed that this complaint should be discussed with Dr Calver who should be asked to approach Ayling. Dr de Caestecker felt that such an approach should come from someone more senior than himself.

3.345 In his evidence to us, Dr Calver recalled that Dr de Caestecker told him that two GPs in the Ashford area had received complaints from their patients when Ayling was working for SEADOC, that those complaints were both of a sexual nature, but unfortunately neither had felt able to put their complaint in writing. Although Dr Calver recalled that one of the GPs was Dr Moffat, he could not remember that name of the other. He recalled that one examination was inappropriate for the condition and that the other examination was done in an inappropriate manner. He pointed out that this was fourth-hand information and that he had nothing in writing.

3.346   Notwithstanding this, Dr Calver felt that he would speak to Ayling in general terms and give him advice that would enable patients to be protected and not put his career at risk. Dr Calver felt that his first approach should be to speak to the LMC and he believed that he spoke to Dr Ashton, then its Assistant Medical Secretary. Dr Calver said that, once he started talking about the nature of the complaints, it became quite obvious from the feedback that the LMC knew who was being discussed. One of the comments that shocked and surprised him was *"Is he the Doctor that examines without gloves, the man from Cheriton?"*. At this stage Ayling's name had not been mentioned.

3.347   Dr Calver had an opportunity to talk to Ayling at SEADOC and expressed the concerns that had been raised to him. He warned Ayling that complaints had been made about inappropriate examinations for the presenting conditions of some female patients while he was working for SEADOC. Ayling firmly rejected any idea of wrongdoing and quite vehemently defended his actions as being according to *"best practice"*. He was upset that these accusations had been made and he had heard about all this "simple rubbish" before. The reference to *"best practice"* was a reference to data sheets in circulation stating that physical examinations should be carried out prior to prescribing oral contraceptives. Although neither of the incidents raised with SEADOC appeared to have anything to do with prescribing oral contraceptives, Dr Calver confirmed that the conversation turned to this subject after he had put to Ayling the two SEADOC incidents; Ayling *"took the conversation to a different area"*.

3.348   Dr Calver did not document his conversation with Ayling because he felt he was helping a colleague in an informal way. But he reported the conversation he had had with Ayling back to the LMC and to Dr de Caestecker. He was unaware of any action taken by the LMC. So far as SEADOC were concerned, both he and Dr de Caestecker felt that as he had brought the matter to the attention of Ayling and the LMC and in the absence of a written complaint, there was nothing more they could do. Dr de Caestecker accepted that he had not instituted any checking mechanism to assure that Ayling's behaviour had changed.

Conclusion

3.349   We are concerned about a number of features in the SEADOC aspect of the Ayling story:

3.350   First, SEADOC had no system for recording a series of complaints against a particular doctor. When a complaint was received, there was no simple way of checking how many complaints and of what nature had been received about an individual. No action seems to have been taken about the fact that the number of complaints about Ayling was significantly higher than the average for GPs working for SEADOC.

3.351 Secondly, the whole emphasis was on an informal approach, notwithstanding the potential gravity of certain complaints.

3.352 Third, Dr Calver allowed Ayling to deflect questioning about the complaints by changing the subject under discussion. We believe that this should have alerted him to the possibility that, although no complaint had been put formally in writing, there was a matter of substance, which needed investigation.

3.353 Finally, Dr de Caestecker was prepared to let the matter drop once he had heard back from Dr Calver, notwithstanding the serious nature of the complaints. He did not institute any mechanism to monitor Ayling's future behaviour.

E) EVENTS – 1998 TO 2000

Introduction

3.354 In this section, we deal with the period from 1998, when the East Kent Health Authority (EKHA) first received a formal complaint about Ayling, until 2000 when Ayling's criminal trial took place.

3.355 From February 1998 onwards, the EKHA and the GMC received an escalating number of complaints against Ayling. These complaints, and the investigations which they triggered, led directly to referrals to the Police; which in turn led to a Police investigation and to Ayling's arrest on 11th November 1998.

3.356 The history of events from 1998 onwards is complex as further patients came forward to tell their stories. In this section of our Report we do not set out a full chronology, but rather we seek to consider the actions of the EKHA from the date of the first complaint about Ayling's serious sexualised behaviour. We consider the actions taken in the light of the decision of the High Court to vary Ayling's bail conditions so that he could continue to practise subject to certain restrictions. Finally, we review the decision of the Guildhall Street practice to merge with that of Ayling and the support given by the EKHA for this merger in the light of the revelations that were unfolding about Ayling.

3.357 We heard oral evidence from three key officers of the EKHA and three witnesses from the Guildhall Street practice:

- Mark Outhwaite – The Chief Executive;
- Jacqueline ('Jacqui') Stewart – The Director of Healthcare Development, with responsibility for Primary Care; and
- Cathy Bolton – The Secretary to the Board
- Dr Hossain – Senior Partner in 1998;
- Dr Khine-Smith – one of the other partners; and
- Hilary Goodburn – Guildhall Street Practice Manager.

The Initial Receipt and Handling of Complaints about Ayling

3.358   Jacqui Stewart told us that until 1998 there was nothing about Ayling's practice that singled him out to the EKHA. Although there was some concern about certain aspects of his prescribing, particularly of drugs to treat asthma and of methadone, he was considered to be *"one of the average GPs locally"*.

3.359   The first detailed consideration of Ayling's practice was sparked off by a single patient's complaint, sent to the EKHA on 23rd February 1998. It described in compelling detail two consultations with Ayling at his Surgery in Cheriton High Street, during which he performed humiliating internal examinations and unnecessary breast examinations. On the second occasion Ayling was said to have had an erection. He was subsequently convicted of indecently assaulting the patient.

3.360   The extreme seriousness of the complaint was recognised immediately by the EKHA and the Medical Adviser, Dr Anthony Snell, agreed that it should be referred directly to the GMC, subject to the patient's consent.

3.361   On 12th March 1998 the EKHA received a second letter of complaint about Ayling. The patient alleged that she had undergone repeated internal examinations and had been asked unprofessional personal questions. This complaint was also referred to the GMC with the patient's consent. This complaint too eventually led to criminal charges; Ayling was convicted on one count and acquitted upon another. On 1st June 1998, a third complaint was received, alleging clinical mismanagement by Ayling, who was said to have prescribed drugs to which the patient was allergic.

3.362   At this stage the EKHA initiated the procedures of the Poorly Performing Doctors Panel. This was set up in 1997 (following the publication of a report commissioned by the DH "Measures to assist GPs whose performance gives cause for concern" and the introduction of new performance procedures by the GMC) and was a sub-committee of the EKHA with membership representing general practice education, the LMC and the Health Authority. Under the Panel's protocol, its advisers, Dr Snell and Dr John Ashton, the Clerk of the Kent LMC, saw Ayling at the LMC's offices on 14th July 1998. He was informed for the first time about two complaints under consideration by the GMC and was asked to describe his practice in relation to intimate examinations. He was then strongly advised to make use of a chaperone and to provide covers for his patients. Ayling made no comment about the third complaint of drug mismanagement. The purpose of the Poorly Peforming Doctors Panel was to protect patients, but also to operate in a supportive manner towards doctors and to encourage remedial, educational reform in cases where deficiencies were identified. Any action beyond making arrangements for educational support (such as a referral to the GMC) would have needed to be ratified by the EKHA.

3.363   Thereafter, on 30th July 1998, the EKHA Reference Committee considered all three complaints and decided to refer the third (the only one that was not barred under the 13 week time limit) to the Medical Discipline Committee.

3.364 A formal visit to Ayling's surgery then took place on 6th August 1998, looking primarily at clinical issues and practice administration. The EKHA Poorly Performing Doctor Panel subsequently met in late September and the decision was made to refer Ayling to the GMC on the basis of professional misconduct and poor practice. Details of the decision were sent to the GMC in a report on 1st October 1998, which stated that the Associate Adviser in General Practice considered that educational input was unlikely to lead to improvement in Ayling's practice. The EKHA also began to draw up papers for an NHS Tribunal hearing.

3.365 Meanwhile, on the 11th September 1998, a fourth complaint was received by the EKHA, alleging that Ayling had performed an inappropriate breast examination in an intrusive and abusive manner on 6th September 1998. No chaperone had been offered or present. There was considerable concern within the EKHA that this should have happened after Ayling had been given a strong warning by Dr Snell and Dr Ashton only two months previously. The immediate response was to call the patient and advise her to report this matter to the Police, as well as the GMC.

3.366 At this point, the EKHA had various possible routes of action in response to the substance of the complaints:

- to deal with matters themselves through their own internal procedures. However they felt these to be insufficient to deal with such serious complaints, bearing in mind that the Authority could not suspend or remove from practice a GP, who was an independent contractor to the NHS.
- to rely upon a Police investigation – while this was the obvious action to take in such circumstances, it had the disadvantage that the Police were very often unhappy for other bodies to take action before a criminal trial for fear that the witness evidence could be contaminated.
- to refer Ayling to the General Medical Council – which had and retains the power to remove any medical practitioner from its Register who is found guilty of professional misconduct.
- to refer Ayling to an NHS Tribunal – which had the power to suspend and disqualify a practitioner from service, but was seen as procedurally cumbersome and on occasions seen as more concerned with protecting the doctor than the patient.

3.367 However, by September 1998, a Police investigation had commenced. Two things, in particular, widened the circle of complainants.

3.368 The first was that the EKHA learnt about the history of patients seeking to transfer from Ayling's surgery to the White House surgery. On 5th November 1998, Dr Anderson had telephoned Dr Snell, after taking advice from his medical defence organisation on how to respond to the serious concerns about Ayling's conduct from patients seeking to transfer to the White House surgery. They were able to speak the following day when Dr Anderson agreed to hand over the names of the relevant patients, subject to their consent. On Monday 11th November 1998, the names of five patients were provided to the EKHA and Dr Anderson and his former partner subsequently made statements to the Police.

3.369   The second factor was the publicity about the case in the local media. This followed Ayling's arrest and the charges of four counts of indecent assault, which were laid before the Court on 13th November 1998. The EKHA set up a confidential helpline. They sent out details of the line, and of back-up arrangements for patient counselling, to all local GPs. The following day, calls to the helpline started up and a number of former patients gave statements to both the Police and the EKHA as a result.

Referral to the General Medical Council

3.370   The first and second patients to complain to the EKHA about Ayling's conduct in March 1998 had also sent letters directly to the GMC. Further copies of their complaints were forwarded to the GMC by the EKHA on 11th March and 21st April 1998 respectively. The GMC acknowledged these letters immediately and gave assurances in April and May that the matters were being dealt with. However, it was not until 16th June 1998, that the GMC sent a letter to the EKHA stating that there were possible grounds for action under the fitness to practise procedures in relation to the first complaint, but that further details were needed from both patients. Letters were also sent directly to the patients themselves, requesting further information.

3.371   Understandably, the EKHA became increasingly frustrated with the perceived inactivity on the part of the GMC and, following the third complaint about Ayling's sexual conduct, Mr Outhwaite wrote to them on 22nd September 1998 expressing the Health Authority's concern and asking that the process of investigation be expedited.

3.372   In November 1998 Cathy Bolton telephoned the GMC to check their progress, and on 27th November 1998 the GMC wrote to say that they were going to await the outcome of the criminal proceedings before considering further what disciplinary action would be merited. In the six months between June and November, the GMC were undertaking the further investigations their procedures required, as well as receiving a further complaint which necessitated their taking legal advice. In late October, at the point at which the Preliminary Proceedings Committee would have begun their consideration, the GMC learnt that Ayling had been arrested.

3.373   In his evidence to us, Mr Finlay Scott, the Chief Executive of the GMC, accepted that there had been a delay in acknowledging the complaints and giving them early consideration. This should not have taken until June 1998. However, he pointed out that during 1998 the organisation was suffering from a huge workload because of events at the Bristol Royal Infirmary. He stated that the number of referrals had doubled since 1995. But he freely acknowledged that things had just taken too long, although he also doubted whether the GMC would have been able to justify imposing restrictions on Ayling's ability to practise at such an early stage of a relatively complex case.

The NHS Tribunal

3.374   The EKHA had submitted their application to the Tribunal for Ayling's interim suspension on 10th November 1998. However, the next day Ayling was arrested. As a result, the Chairman of the Tribunal telephoned on 19th November 1998 to ask why the EKHA wanted to apply for an interim suspension, particularly as Ayling would be likely to object to the application on the grounds that the criminal proceedings should take precedence. At that stage Ayling's bail conditions were that he could not practise as a GP and so this seemed reasonable.

3.375 However, Ayling successfully appealed against these restrictions and the High Court granted him permission to practise provided that a chaperone was present during the examination of female patients. (The bail conditions are discussed in detail below.) As a result of this, the EKHA asked for their application to the Tribunal to continue and a hearing was fixed for 17th December 1998. When this hearing was subsequently adjourned as a result of various procedural difficulties, the EKHA's legal representative advised the EKHA that, given the High Court had overturned the bail conditions, it would be very difficult to argue that the NHS Tribunal should grant an Interim Suspension Order. He felt that the Tribunal would not want to 'second-guess' the High Court. The EKHA was asked to gather further patient evidence by seeking access to the statements being gathered by the Police and also advised to seek expert advice on the clinical aspects of the claims being made. It was hoped that these steps would strengthen the case for suspension.

3.376 The Inquiry heard of two difficulties associated with subsequent events. The first of these was the very limited information provided to patients. One witness told the Inquiry that she received a letter in the first week of November 1998 telling her of the Tribunal, but not its date; was then told in a letter in January 1999 that the Tribunal had been adjourned, but not why; and subsequently heard nothing until a year later, in January 2001, after the criminal trial. At no point was she given a history of the Tribunal proceedings.

3.377 The second difficulty was that the Police refused to allow their evidence to be used by the EKHA for the Tribunal, because of their concern that its force in the criminal trial would be weakened by rehearsal in another set of proceedings. The problems posed to employing and regulatory bodies in their investigations of alleged misconduct by the priority given to investigations by criminal justice organisations are explored elsewhere in this Report, but the immediate effect in June 1999 was that the EKHA withdrew their application to the NHS Tribunal. A further factor in this decision was the lack of any evidence that Ayling was not observing the conditions of his bail or that the patients were not adequately protected by those conditions.

The Bail Conditions
3.378 The EKHA had not been told that Ayling was appealing the bail conditions set by the Magistrates' Court until Friday 20th November 1998 – one working day before the High Court hearing. A meeting took place that evening to discuss the situation. However, there was no time to take legal advice and insufficient opportunity to consider whether it would be valuable for representatives of the EKHA to attend Court and assist the Crown Prosecution Service in their defence of the appeal.

3.379 Though not the fault of the EKHA, this was highly unfortunate, since their presence at the hearing could have made a significant contribution to any submissions relating to the restrictions to be placed on Ayling's opportunities to examine female patients. First, they could have appraised the Court of Ayling's history of ignoring advice as to the use of chaperones. Secondly, they might have assisted the Court towards setting a more explicit requirement relating to the nursing qualifications of the chaperone who should accompany Ayling at any examinations.

3.380 In the event, the conditions imposed by the High Court allowed Ayling to examine female patients in the presence of a *'qualified nurse'* – a term which was not defined by the Court and which was therefore subject to varied interpretations. The EKHA took the view that the condition required the employment of a fully qualified state-enrolled or state-registered nurse, with sufficient experience and authority to fulfil the role of an independent chaperone. Ayling himself disagreed, rejecting any interference by the EKHA and employing a modestly qualified (Grade B) Nursing Auxiliary. In Annex 7 we set out details of nurse registration and qualifications in 1998.

3.381 Additional restrictions were further ordered by the High Court. These included a prohibition on contacting any prosecution witnesses; on accessing any patient medical records, unless needed for the purpose of providing medical services to a patient and if the record was handed to him by a receptionist. Finally, Ayling was not to perform any clinical examinations or house visits when acting for SEADOC.

3.382 Although the Police had formal responsibility for enforcing Ayling's bail conditions, in practice it was left to the EKHA to provide funding and address any concerns about the adequacy of his chaperoning arrangements.

3.383 Following the merger of Ayling's practice with that of the Guildhall Street practice, the EKHA had some reassurance in the involvement of Ayling's new practice manager, Hilary Goodburn. A trial merger had begun to operate on 1 October 1998, i.e. before Ayling's arrest. However neither the EKHA nor Hilary Goodburn were familiar with such a situation and neither had formal powers of compulsion over Ayling.

3.384 To her credit, Hilary Goodburn, took a number of prudent steps to ensure compliance with Ayling's bail conditions. These included a change of locks at Cheriton High Street so that he was no longer in possession of keys to the building; and the removal of the hard drive from his practice computer to safeguard historic patient data. She altered Ayling's consulting room to be nearer the reception to facilitate monitoring; and she ensured that the four other partners undertook all home visits to his female patients.

3.385 She arranged for all pre-planned examinations of his female patients to be undertaken by other partners and staff at Guildhall Street and provided five surgery sessions weekly by other partners at Cheriton High Street. She also arranged for the Practice Nurse to act as the chaperone on three mornings a week and for the chaperone funded by EKHA to cover the other two mornings and afternoon surgeries. All this was done within three to four days of the High Court decision.

3.386   Hilary Goodburn was also surprised about the use of a nursing auxiliary as a chaperone by Ayling, but she did endeavour to ensure that a chaperone was present at all times when he needed to conduct intimate examinations on his female patients. She visited each member of staff to inform them of the nature of the conditions and arranged for large posters to be placed in the waiting room, toilets, Ayling's consulting room and the nurses' treatment room, explaining that female patients could expect a chaperone for intimate examinations. She called at Ayling's surgery almost every day, varying the times of her visits. She received no complaints that Ayling was not using the chaperone.

3.387   However, as early as 3rd December 1998, the EKHA received a telephone call from community nurses attached to Ayling's practice expressing concern that he was using a Grade B nurse as a chaperone – i.e. someone with no statutory nursing or midwifery qualifications. The next day a letter was sent by Ayling's solicitors to the Crown Prosecution Service referring to the fact that EKHA has queried whether the chaperone met the bail conditions and expressing their gratitude that the CPS had confirmed that they were entirely happy with the situation. This letter resulted from Mrs Stewart contacting Ayling about making arrangements for the chaperone and his telling her that it was none of her business. Whilst the EKHA offered to fund a more experienced (Grade D) nurse, this offer was rejected, on instructions, by Ayling's solicitor. Further concerns about the adequacy of the chaperone's qualifications were expressed in January 1999 by employees of the East Kent Community NHS Trust. The EKHA talked to the Trust and suggested that they communicate directly with the Police. However, once again Ayling refused to discuss the matter with the Authority. The EKHA's reaction was that it had done all it could. Nevertheless, discussions took place with their solicitors about applying to vary the conditions so as to impose the requirement that a Grade D registered nurse be used as a chaperone. They were advised that little could be done to vary the decision of the High Court.

3.388   As we have stated above, Mrs Goodburn, or the new merged practice staff, received no complaints from patients about breaches of the bail conditions. Nor did the EKHA. However, two patients did tell the Inquiry that they now considered that the bail conditions had been breached. One was a long-standing patient of Ayling's, who complained that although she knew about the charges against Ayling she was not made aware of the bail conditions and suggested that intimate examinations were carried out on three occasions without a chaperone being present. A second patient joined the surgery in 2000. She agreed that a female nurse had been present when she attended for an examination, but complained that she was sent out of the room from time to time.

3.389   By the end of 1998 the number of criminal charges faced by Ayling had increased substantially, from four to twelve. The EKHA therefore discussed the possibility of returning to Court with the two Police Officers responsible for the criminal investigation. Despite the concerns about the qualifications of the chaperone employed at times by Ayling no such application was made and it appears that no formal contact was initiated between the EKHA's solicitors and the Crown Prosecution Service.

Help for Patients Provided by EKHA

3.390   Prior to Ayling's arrest the EKHA had set up a helpline and had arranged for the Psychology Department of the East Kent Community Trust to give support and counselling to any callers requiring it. When Ayling was arrested, the EKHA arranged for publicity in the local media, giving details of the helpline which went live immediately.

3.391   All the staff answering calls were female. After the initial call had been received, either Jacqui Stewart or Cathy Bolton went to interview the complainant in person and discussed the option of referring the complaint to the Police and/or the NHS Tribunal. The interviewer asked for details of what had happened and then sent out a letter to the complainant confirming what had been discussed and enclosing a draft statement and consent form authorising the disclosure of medical records. After this had been done, there was no further close contact with the patients but they were provided with the direct dial and mobile phone numbers of Jacqui Stewart and Cathy Bolton.

The Merger of Ayling's Practice with the Guildhall St Practice

3.392   Ayling was always due to retire in November 2001 when he reached the age of 70. Towards the end of 1997, he therefore asked Dr Hossain, the senior partner at the Guildhall Street surgery, if they could help out with his practice on his retirement. Hilary Goodburn told Dr Hossain that, if he were to inherit Ayling's practice list, he would have to be in partnership with Ayling for at least a year. On the retirement of a single-handed practitioner it was common for surgeries to be linked up beforehand to provide a smooth transition for patients and also attract additional patients to the new practice.

3.393   The Guildhall Street practice held a number of partners' meetings on the proposed merger, including one with Ayling himself in April 1998. In the end, they decided to merge; although Dr Khine-Smith had reservations about the extra workload, particularly in the areas for which she had primary responsibility – children's and women's health- and she did not support the proposed merger.

3.394   There was a further meeting with Ayling in July or August 1998, at the end of which he mentioned complaints by patients and that he was being investigated by the EKHA and said that he might have to take time off from the practice. As a result Hilary Goodburn spoke to Dr Hossain who told her that he was aware that more than one complaint against Ayling was being investigated by the EKHA. He was not aware of the details of the complaints and asked her to set up a meeting with the Health Authority.

3.395   Hilary Goodburn recalls that both the LMC and the EKHA readily made themselves available for this meeting, which focused on whether the LMC would allow the EKHA to permit the partners to inherit Ayling's patient list if the partnership had been in existence for less than one year. She also asked for the release of funds to bring Ayling's building up to date. She says that Jacqui Stewart used words to the effect *"Ayling will not be practising for very long – six months at most"*. For her part Jacqui Stewart had no record or any specific recollection of this meeting but does recall at some point in late 1998 the identification of the need to refurbish the building housing Ayling's practice.

3.396   At the beginning of September 1998 the Guildhall Street partners decided to support Ayling for a three-month trial period starting on 1st October 1998 prior to a formal merger and to provide cover for Ayling's patients. They were unaware at this stage that Ayling was being investigated by the Police. The first that anyone at Guildhall Street knew of the Police investigation was when they heard of Ayling's arrest on 11th November 1998.

3.397   On the day of Ayling's arrest Hilary Goodburn telephoned EKHA at about 9.15am and was told to transfer all press and patient queries to their Press and Publicity Department. A locum arrived in the afternoon, presumably arranged by Ayling, and the Guildhall Street practice drew up an emergency rota for partners to cover Ayling's surgery. This was soon extended to include a Dr Leyton who had been asked by the EKHA to attend Ayling's patients. Dr Leyton arrived on Monday 23rd November 1998, the day of Ayling's appeal against his bail conditions. When Dr Leyton came in the following morning she found that Ayling was back; he then dismissed her.

3.498   The full merger took effect on 1st January 1999 and the EKHA sent a standard letter to Ayling's patients informing them of the changes – but making no mention of the circumstances relating to his arrest. In normal circumstances when one practice was effectively taking over the practice of someone who was soon to retire, such a letter would be sent only to the patients of the latter practice. However, in the light of the fact that Ayling had by then been charged and was on bail with conditions attached, it is unfortunate that the Guildhall Street patients were not informed

3.499   An important point here is the absence of any protocol or guidance on how to communicate with patients whose GP has been charged with an offence that clearly is related to their professional behaviour. It seems to us that patients must have a right to know of the facts, whilst recognising that there is a balance to be struck that reflects the presumption of innocence. As this will always be a difficult decision, it is an area where some clear guidance is essential as an aid to practice managers.

3.400   One of the Guildhall Street patients gave compelling evidence to the Inquiry that she should have been informed of Ayling's arrival, having deliberately avoided registering with him following an unpleasant breast examination at his surgery. Given that Ayling had been charged with a number of sexual offences, it would have been far preferable if all his patients had been given a proper opportunity to choose whether to attend consultations with him.

3.401   Although the circumstances of the merger were difficult for both the EKHA and the Guildhall Street surgery, it is understandable that they proceeded with it. While it is clear that the surgery was under some pressure from the EKHA to continue with the merger, there were obvious financial benefits for the new practice as it inherited Ayling's list of patients. From the perspective of the EKHA, with the prospect of Ayling's conviction and the certainty of his retirement in any event in 2001, there were strong incentives to provide continuity of treatment for patients who might otherwise have struggled to find themselves a new general practitioner.

Ayling's Conviction and the GMC's Ruling

3.402   Ayling's trial was delayed substantially as further investigations were pursued when new charges were added to the indictment. It finally commenced on 16th October 2000 and concluded on 20th December 2000. Ayling was found guilty of twelve counts of indecent assault and sentenced to four years imprisonment. He was found not guilty on a further nine charges, and the Court ordered fourteen other charges to remain on the file.

3.403   The GMC did not formally resume its consideration of Ayling's case until January 2001. Its Interim Orders Committee met on 12th January 2001 and suspended Ayling's licence to practice for eighteen months. His case was then referred to the Preliminary Proceedings Committee which met on 17th January 2001 and referred the case on to the Professional Conduct Committee. Ayling's name was finally erased from the Medical Register on 14th July 2001.

Conclusion

3.404   The Inquiry commends the efforts made by the EKHA to set up the helpline and to ensure that the initial contact with patients who telephoned was made as comfortable as possible in the circumstances.

3.405   We also have considerable sympathy with the dilemma that the EKHA faced following Ayling's successful appeal against his bail conditions. However, we agree with Mark Outhwaite that it would have been preferable if the organisation had considered applying to the High Court, through the CPS, to reconsider the bail conditions when the charges against Ayling increased considerably.

3.406   The EKHA might also have adopted a more proactive approach to communicating with the patients after the initial interview. It was important to keep them informed of what was happening over such a long period and in this respect a number of patients contrasted the approach of the Authority with that of the Police. Certainly we feel that a letter should have been sent to the Guildhall Street patients about the merger. The latter's partners could have taken a much more active interest in the problems caused by Ayling's advent and not delegated them to the surgery's practice manager.

3.407 However, we consider that the most important lessons to be learnt from this episode concern the difficulties involved when criminal proceedings are pending and professional or disciplinary action is required to protect patient safety. While we accept the need to avoid contaminating criminal proceedings it is clearly unacceptable for patients to be exposed to an unnecessary risk of injury or harm. We understand that Primary Care Trusts (PCTs) now have powers to suspend practitioners. In our view it is vital that PCTs feel able to exercise this new responsibility and that they can demonstrate justifiable use of this authority.

CHAPTER 4
ORGANISATIONAL CULTURE

Introduction

4.1   In previous sections we have described a number of attempts by both patients and staff to raise concerns about the manner or conduct of Clifford Ayling over the years he was in practice, and we have commented on the individuals who could and should have acted on the information then available. It was not until 1998 that complaints about Ayling were investigated and taken seriously. From 1971 until 1998, we have identified a number of missed opportunities when concerns and complaints about Ayling might have been acted on. In this section we look at some of the underlying causes within the culture and systems of the NHS in those years, which seem to us to be as significant in the creation of the missed opportunities and perhaps even more so than the actions of individuals at the time.

4.2   In Chapter 5 we also look at and comment on the complaints procedures in place in the NHS in the years covered by our terms of reference. In relation to underlying causes for missed opportunities we have the following observations to make.

Hearing Patient Voices

4.3   The numbers of patients who told the Inquiry of their unhappiness or distress following treatment by Clifford Ayling was greatly in excess of those who made a contemporaneous complaint, or sought to raise their concerns informally at the time. Rather, patients were, throughout the course of the events studied by the Inquiry, reluctant to complain. A trust in the integrity, honesty and good faith of a doctor was, and remains, a fundamental element of the relationship between patient and doctor. It was a basic and deep belief, shared by doctors and patients alike, that doctors acted in the patient's best interests. Clear and convincing evidence could be needed, before this belief would be questioned – either by patients and other staff members who they might approach. Furthermore, there was a general reluctance amongst patients to challenge a professional. Doctors, as skilled professionals, were widely thought to 'know best'.

> "I can't just ring somebody up to say my doctor's done this. It's not the done sort of thing."

> "I did not voice my concerns at the time because, as a patient, I felt I should trust my doctor."

> "Although I did not like being asked to take all my clothes off I assumed that the examinations were necessary for my health."

4.4   With limited or no previous information of similar situations, it was hard for patients to know whether what they had experienced was normal or justified.

> "I was young and inexperienced and I had nothing to compare this treatment to."

"I did not make a complaint, because although I found these examinations unpleasant, I did not realise that they were unnecessary. Ayling was the only doctor I had visited for contraceptive advice."

4.5   As one nurse in a family planning clinic commented:

"I think that self-doubt about whether any abuse had taken place would probably have been the major factor that would have held, and probably continues to hold, people back from making a complaint in these types of circumstances."

4.6   Others were concerned that they would not be believed, if their word was pitted against that of a doctor. There was a worry about launching a complaint against someone whom they might have to see again, or being labelled a 'complainer', or being removed from a GP's list. To one patient, who described her treatment:

"I was very worried about doing this because I was worried that if I made an accusation or caused trouble that I might be branded as a troublemaker and I might not be able to get into another doctor's practice."

4.7   Another identified two concerns:

"…one, that you may have to see them again, and secondly, you do not want to appear as a habitual complainee, especially about doctors."

4.8   In a small community, to complain might have repercussions:

"[Relatives] were patients of his as well and you sort of have this feeling that you're going to open up a great big hornet's nest."

4.9   In the case of serious sexualised behaviour, this generalised reluctance to complain took on an added dimension. Patients were reluctant to speak of a private, intimate and potentially highly embarrassing situation.

"The whole thing made me feel disgusted and dirty, so I decided not to report the matter"

"It was a very humiliating experience. As a result I did not take the matter any further."

4.10   One nurse spoke of an episode in which she had offered her support to a woman, to enable her to make a formal complaint, but:

"It was quite clear that she just wanted to get out of the clinic."

4.11   Patients felt that they would not be believed if they spoke out, and were afraid that the experience of complaining would be difficult and distressing. Most of the patients who spoke to the Inquiry had no idea, and no means of finding out, that other women had complained of similar experiences. If they had known that they were not alone, they might have been more ready to speak out. But "I couldn't do it on my own".

4.12   Without a formal complaint, the patient experience was unlikely to be examined by those in authority. Systems for capturing patient experience, feedback and comment were almost wholly lacking in the NHS at the time. One patient commented:

> "I feel that I would have made more of an issue of my treatment if there had been a means for expressing my complaint in a less confrontational way."

4.13　Patients lacked knowledge of the complaints procedures, and did not know who to complain to. In the early days especially, the complaints process was not publicised. The first mention of publicity for procedures (other than the information contained on NHS cards) was of the posters that were put up in the South East Kent Hospitals from 1991 onwards.

4.14　If patients did make their way to the right starting point, being told by staff to put complaints in writing discouraged them. For reasons which included the perceived effort and eloquence required and the very subject matter and sensitivity of any such complaint, this was often enough to dissuade patients from pursuing the matter further. Mr David Astley stated:

> "The NHS complaints procedure … relies predominantly on people writing their complaint. "Please put it in writing" I can hear being said on many occasions in the past. I think we have to remember that many of our clientele are not able to write clearly, a clear letter explaining all their feelings because, as we know, some of the incidents that have occurred are deep-seated and extremely difficult to express orally, never mind in writing. So I think to have available a person, a friendly face, someone who could say, "Can I help you? What is the problem?" someone good at listening, someone able to understand what the issues are, I think could have made a significant contribution."

Support for Patients

4.15　Instead, there was an almost complete lack of support available to patients who might have wished to raise a concern, or might have complained. Many patients from whom the Inquiry has heard either tried, or would have liked, to 'test' their experiences in a safe environment before deciding what action to take. They needed to be able to talk to a sympathetic individual, probably a healthcare worker, who was in a position to tell them if what they had experienced was something to be concerned about, or if it was entirely normal.

4.16　One patient told the Inquiry that she would have liked to have approached her own GP:

> "I would have liked him to have reassured me that this was not common practice for a doctor to have allowed this – to have behaved that way in the hospital and treated me like that."

4.17　For many, this 'safe' confidante was not available. There was no formal or 'sign-posted' route to such a person. Staff members to whom patients spoke were, no doubt, well meaning. But the mind-set which is discussed below meant that their experiences were generally discounted or their attempts rebuffed.

4.18   The local Community Health Council (CHC) might, in theory, have provided such a 'safe' source of support. However, it appeared that (despite the excellent work which it did do) it was not generally 'visible' in the community, and was not widely known about. The Inquiry has set out the stories of those women whom it heard either complained, or sought to voice a concern. Only in one case, was any contact made with the CHC. Another woman knew of it, but did not choose to seek its assistance. Such a history is a measure of the challenge faced by the successors to the CHC, to make their organisations visible and accessible to patients. This is a particular issue in the primary care setting, where the Patient Advice and Liaison Service (PALS) cannot be located in every surgery.

4.19   Mark Outhwaite spoke of the need for the NHS to think carefully about: "how we provide those non-threatening initial contacts, but it does not suddenly trigger a whole panoply of official letters and everything else."

4.20   There was a general feeling amongst the women who contributed to the Inquiry that it was wrong that the person who made the complaint should also have to take up the burden of pursuing it. The person to whom the complaint was made should take up that role, helping the patient with tasks such as making a written statement, if one was required. If the NHS is to be seen to value complaints, it has to facilitate them.

4.21   In the GP surgery's setting, there was no independent figure to complain to. The Practice Administrator was Mrs Ayling, who was employed by her husband. It is not a reflection on Mrs Ayling personally to say that she was not seen as an independent figure. Further, we consider that, particularly in a small practice, most surgery staff would have been seen as closely identified with the interests of the practice and its partners, who employed them. The experience of the Ayling patients is supported by the results of a survey, conducted in 1999, by the Public Law Project "Cause for Complaint" (Wallace/Mulcahy, 1999), which identified similar concerns about the requirement to complain directly to the practice.

4.22   The restrictive time limits applied in the primary care setting until at least 1996 caused difficulties for one patient in pursuing her complaint against another GP. More fundamentally, her decision as to which complaint to pursue, out of a number of complaints, was determined by the complexity of the system. She had been told by the CHC that her complaints needed to be sent to three addresses: one for complaints against GPs in the Medway area, one for hospital treatment in Thanet and the last for hospital treatment in the Medway area. As a result, she pursued only one:

        "We had been given three different bodies to write to and we did not feel up to making numerous complaints to many different bodies."

4.23   The complaints procedure reflected the organisational structure of the NHS, not the patient's experience of treatment and care.

4.24   However, although there were many comments made to the Inquiry about the deficiencies of the formal procedures, particularly by healthcare staff who had seen them in operation, it was not these deficiencies which handicapped the women from whom the Inquiry has heard. Rather, the

112

two major handicaps were the difficulty in accessing a complaints procedure in the first place; and the burden placed on a complainant, to 'prosecute' a complaint.

Complaints Handling

4.25   We discuss in more detail in the next section of our Report complaints procedures and our views on the inherent barriers to both patients and staff in accessing and using these procedures. But in addition to these there were cultural issues, which apparently mitigated against the prompt and open handling of complaints which were made.

4.26   When formal complaints were received, the investigations that the Inquiry observed were often protracted or slow. The professional view was that investigations should not involve non-medically qualified people if a clinical issue was at stake. The view of a layperson, or a manager, was not seen as a valuable contribution. If a complaint was made, there was all too often a lack of feedback about the results of a complaint. This applied to staff too. The case of Patient I was an exception: the patient there did receive a clear response to her complaint.

4.27   The fear that patients had, that their word would not be believed, was not unjustified. Speaking of procedures in the early 1980s, a witness commented: 'The emphasis was very much on giving doctors the benefit of the doubt and protecting them against possible unwarranted accusations from their employers and from patients."

4.28   The Inquiry heard the account of one patient who did make a formal complaint to her consultant about Ayling. The consultant was content to see Ayling and to accept his version of events without wider enquiry of, for example, potential witnesses such as nursing staff, and to relay this to the patient's GP. This lack of a truly inquisitive, or inquisitorial approach can also be seen in the case of a staff complaint where the incident which was the subject of a formal complaint was witnessed by a nurse who was able to provide a statement to the Police in 1999, and to the Inquiry. Yet at the time her evidence was either not obtained, or not relied upon, when deciding to accept Ayling's assurances that there had been a "misunderstanding".

4.29   The absence of an inquisitive mindset was reflected in staff reports of concerns as well. One nurse who worked in family planning clinics stated:

> "I told my managers about the concerns raised by clients about Dr Ayling. In general, their response was that clients had to put their concerns in writing for them to be able to take any action."

4.30   A defensive response to complaints was a product of a culture that saw complaints as a challenge, rather than a source of information and an opportunity to learn from that information. Thus, when 'local resolution' was introduced as part of the 1996 reforms to the NHS complaints procedures, a number of practices "found it difficult not to be defensive about complaints and initially went through the motions because it was a requirement of their terms of service, rather than because they felt it would be helpful."

Clinical Freedom and Self Regulation

4.31   If patients were reluctant to speak, doctors and other professionals within the NHS were reluctant to hear. Mark Outhwaite commented on the problems of the complaints procedure, from 1989–1993:

> "…I felt that the procedures were more heavily weighted in favour of the doctor rather than the patient. This was rooted in the predominant culture of the time of 'doctor knows best', the presumption of the effectiveness of self-regulation and an inherent professional defensiveness when challenged."

4.32   The freedom of doctors to regulate their practice formed an integral part of the settlement reached with the professions when the NHS was founded. The doctor's individual clinical autonomy meant that he or she had the responsibility for decisions taken in treating the patient. The underlying assumption was that doctors were skilled professionals working for the benefit of their patients. The "Three Wise Men" procedure within hospitals invoked to tackle concerns about Ayling's conduct in 1980 is a prime example of this cultural approach, with the GMC acting as a 'long-stop' in cases of proven examples of professional misconduct.

4.33   Because they were trusted professionals, they were the best judges of their own skills and professional development needs. Concerns for quality in practice were slow to emerge. The RCN told the Inquiry: "During the 1970s there was no expectation that patients would be provided with care that was not adequate." To speak of supervision or performance management by managers, during this period, would be not merely inaccurate but anachronistic. For the major part of the period under consideration by the Inquiry, the accepted role of managers was to provide clinicians with the setting and support needed to treat patients, but not to interfere with their judgments. On the contrary, the prevailing culture was for consultants to be seen as independent of management and the more idiosyncratic, the better. At the Inquiry David Astley stated:

> "But certainly, in the time the Inquiry is looking back on, the more idiosyncratic and the more – in a sense – the loner the consultant, often the way more that person will be championed as being an excellent consultant; that is part of the behaviour-set that was appropriate at the time: to be seen to be independent, independent of management and working to the best interests of your patients. That was the culture that was pervading at the time. It is not any more."

4.34   Mark Outhwaite explained, that from his perspective as an NHS manager he perceived that the prevailing culture amongst GPs was that:

> "… at that time, and in many years previously, you did not rat on your colleagues. You know, the concept of challenging a peer or raising an issue about your peer outside your peer group was letting the side down.

> "I think also there was a feeling that they were professionals and therefore professional self-regulation was an important duty which had to be done. How well that was undertaken varied, depending upon the diligence of the LMC and peer group. It was not something that is

unique to general practice, as we have seen from other problems in other parts of the country as well as in East Kent. There was not a culture of sharing concerns. General practice is an extremely parochial affair. You move to a practice and you practice there virtually for life. That is changing, but it is – it is a very tight-knit community and clearly a GP is going to be concerned if he says something about a colleague, to which there is what he might think too much of a knee-jerk reaction from management, how is he going to deal with the fact that he is going to be living next to that colleague or doing out-of-hours cover with that colleague for the next 20 years."

4.35   The introduction of 'general management' from 1984 made little immediate difference. Few doctors entered management. The Inquiry was told by one who did that she was seen as having crossed to the 'other side'. Dr Voysey spoke of her relationship with her former consultant colleagues when she became Unit General Manager:

"Well, I rather thought that they would help me in my managerial role and the first time I attended a Medical Staff Committee in my new role as manager I actually said, "Now, you're all going to help me to do this, aren't you?" And in unison they smiled at me and said, "No, you're a manager now. You can tell us what you want to do and we will tell you whether we like it or not".

4.36   When the post of Medical Director was introduced within Trusts from 1991 onwards, this was the first time that a doctor was given the responsibility to investigate and challenge poor performance by his peers. The importance of the position can also be seen as a measure of the restricted powers of managers, at that time. It needed an influential clinician, respected by his peers, to investigate and manage concerns about performance effectively. One general manager reported to the Inquiry that, without substantial pre-existing evidence of misconduct or incompetence, a doctor's peers, who had the task of considering the accusation, were unlikely to assist or even acquiesce in any fact-finding exercise or investigation.

4.37   Doctors' reluctance to criticise colleagues had (and continues to have) many roots. One strand derives from an understanding of medical uncertainties, that there are often no sure answers in medicine and more than one reasonable way to tackle a problem. Another, allied strand is the perception that each doctor is similarly vulnerable to challenge, to error and to blame: so 'there but for the grace of God go I".

4.38   Thus, as Dr Sarkhel made plain, not only could he not state unequivocally that Ayling's practice was unreasonable, but his own too could be susceptible to challenge too: "I'm not the only doctor... specialising in genito-urinary medicine or whatever. My practice could be criticised quite easily…"

4.39   These reactions were not unique to east Kent. A GP quoted in Rosenthal's study of 'The Incompetent Doctor' said:

"If we criticise, we'll be criticised. It's all so marginal; it's difficult. GPs are not good at confronting a colleague, and those who are incompetent isolate themselves. If we all complained about each other all the time, we're all vulnerable."

4.40   Forgiveness, rather than confrontation, was a likely response to such pressures. Furthermore, if doctors were wary of criticising one another, it was even more likely that criticism by lay people would not be recognised as valid. Deference to doctors' professional experience and views was deeply rooted. Fedelma Winkler, Chief Executive of the Kent Family Health Services Authority from 1993 to 1995, told the Inquiry of the difficulties in re-shaping disciplinary procedures for GPs. She regarded them as being dominated by the professionals:

> "So we have to also bear that in mind when we are actually training non-professionals to engage in this kind of work, that there has to be a lot of support and development of the culture for the lay members as well, because they very often tend to seek a professional view of something that is not an issue."

4.41   A patient's complaint was, and remains, a major threat to a doctor's self image, or social identity, as a caring and competent professional. Professor Forsythe, Area Medical Officer, Kent AHA, commented:

> "by and large, the medical profession feels a sense of total failure when they are criticised and cannot see the benefit in criticism actually improving the overall quality of the service."

Staff Hierarchies

4.42   The staff that were in the best position to judge Ayling's hospital practice were those who worked most closely with him, on a day-to-day basis. Few were doctors: most were nurses or midwives. The Inquiry heard that, during the 1970s and 1980s, nurses and midwives were reluctant to criticise doctors. There was a professional hierarchy. Observing its rules, nurses or midwives would not feel able to challenge or question doctors. Heather Nightingale Area Nurse (Personnel) Kent AHA commented:

> " it is quite a thing for one professional to make a challenge to another professional, [particularly] when the medical profession was thought to be more senior than the nurse."

4.43   To another member of staff:

> "…you think that doctors are above reproach. I certainly did … 20 years ago. They were the Gods of the hospital, if you like, and I personally wouldn't have challenged any of them."

4.44   Jennifer Cook, Staff Midwife/Sister, Thanet District Hospital, told the Inquiry that her recollection was that challenges from an enrolled nurse were fruitless:

> "If you challenged him, which we did, he would say, "I have my own protocols to follow and this is my practice. I'm the doctor. You called me. This is what I want to do.""

4.45   Moreover, she did not consider that she could necessarily look for support from her senior officers:

116

"People above staff midwife level, staff nurse level, remained aloof, were almost a different society to the rest of the juniors."

4.46 But such senior staff had difficulties too:

"We were always made to feel that it wasn't our place to speak directly to the doctor, whatever the concern."

4.47 In sum:

"In those days doctors worked in their preferred way under the umbrella of "clinical freedom" and clinical practice were not evidence based as it is today. It would have been very difficult for a midwife to complain to him about his conduct, let alone a nursing auxiliary to challenge this practice."

4.48 Doctors had the power to make nurses' or midwives' lives very difficult. This coupled with an environment in which complaints were not welcomed, and no action appeared to follow even if a concern was voiced by a member of staff, discouraged staff from raising or pursing issues further, or getting involved in disputes. Rather, they would fall back on the use of those protective mechanisms which they had the power to implement. For example, ensuring that hospital policy on the use of chaperones was followed; and providing blankets for patients.

4.49 This same hierarchy was evident amongst doctors when training. The Inquiry received written evidence from a medical student, who had worked alongside Ayling and observed his behaviour and the response this evoked from patients. She would not have considered reporting this, and would not have been asked her opinion of Ayling's approach to patients. Neither would the patients. Junior doctors depended on references from consultants to obtain their next job.

Lack of Openness
4.50 The cultural lack of openness was compounded by the absence of structural guarantees of protection to those who did raise unpopular issues. There was no formal system for staff to raise concerns during the 1970s and 1980s. Instead, any member of staff with a concern was expected simply to raise this with their superior. It was presumed that staff would know that this was the right thing to do. This system of reporting information up the chain of command, instead of one having a person designated as dealing with these complaints, relied on the personal qualities of the complainant's superiors for its success. If concerns were raised, they were rarely discussed with those who had raised them, and there was a lack of feedback as to the results. This, too, discouraged any practice of raising concerns.

4.51 It was not until 1993 that the first guidance on speaking out about concerns was published. This required that procedures should be established to enable concerns to be voiced, both informally and formally and stated that the working culture of the NHS should foster openness. At that time, the context was mainly concerns about so-called 'gagging clauses' in new Trust contracts, and had no direct application to general practitioners. There was no central guidance on adverse incident reporting schemes. In

1998, the Public Disclosure Act provided the first guarantees of protection if 'protected disclosures' were made, and required Trusts to develop policies upon the subject. More detail about 'whistleblowing' in the NHS is given in Annex 8.

4.52 Throughout the period of the Inquiry, we heard of no formal training for staff in how to handle the expression of concerns and complaints by patients, whether at the front line or at the top of the management structure. Thus nursing staff in the family planning services were not empowered to act on the concerns they heard from patients and had to refer these to their managers for advice on how to respond, and equally, it would seem that in 1992 Merle Darling, as Director of Nursing for the South East Kent Hospitals, was simply given the responsibility for managing the hospitals' complaints procedure. The need for specific training in handling complaints has now been acknowledged in the most recent proposals for improving the NHS complaints system.

A Failure to Hear

4.53 Allegations of abuse were rationalised as "misunderstandings" (as was the incident with the student nurse in 1992), explained as "old-fashioned practice" (as Penny Jed told patients who were concerned about Ayling's practice of conducting vaginal examinations in early pregnancy) or were presented as action taken for "the patient's own good" (as Mr Patterson told Patient D and her parents). We recognise this as another form of deference to doctors.

4.54 Below the level of a formal complaint, there were generalised concerns expressed by both patients and staff about Ayling. During the course of the Inquiry, witnesses who had been told on more than one occasion of concerns about Ayling were deeply remorseful that they had not recognised what they had been told. As Mr Patterson said to us, he had been naïve in his views in 1981 over what Patient D had told him about Ayling's sexualised comments. Penny Jed reiterated to us that she had had "no insight" into what patients were telling her when confronted by the evidence from Ayling's former patients about the concerns which they believed they had put to her, and at the time did not think to explore any further with them the "dislike" or "uncomfortable feelings" they gave as reasons for wishing to change GPs.

4.55 Mr Patterson, perhaps, put this failure to hear most explicitly when he acknowledged to the Inquiry that midwives might have expressed their concerns in a "coded" way which he had not "read".

Lack of Clear Professional Guidance

4.56 GMC guidance existed from 1987 onwards on the duty to report concerns about a colleague whose performance or conduct threatened patient safety (to use a modern term). However, early versions did not speak with a clear or unequivocal voice. Until 1992, this advice was hidden under a title, "Disparagement of professional colleagues", which conveyed the respect for professional solidarity and caution, rather than patient safety. Whilst a less cautious heading was substituted in 1992, "Comment about professional colleagues", it was not until the publication of "Good

Medical Practice" in 1995, that the advice became unequivocal. Under the heading *"Your duty to protect all patients"* this stated:

> "You must protect patients when you believe that a doctor's or other colleague's health, conduct or performance is a threat to them."

4.57   Witnesses such as Dr Pickering said that there was a general feeling that you should not make allegations, or launch an investigation, without concrete evidence. Acting on insufficient evidence might lead to accusations of defamation of character. A patient's word – especially if not in writing – was not sufficient 'evidence'.

4.58   Professional guidance to nurses and midwives did not provide clear guidance on what to do if a fellow-professional was suspected to be a risk to patients, either. The nursing regulatory body did not publish its first Code of Conduct until the early 1980s. This Code was based on ethical concepts, none of which presupposed the need to report fellow health workers. No reference to the need to report fellow workers for unprofessional or abusive behaviour therefore exists within this Code. The third Code, published a decade later in 1992, was the first to reflect the societal decline in the absolute trust that had been placed in health care staff. Clause 13 required, for the first time that nurses:

> "…report to an appropriate person or authority where it appears that the health or safety of colleagues is at risk, as such circumstances may compromise standards of practice or care."

4.59   Furthermore, the Inquiry heard complaints that the GMC was remote, and reluctant to take action. 'Solid' evidence was required and written complaints were not always adequately followed up, thus discouraging recourse to the GMC. When Dr Voysey dealt with the patient complaint received in 1987:

> "…my feeling was that the GMC would pay no attention whatsoever to an unsubstantiated verbal complaint, against somebody who until then had had no suggestion of improper conduct of this nature."

4.60   During his evidence to the Inquiry Professor Forsythe stated that:

> "By and large I supported the General Medical Council view that it is the job of the employer to deal with their employee as a matter of first importance, and so they would often await the outcome of the – what evidence the employer was going to do with the problem doctor before they would move, but over and beyond that their speed of reaction was quite appalling in the old days. It is better now because they are running in parallel professional misconduct sessions."

4.61   The history of the development of a code of professional accountability for nurses and midwives is given in Annex 9.

Patient Confidentiality

4.62   Dr Anderson, a GP at the White House surgery, stressed to the Inquiry the conflict between the GMC's advice to report concerns about colleagues' performance or conduct, and its advice that patient confidentiality must be respected, if the patient was capable of giving or withholding her consent to disclosure. Speaking of the latter advice, he said:

> "I think it boldly states that if the patient is incapable of giving consent, then you should do something, and if the patient is capable of giving consent, then you would be in breach of GMC guidance were you to do it without their consent."

4.63   He wrote:

> "Pre-1994 I believe that the onus was on the patient to make the complaint to the FPC, GMC or the Police. It was therefore their choice, and without their consent a doctor could do little… It is still the case today that a doctor can do little to take the matter further without the consent of the patient"

4.64   To Dr Maitra:

> "if I do forward anything without the consent of the people, I would breach the law… I couldn't do anything without patient's consent"

4.65   To Dr Calver:

> "I would also have required the patient to put the complaint in writing and authorise me to take action on their behalf before I would feel able to act, so as to protect patient confidentiality."

4.66   This was partly an issue of patient autonomy and choice:

> "It is ultimately up to the patient to decide whether they wish to take the matter further."

4.67   Although in 1999, the Courts took the view that patient data that had been anonymised was no longer subject to a duty of confidence,[1] this was not clearly recognised before that date. For example, in its guidance upon the implementation of the 1996 complaints procedures, the NHS Executive wrote:

> "Where anonymised information about patients and/or third parties would suffice, identifiable information should be omitted. Anonymisation does not of itself remove the legal duty of confidence but, where all reasonable steps are taken to ensure that the recipient is unable to trace the patient/third party identity, it may be passed on for a justifiable purpose. Where a patient or third party has expressly refused permission for the use of information, then it can only be used where there is an overriding public interest in doing so."

4.68   During the Inquiry, patients suggested that there needed to be a wider recognition that patient safety was more important that patient confidentiality.

Disciplinary Procedures

4.69   Disciplinary procedures were complex, time-consuming and expensive to operate. The standard of proof for establishing misconduct on the part of a

1   *R v Department of Health ex parte Source Informatics Ltd* (2000) 1 All ER 786: (2000) 52 BMLR 65: (2000) 2 WLR 940.

doctor was 'beyond reasonable doubt' so as to match the tests applied by the GMC. 'Exporting' a problem was one solution with certainty of outcome. As Professor Forsythe commented: "To deny a problem is easier if responsibility for dealing with it lies at another level."

4.70 'Exporting' a problem ensured that a doctor causing concern no longer worked within one's own organisation, but did not address wider issues of protecting future patients; and it encouraged an attitude to 'work around' a problem rather than tackling it vigorously. The decision made in 1993 by the South East Kent Hospitals not to renew Ayling's contract, and the emphasis placed in subsequent correspondence with Ayling's medical defence organisation on the absence of any disciplinary action associated with this decision, is an example we identified of this expedient approach to resolving problems. As Dr Ann Farebrother said to us, in dealing with allegations about Ayling's approach to patients attending the family planning services, she "took the easy way out" in removing his name from the list of approved locum doctors for the service.

4.71 The NHS reforms of 1992 increased the authority at hospital level to tackle problems of performance amongst clinicians, and the appointment of Medical Directors enhanced this. As Dr Padley explained:

> "The reason I wanted to be a medical director to take it forward is because I felt that around that sort of time the systems that these people were trying to use and the way the Health Service was operating, and the controls and performance management of doctors was very lacking and it was very difficult for people to make any progress, given the way things were arranged. Trust status actually did improve this a great deal."

4.72 There were very few policies on the appropriateness of suspension. In 1987, there appeared to be none within the KCH – but there is no reason to think that this was out of line with prevailing NHS practice. As far as we know, guidance on suspensions was not generally given until the Department of Health issued main guidance in a circular sent out in 1994.

4.73 In the general practice setting, the picture was no better. In 1998, complaints reached the EKHA and it decided to take action against Ayling. However, the EKHA lacked the power to suspend him prior to his trial or removal from the medical register. To achieve suspension, it had to persuade the NHS Tribunal to act. But to Mr Outhwaite – the NHS Tribunal "was an even more complex set of processes than the GMC." He continued:

> "...the general view within the land of Family Health Service Authority, and indeed our predecessor to the family practitioners committees was that the NHS Tribunal was the last vestige of a set of practices and approach, which actually was 20 or 30 years out-of-date, and indeed certainly the experience of other FHSAs, who had taken issues to the Tribunal, was that the Tribunal seemed to be more concerned with protecting the doctor rather than the patient. And so the reservations I had was I was not entirely hopeful that we were going to get any form of speedy resolution than that being offered by the GMC."

4.74   The limitations of the mechanisms then in place, and the lack of a
        sustained focus upon patient safety, are illustrated too by the events
        surrounding Dr Harold Shipman's suspension from practice. According to
        the Shipman Inquiry's First Report:

> *"The Police had been attempting for some time to prevent Shipman
> from continuing to practise. They had informed the GMC of the
> position in August 1998 but were told that the GMC could do nothing
> until Shipman had been convicted of an offence. On 18th August, the
> West Pennine Health Authority contacted the NHS Tribunal, which
> had power to suspend him, but a hearing by the Tribunal could not be
> arranged before 29th September. After that hearing, the Tribunal's
> decision to suspend Shipman from practice was not communicated to
> the Health Authority until 15th October. The Health Authority was
> able to take control of the practice only after the expiration of the
> period for an appeal against that decision, on 29th October 1998."*

4.75   In the criminal process which begun in late 1998, the EKHA took 'second
        place' behind the Police and Crown Prosecution Services. Co-ordination
        was, on the whole, reasonable, but in the critical case of Ayling's
        application for bail before the High Court, communications failed. The
        Health Authority was given late notice of the application, and was not able
        to contribute its own expertise or views on the proposed bail arrangements
        – despite the fact that it would subsequently be asked to play a major role
        in making them 'work'.

Preference for the Use of Informal Systems

4.76   Medical sociologists have observed that doctors, like other professions,
        develop informal systems to deal with "problem" colleagues.[2] Methods
        include not only the 'quiet word' but also protective mechanisms such as
        shifting work, or certain types of work, away from a weaker colleague.
        Such informal methods are more commonly used than formal ones –
        partly because of the difficulties in invoking formal procedures, but also
        because formal action almost inevitably means raising the problem
        outside professional ranks, by bringing it to the attention of managers.
        Formal systems are "fallbacks", invoked only when nothing else works
        and the problem is too disruptive to be tolerated.

4.77   The preference for informal methods can been seen repeatedly during the
        course of the Ayling story. In the general practice community, it led to a
        number of attempts to 'have a word' with Ayling such as the interventions
        of Dr Montgomery and Dr Calver, as well as the attempt to invoke the
        assistance of the LMC, via Dr Robinson. The events we have described
        can be set against research findings, in the form of the view of a regional
        general practice advisor, quoted by Rosenthal:

4.78   "Problems go on for a very long time. Other GPs may be suspicious but
        they don't want to delve too deeply because if they know too much, they
        will have to take action. So the problem may go on for a very long time. It

---

2   Rosenthal, M: "Dealing with Medical Malpractice: the British and Swedish Experience."
        (1987) London: Tavistock.

has to be absolutely catastrophic and threatening patient harm for someone to interfere."[3]

4.79   In the hospital sector, it took the form of the decision to direct the complaint from Patient C and her husband to the "Three Wise Men" or Special Professional Panel. As a confidential and peer-led body, the "Three Wise Men" were a semi-formal system, discreet and low-key compared to the formal complaints process. As Mr Astley explained, "it was a confidential procedure." As a result, feedback to patients about any investigation was unlikely:

> "I think where the NHS's complaints procedure was in place and there was feedback required to a patient, that may happen regarding a medical staff, but in relation to the use of the "Three Wise Men" procedure, I think the likelihood of any feedback to the patients is very unlikely."

Absence of Audit, Supervision or Performance Management

4.80   In the hospital setting, Ayling was an employee and was nominally subject to the direction of management. However, the self-regulating status of clinicians meant that, throughout the period of his hospital career, managers did not have an accepted right to intervene in clinical affairs. Rather, each clinician was responsible for the adequacy of his or her own professional practice and for keeping abreast of medical developments.

4.81   There were no appraisal or assessment schemes in operation in the hospital setting at the time, and no formal or structured requirements to take part in any form of continuing professional development (although applications for study leave to attend conferences and meetings were made periodically by Ayling throughout the 1970s and 1980s when employed at Thanet and Canterbury Hospitals, and approved by the hospital authorities). When audit meetings were first introduced at Thanet and Canterbury – and the Inquiry heard that they were first introduced, in the form of perinatal mortality and morbidity meetings – these followed the predominant model of the time. Audit was an educational process, confidential and peer-led. It aimed to improve clinical practice by discussion and example. But it lacked 'follow-up' systems to ensure that lessons were both learned and implemented. Doctors tended to audit what was easy to study rather than what was important. Furthermore, 'soft' issues concerning patient experiences were regarded as a lower priority than 'hard' issues concerning adverse clinical events.

Clinical Assistants

4.82   Detail on the role and employment of clinical assistants in the NHS is set out in Annex 3 but the status of clinical assistants within the hospital hierarchy in Kent caused confusion. As Professor Forsythe said at the Inquiry:

> "Clinical assistants, of course, were a very peculiar post in my day. …they were neither a training job or a proper career job and they usually had limited contracts. The amount of them that existed varied

---

3   Quoted in Rosenthal, M: "The Incompetent Doctor: Behind Closed Doors" (1995) Buckingham: Open University Press.

enormously across the NHS. In East Kent, it was a rather (inaudible) they were very prevalent."

4.83   Their status within the medical hierarchy was generally seen as being of roughly the same level as a registrar, though some thought of them as being more closely equivalent to a senior house officer. They were not, however, training posts.

4.84   As a clinical assistant, Ayling was responsible for the care of patients who were under the overall supervision of a consultant. However, the Inquiry heard that these consultants did not consider themselves responsible for supervising Ayling's clinical performance, once his training had come to an end. At that point, he was regarded as a professional capable of operating independently, and calling for consultant help when it was needed. As Mr Fullman said, he had supervised Ayling whilst still a registrar and satisfied himself of his competence. But he had then;

> "…obtained the MRCOG, which is the United Kingdom specialist qualification for obstetricians and gynaecologists. He was therefore considered to be a trained obstetrician and gynaecologist, so we would not supervise him."

4.85   Further, as time went on, he was increasingly regarded as an experienced practitioner, and was elected to Fellowship of the Royal College of Obstetricians and Gynaecologists in 1985.

4.86   The lack of clarity as to responsibility for Ayling's performance was compounded by his move into general practice. Thus, in 1993, there was confusion as to whether any report to the GMC, or other action, should be initiated by his employers within the hospital sector, or the KFHSA, as the body with responsibility for commissioning family health services and which had some oversight of local GPs.

Workload

4.87   The Inquiry heard that Ayling was useful. He filled a gap, being willing to provide essential emergency cover at weekends. He enabled clinical services to be maintained, as is evident in his re-employment as a clinical assistant in colposcopy in 1987 at Thanet Hospital and for services to be provided on a number of hospital sites, as is apparent from the circumstances of his employment by South East Kent Hospitals to provide cover for consultant staff at the smaller hospitals in the Unit.

4.88   The Thanet and KCH hospitals were understaffed, by the standards of the present day, and the consultants were stretched 'thinly'. In such conditions, there appears to have been little peer contact, and limited opportunities for regular peer review or learning. We do not consider that study leave granted on an occasional basis to attend courses, would be an adequate substitute for these informal methods of avoiding the erosion of skills.

4.89   The timing and location of Ayling's sessions increased his clinical isolation. Dr Voysey was asked:

> "Q: Going back to Dr Ayling, you have said in your statement that at no time did you have reason to doubt his competence. Is there any evidence that you are aware of, again in the case of Dr Ayling, that suggested that his clinical skills might not have been as carefully evaluated or scrutinised because of the need to keep him on to provide junior doctor cover?
>
> "A: Unless there was a complaint, I don't think that consultants would have been involved in his work, i.e. most of it was emergency surgery, and I don't remember anybody ever coming to watch and see what he did."

4.90   Isolation was compounded by the number of hours worked. There is evidence that Ayling himself was overworked, at least at times – in particular, after he took on commitments as a general practitioner as well as his hospital sessions.

4.91   The Inquiry found it difficult to believe that Ayling's usefulness did not compromise the ability or the willingness of those who could and should have done so to assess critically the service that he was providing, and the manner in which it was being provided.

Chaperones

4.92   The role of a chaperone in the conduct of intimate examinations was a matter of interest to the Inquiry, not only because of the importance attached to this as part of Ayling's revised bail conditions but also because of the significance attached to this as part of the 'coping' strategies developed by nurses and midwives to handle their concerns about Ayling in the hospital setting, and embarrassment and distress caused to patients and witnessed by nurses in family planning clinics when Ayling apparently ignored the chaperone policy for the service.

4.93   The role of a chaperone is ambiguous. The Inquiry learned of a range of expectations of a chaperone: to protect a patient from humiliation or distress, to support and comfort a patient, to protect a doctor and to identify untoward behaviour. The Inquiry also heard that the presence of a chaperone could be a deterrent to the disclosure of sensitive and important clinical information. Professional advice varies on the use of chaperones. The Royal College of Obstetricians and Gynaecologists (RCOG) advises that 'chaperones should be available'. The GMC advises that 'a chaperone should be offered'. The lack of clear expectation of a chaperone's presence is compounded by the lack of recognised training for the role – the differing interpretations by Ayling and the EKHA over what constituted a 'suitably qualified' person to act as a chaperone in accordance with Ayling's revised bail conditions is illustrative of this. An 'unqualified' chaperone is not well placed to intervene in an inappropriate clinical examination: they may offer protection against acts of gross indecency but not a more subtle form of abuse or misuse of a professional position.

4.94   Furthermore, the capacity within a GP surgery to provide a chaperone when requested is limited so that, for example, as Ayling indicated at his criminal trial, if the practice nurse was unavailable, a practice receptionist would be called on to provide a chaperone for patients if required. Staff resources are clearly a limiting factor on the routine availability of chaperones in the GP surgery although it was made clear to the Inquiry that staffing levels in the hospital setting could also pose problems.

4.95   The presence of a chaperone did not, the Inquiry was told, apparently prevent Ayling from acting unprofessionally and nor did the presence of more senior nursing and midwifery staff apparently deter him from making distasteful and unprofessional comments. Furthermore, even after the presence of a chaperone was mandated by Ayling's revised bail conditions in 1998, the Inquiry was told by one patient that the chaperone who was present at her consultation with Ayling in 2000 was sent out of the room by him from time to time.

Independent Contractor Status

4.96   Until the 1990s, the FPC was basically an administrative body, dealing with 'pay and rations' and little else. It had no responsibility for the management of GP performance and standards.

4.97   In 1990, the KFHSA was introduced as a new organisation with a new function. The concept of management was introduced for the first time. However, the new systems took some time to take effect, both structurally and culturally. Furthermore, the changes introduced were limited. The KFHSA and then the EKHA still possessed limited powers of oversight. This was reflected, for example, in the limited access that Health Authorities had to practices, which meant (for instance) that they could not scrutinise the complaints made about them. GPs' annual reports were meant to include statistics on the number of complaints made to the practice. But the figures were not always reliable, and, in any event, information about the bare numbers was of little value in identifying problems. There was little monitoring of GPs' performance. The only routine monitoring was by way of prescribing analyses, which were based on cost only. The EKHA could only make recommendations, or, where there were breaches of regulations, report these to the necessary bodies.

> "In the case of primary care the independent contractor status made things more complex and the room for manoeuvre locally was constrained to that which would be negotiated with Local Medical Committees."

> "Their contract was negotiated centrally, and our ability to work with them locally was constrained, the Red Book which sort of governed how they were paid and other things was fairly circumscribed and, therefore, if you wanted to do anything out of the ordinary, then that was a relationship you had to negotiate with people like the LMC."

Local Medical Committee

4.98   A Local Medical Committee (LMC) was (and remains) the body recognised by successive NHS Acts as the professional organisation representing GPs to the FPC (and its successors). Its membership is elected by local GPs, and its funding is largely derived from a compulsory annual statutory levy on those GPs. LMCs have a statutory role in the handling of concerns and complaints about the performance or conduct of

GPs in their area, particularly in respect of proposed action over specific problems of compliance with the terms and conditions of the national contract. FPCs and their successors have a statutory duty to consult the LMC on matters affecting GPs' terms of service, complaints and the investigation of certain matters of professional conduct. As Professor Forsythe told the Inquiry:

> "The LMC has a dual role being both the doctors' friend and also has a role to ensure that problems with defaulting GPs are addressed…it has rather an ambiguous relationship with the NHS."

4.99   The part played by the LMC in the Ayling story was illustrative of this ambiguity.

4.100 On two occasions, GPs who had concerns about Ayling's clinical practices spoke to the Secretary of the LMC. Dr Pickering went to the LMC in 1993 with the information from the transfer interviews at the White House surgery. Dr Calver similarly spoke with the LMC in around 1996 when he received troubling information via SEADOC about Ayling. The response of the LMC to Dr Pickering was to offer a reassurance (subsequently proved to be false) that action was being taken. Dr Calver was shocked and surprised that the LMC was already well aware of the problem over Ayling's clinical practice. Certainly Dr Pickering believed that by informing the LMC of the concerns about Ayling, he had passed the responsibility for further action on to an appropriate authority However, it does not appear that the LMC ever contacted the FHSA to pass on their knowledge about Ayling or the specific information given to them by Drs Pickering and Calver.

4.101 In his evidence to the Inquiry, Professor Forsythe observed that LMCs;

> "…have a statutory responsibility that the Family Practitioner Committee have to deal with them, but, from the GP's point of view they were almost their friend and counsel in helping them with problems. So in that sense, the Local Medical Committee – you could never be quite sure whether they were thinking of more of the GP's needs or whether the organisational needs were more important."

4.102 The statutory role of the LMC is reactive rather than proactive. It has the right to be consulted over the development of policies and procedures which would affect its GPs, such as the introduction of the complaints procedure described by Fedelma Winkler in 1996, and it will vigorously support individual doctors in difficulty. But it is also identified as a body to which GPs might take perceived problems of professional or ethical conduct in their colleagues. Thus, when Dr Anderson consulted his medical defence organisation in 1998 about what he should do with the information he held from the White House surgery transfer interviews, he was asked if the LMC had been approached. Over the years, GMC guidance to doctors on their professional responsibilities has also identified the LMC as a source of advice. But there does not appear to be any commensurate guidance for LMCs on what responsibility they might have to act on information concerning patient safety.

4.103   As Mark Oithwaite commented to the Inquiry:

> "...they were jealous guardians of other doctors, [of] independent contractor status. The nature of LMC interventions differed depending upon the quality of both the Secretary of the LMC and the mandate given to them by the Chair and members of the LMC."

4.104   The Inquiry heard that the practice of LMCs with regard to sharing information with other organisations has varied, and continues to vary, considerably across the country. LMCs stand outside the accountability framework of the NHS and so are not answerable to the NHS for the decisions they make.

Single Handed Practitioners

4.105   We have discussed the limited supervision of Ayling's work as a clinical assistant. As a single-handed general practitioner, Ayling lacked colleagues with whom he could have exchanged ideas and information on a daily basis. This would have been an important means of up-dating clinical knowledge and practice – an informal form of 'peer review'. We do not consider that the fact that Dr Ribet, who had retired as a partner but continued to carry out a number of weekly sessions at the practice, filled this gap.

Family Planning Services

4.106   Family Planning clinics have historically been organised on a 'sessional' basis, with few, if any, full-time doctors employed, and most doctors providing only a limited number of sessions per week. This made it difficult to judge whether doctors were following appropriate and adequate procedures, as in the case of Ayling. Ayling's behaviour in the family planning clinic setting was a particularly acute example of the wider problem faced by the NHS in 'pooling' information about doctors who worked across a number of sectors.

Organisational Change

4.107   During the period of the Inquiry, but from the late 1980s in particular, the NHS has undergone a number of significant reorganisations. There have been significant changes in roles and in the personnel which have filled them. Any such re-organisation, whilst aimed at improving patient care, is likely to have unintended side effects.

4.108   Although Ayling's position within east Kent as a GP and as a clinical assistant was itself untouched by NHS reorganisations, we believe the consequences of these were apparent in the way the concerns about Ayling were handled. The demise of the Kent AHA in 1984 meant that there was no overarching body at which similar problems in the hospitals in its DHAs might be recognised, and the emphasis on independent management units even within DHAs such as the Canterbury and Thanet DHA disinclined their managers to share information.

4.109   When the new roles of Medical Advisor to the FHSAs and Medical Directors within Trusts were established in 1990/1991, the new incumbents had to define their roles. Dr Savege spoke of the lack of definition of his role when he began:

> "I went into post with almost a clean sheet of paper and the role developed as experience developed."

Information Sharing

4.110   One of the consequences of the re-organisations, and the shifts in personnel which accompanied them, was a loss of 'corporate memory'. The Inquiry was told that many people who might be sources of knowledge or history had taken opportunities to move or been made redundant. Filing systems were fragmented by a series of moves and handovers to different successor organisations.

4.111   A key example of this fragmentation can be seen in the EKHA's knowledge of events of 1991–1993. When in early 1998, complaints about Ayling were made, it was not able to make any links with the events of 1991–1993, as the KFHSA's file on the matter had not been transferred to the new health authority. If the EKHA had had this information at the time when they made the initial referral to the GMC, it would have helped to establish a pattern of behaviour.

4.112   Separate lines of accountability for responding to concerns about doctors in the primary, community and secondary care sectors meant that it was difficult to make connections about the performance of doctors who worked for different organisations. Nor was there clarity on who was responsible for such doctors, if problems about their performance were highlighted. The attempt to share concerns about Ayling derived from the family planning services and the South East Kent Hospitals with the FHSA in 1993, and the relative informality of the process, left an uncertain outcome in terms of responsibility for taking these forward to the GMC with the consequence that no formal action was taken. The Inquiry felt that the FHSA had had the problem passed over to them, despite the evidence, which would have been required to support a referral to the GMC, being located in the hospital and family planning services.

4.113   The Inquiry was told that the creation of Hospital Trusts in the 1990s hardened these fault lines, as some Trusts were more concerned to manage their reputations than to share information about clinical performance or other problems.

4.114   Sharing information proactively on clinical performance was limited to informal professional networks, if shared at all. The response of the LMC to concerns raised by Dr Calver in that they knew of Ayling as the doctor "who didn't wear gloves" when conducting internal examinations is one such example.

Experience of Handling Serious Untoward Incidents Involving Criminal Proceedings

4.115   The situation which faced the EKHA in 1998 was a complicated one, involving many actors. It was also protracted, not being fully resolved until 2000. Co-ordination of the many processes, and the bodies leading each one, was potentially complex. It involved many patients, the GMC, the police, the NHS Tribunal, the Ayling and Guildhall Street surgeries, the Regional Health Authority and the Department of Health. The criminal, NHS and GMC processes competed for priority. Health authority staff lacked not only previous experience of such a situation, but readily available advice on how to handle it. There was a lack of guidelines about sharing information with the police, and, in particular, on the steps which the NHS bodies should take to avoid being accused of contaminating evidence or preventing a fair trial. Mark Outhwaite commented that, although there had been some experience gained locally as a result of dealing with the Rodney Ledward affair, that had lacked the complicating factor of criminal proceedings:

> "Where there have not been criminal issues in play, we have – that has been easier. Certainly with a previous – the Ledward incident, there was a much more open approach to the sharing of information, because at that stage there were not criminal proceedings going on, the clinicians met with women as a patient group, and indeed, we specifically as an authority funded the support to create a patient group, we provided that money. I think, in this particular case, again, it was a worry about contaminating criminal proceedings, and therefore I would go back to my original point about having a clear protocol about who deals with communications: are these individuals treated as complainants in the NHS or potentially are they treated as victims within the police Victim Support Service, or is there some mixture of the two? But that is then effectively communicated."

4.116 The consequence was that patients caught up in this, and staff on the periphery such as the Practice Manager of the Guildhall Street surgery, felt they were left unsupported and uninformed through a lengthy and novel process with an uncertain outcome. Patients in particular commented to the Inquiry on the consistency of support they received from the Police in contrast to that offered by the NHS.

Conclusion

4.117 In the year of Ayling's conviction and imprisonment, the Government produced its plans for a National Health Service that was more responsive to those who pay for and use its services. Many of the themes we have identified as contributing to the handling of complaints and concerns in the NHS of the years covered by our Inquiry's terms of reference have been identified as requiring further or new action and in Chapter 6 we look at the NHS today to assess how the changes that have been introduced since Ayling's trial and conviction might mitigate a repetition of another Ayling. A key feature of action on organisational and process change in the NHS since the publication of the NHS Plan in 2000 is the emphasis placed on putting the patient at the centre of health care services, both in terms of assuring the quality of their care and learning from their experience of care.

CHAPTER 5
HANDLING OF CONCERNS AND COMPLAINTS

Introduction

5.1   We are required by our terms of reference to examine the way the NHS
        handled complaints and concerns about Ayling. In previous sections we
        have commented on the handling of individual complaints which were
        made about Ayling during the period covered by our Inquiry. In this
        section we describe the development of NHS complaints procedures and
        the procedures in place in the NHS during the period Clifford Ayling was
        in practice. We look at how these were applied in the various bodies in east
        Kent with responsibility for Ayling, the barriers for patients and staff in
        raising their concerns and the policies and procedures in the NHS today.

Principles of complaints procedures

5.2   Until 1996, complaints procedures in the hospital and primary care setting
        were significantly different, reflecting the different history of the
        component parts of the NHS.

5.3   For a GP, a complaint would be investigated by the FPC/FHSA under the
        terms of a Medical Service Committee (MSC) which could only
        determine whether or not a GP had, by the actions alleged of him or her,
        breached the terms and conditions of the national contract with the NHS to
        provide adequate medical care. Thus a complaint was assessed primarily
        as a disciplinary matter and non–clinical complaints were effectively
        excluded from the procedure. Most importantly, strict time limits were set
        so that a complaint about matters outside the time limit of 13 weeks of the
        event occurring which gave rise to the complaint could only be considered
        at all if the reasons for the 'delay' in raising a complaint were considered
        justifiable (the Inquiry heard from one patient who had her complaint
        about her GP rejected on these grounds). The complainant was expected to
        present the subject matter of their complaint to the MSC in person at a
        hearing, at which the practitioner would also be present.

5.4   In contrast, complaints in a hospital setting, where care was provided by
        employees, were seen as grievances to be resolved. The 1966 guidance to
        hospitals suggested a four stage process whereby oral/informal
        complaints should be dealt with by front-line staff, written/formal
        complaints by a senior member of the hospital department involved,
        referral if unresolved to the hospital administrator and finally, referral to
        an independent inquiry or for further investigation by a panel of the
        Hospital Management Committee.

5.5   A major review of the hospitals complaints procedures was undertaken in
        1976 by Professor Davies which found that practitioners had failed to take
        complaints seriously; that defensive attitudes to complaints were both
        common and detrimental to staff morale (in this context, we would point to
        the decision by two nursing staff in the Colposcopy Clinic at William
        Harvey Hospital to resign) and tended to repress grievances (and again,
        we draw attention to the evidence presented to the Inquiry by a nurse who

had worked in the Outpatients Department at Thanet Hospital); and that inadequate information was available for staff and patients about complaints procedures and how to access them. The review team also found that hospital staff had operated the procedure to insulate them from criticism (a conclusion also evidenced to us in the course of our Inquiry), that the procedure, by concentrating on principles, was deficient in operational detail and lacked the rigour of any external review. The principles which the team identified as those which should govern complaints handling procedures were that complaints must be properly investigated, a fair review or evaluation of the allegation made and remedial action taken or a reasoned explanation given as to why this was not appropriate.

5.6   The outcome of this review was not issued as guidance for the NHS until 1981, although in the interim the need for publicity about complaints procedures was recognised, as was the need for assistance in making complaints together with the importance of recording complaints. However, the Inquiry was told by witnesses that, for example, it was not until 1991/2 that extensive publicity was given to how and to whom to make a complaint in the hospital setting (see SE Kent Hospitals below) and in the primary care setting, GPs such as Dr Pickering were still advising patients that the source of information on making a complaint was contained in their medical card, despite the apparent publicity organised by the FPC (see Kent FPC and FHSA below). Additionally, as we have set out in preceding sections, the recording of complaints about Ayling in the hospitals in which he worked seemed to us to be desultory.

5.7   The 1981 guidance set out a formal process for DHAs to operate (with referral to the Health Service Commissioner (HSC), a post established in 1973, if a complaint was not resolved at the District level), overseen by health service managers. The Department of Health also recognised that oral/informal complaints could be no less weighty than written/formal complaints and that what constituted a formal complaint should be the wishes of the complainant to have their grievance investigated by a senior member of staff and/or to have a written or oral explanation. The value of meeting with complainants to discuss a complaint as part of the investigation process was also emphasised. However, this procedure did not apply to complaints about family practitioners so, for example, whilst the time limit for making a complaint about hospital and community health care services was set at a year, the 13 week limit was still in place in relation to complaints about GPs.

5.8   This guidance contained the first reference to the right of staff to be fully informed of the details of allegations made about them from the outset and to be given the opportunity to provide an explanation.

5.9   Following the 1976 review, the Joint Consultants Committee of the BMA and Royal Colleges successfully lobbied for a separation of procedures for clinical and non-clinical complaints, which also excluded managerial oversight of the investigation of clinical complaints. The 1981 procedures distinguished between clinical and non-clinical complaints, leaving clinical complaints to be overseen exclusively by clinicians, although an independent professional review (which was seen as a 'clinical consultation' rather than a judicial process) could be convened by the Regional Medical Officer if resolution was not achieved at a DHA level.

5.10   In 1991, the first Patients' Charter was published for the NHS which was a product of the wider recognition of the growing imperative of 'consumer' values in public services. Patients' rights and responsibilities in the NHS were defined for the first time, including the right to have complaints about hospital care investigated and to receive a full written reply from the hospital's Chief Executive.

5.11   The 1981 procedures remained in place until 1996, when a common two-stage procedure for dealing with all complaints about hospital and primary care services was introduced. This followed a further review of NHS complaints procedures, chaired by Professor Wilson. The Wilson Committee identified a number of deficiencies with the previous complaints procedures: lack of knowledge about how to complain, ways in which people were deterred from complaining, lack of satisfactory responses and ways in which complaints were handled which appeared to increase rather than reduce a complainant's sense of grievance. Principles for handling complaints articulated by the Wilson Committee and embedded in the new procedures were that grievances were best resolved at a local level by those responsible for the services being complained about, that resolution and satisfaction were most likely to be secured with rapid, personal and informal responses and that appeals from a local level should be the exception and agreed locally. For primary care, this guidance finally acknowledged the distinction between complaints procedures and disciplinary procedures and gave patients the right to complain directly about their GP and removed the 13-week time limit.

5.12   All hospital Trusts, GP practices and health authorities were required to put in place the two stage procedure: local resolution and referral to a convenor for a decision as to whether an independent review panel would assist in resolving disputed issues. However, GPs were not required to report to the DHA the subject matter of complaints which had been satisfactorily resolved at the practice level, but simply the number of such complaints.

5.13   At the same time, the role of the HSC was extended to include clinical complaints and all primary care services.

5.14   In summary, we would characterise the principles underlying the various procedures for handling complaints and concerns over the period of the Inquiry's terms of reference as:

- significantly different philosophies underpinning complaints about hospital staff and GPs, although a patient might have concerns about the management of their related care in both settings
- procedures driven by process rather than outcome
- the slow emergence of managerial responsibility for the investigation of complaints and a recognition of their value in assessing quality of care

- a relatively recent acknowledgement of complaints as a way for patients to become better informed about their care
- an emphasis on informal resolution close to the source of the complaint with limited external scrutiny
- a reliance on professional self-regulation

5.15   We discuss below the barriers these formed to making complaints whilst Ayling was practising.

Responsibility for Complaints procedures in East Kent

Kent Family Practitioner Committee (FPC) and Family Health Services Authority (FHSA)

5.16   As described above, formal complaints about Ayling as a GP would have had been considered by the Kent FPC/FHSA until 1996 as a matter for consideration by a MSC, had they been made within the set time limit. Membership of the MSC was balanced between lay members of the FPC/FHSA and professional members nominated by the Local Medical Committee. In effect, a practitioner's actions would have been judged by his peers.

5.17   The organisation of Service Committees was the responsibility of the Administrator and subsequently the General Manager. From the time Ayling entered general practice in 1981 until 1985, Kenneth Holman was the Administrator. He was succeeded by his deputy, David Homeshaw who was in turn succeeded by the FHSA's Medical Director, Dr Peter Savege, in October 1992. Dr Savege remained the acting Chief Executive of the FHSA until April 1993 when Fedelm Winkler was appointed as Chief Executive.

5.18   In 1996, the Kent FHSA was abolished and its responsibilities transferred to new DHAs. Mark Outhwaite was appointed as Chief Executive of the East Kent DHA and remained in this post until 2002. The Director of Corporate Affairs, Richard Murrells, was responsible to the Chief Executive for handling complaints and his team included a Complaints Manager, Cathy Bolton. All complaints were channelled through the complaints team in order to ensure a central overview of their management and handling. The Director of Healthcare Development had the responsibility for the administration of the statutory and regulatory functions relating to primary care practitioners, including disciplinary issues. From 1996, Jacqui Stewart held this post.

5.19   Information on how to make a complaint was printed on the medical card issued to every NHS patient registered with a GP, and additionally was available from libraries, post offices, Citizens Advice Bureaux, general practitioners, the Kent FPC/FHSA and Community Health Councils. Until 1996, there was no requirement for GPs to display or provide information on complaints procedures.

5.20   If a patient contacted the FPC/FHSA, they would be informed that their complaint would have to be in writing before it could be dealt with, which was required by the regulations governing Service Committees.

5.21   In 1987 or early 1988, the FPC implemented an informal complaints procedure, which was designed to enable the investigation of complaints which did not apparently concern a potential breach of a GP's contractual terms and to make complaints procedures more accessible.

5.22   If a complainant wished to have a complaint considered informally, a conciliator would meet with the complainant and the practitioner, separately. The conciliator would be provided with all relevant correspondence between the FPC and the complainant, and could refer the complaint back to the formal process if he or she judged it inappropriate to attempt conciliation.

5.23   At the end of the process, the conciliator would submit a formal report to the FPC and the complainant outlining the result. No details of the conciliation process were made public and any notes destroyed. The complainant would be asked to sign a formal confirmation of their satisfaction with the outcome, and if they remained unsatisfied they could request that their complaint be considered through the formal process, if it was judged to allege a potential breach of a GP's terms and conditions of service.

5.24   In 1993, the Kent FHSA initiated a pilot programme for a practice-based complaints procedure and from this developed a Kent-wide model which was a precursor to the national model introduced in 1996. The Kent FHSA would accredit practices with staff trained in handling complaints, and each practice would display notices explaining the complaints procedure. The practice would explain to a dissatisfied patient that although they had the right to an investigation by the FHSA, the practice would seek to investigate and resolve complaints within the practice. In exchange, Kent FHSA would refer all complaints back to the practice for resolution unless the patient disagreed. This scheme was supported by the Kent LMC and CHCs.

5.25   The scheme was rolled out across Kent during 1994 and 1995, with the FHSA Complaints Manager and the LMC Secretary developing a training package which included forms, checklists and model response letters. Following training, a practice would have a trial period and would only be certified following an additional assessment.

Kent & Canterbury and Thanet Hospitals

5.26   The Inquiry has been given no details of the staff responsible for handling complaints at the Kent & Canterbury and Thanet Hospitals whilst Ayling was employed as a clinical assistant in these hospitals from 1974–1988, nor of the application of complaints procedures in these hospitals.

South East Kent Hospitals

5.27   Within the William Harvey Hospital, where Ayling was a clinical assistant from 1984 until 1993, the Director of Nursing Services, Stella James, had the responsibility for complaints procedures from 1985 until 1990. From 1989 until 1991, Mrs Gwynneth Richards was the Unit General Manager of the South East Kent Hospitals Unit, and was based at the William Harvey Hospital. She took on directly the responsibility for handling complaints. In 1991, Mark Addison was appointed UGM and remained so until he was appointed as Chief Executive of the new South Kent Hospitals NHS Trust in 1994.

5.28   Mark Addison delegated the responsibility for handling complaints to Mrs Merle Darling. Mrs Darling had been the Assistant Director of Nursing Services (Midwifery and Paediatrics) of the SE Kent DHA from 1984–1989 and in 1989 she became the Director of Nursing Services and Quality Assurance for the South East Kent Hospitals Unit. In 1991 she became responsible for the handling of all complaints within the Unit.

5.29   Mrs Darling's recollection was that prior to 1991 and the publication of the Patients' Charter there had been no formal procedure for handling complaints. At that point, posters were put up advising patients that if they were dissatisfied with their care, they should write to her. From then the percentage of written, as oppose to verbal, complaints increased. She would acknowledge and investigate the complaints, and draft a reply for Mark Addison (who would sign the final letter) with whom she had a weekly meeting. Complaints were usually on the agenda in these meetings and she kept him informed about every formal complaint with which she dealt.

Barriers to Making Complaints – Patients
5.30   Within primary care, we have concluded that there were three major systemic barriers to patients feeling confident about making a complaint about Ayling's conduct of examinations in his surgery.

5.31   First, until 1996, the most evident barrier to making a complaint about a GP was the narrow definition of a complaint i.e. it had to allege that a GP had breached the terms and conditions of the national contract, and the formality of the process.

5.32   Complaints which might have reached the FPC or FHSA would have been required to be in writing and within 13 weeks of the events occurring about which a complaint was being made. The Inquiry heard from a patient whose complaints was deemed to be 'out of time' and therefore rejected.

5.33   A preliminary judgement then would have to have been made as to whether a complaint about the way in which for example, Ayling conducted his examinations suggested that this was a breach of the regulations governing his contract with the NHS in order to proceed to a hearing of the MSC. In the Inquiry's exploration of the complaint made by Patient F, it was apparent that the way in which her complaint was expressed did not suggest to its recipient that this was such a matter. The MSC would then have to determine through questioning both the patient and practitioner whether there was evidence of sufficient clarity to justify disciplinary action, bearing in mind that the practitioner had the right of appeal against the MSC's decision. The Inquiry has heard that Ayling was perceived to be an isolated and old-fashioned GP, and in Annex 1 we have set out an informed view of the gradual changes in clinical practice in relation to, for example, the prescribing of oral contraceptives and the determination of pregnancy. Ayling's clinical practices could have been defended in the professional context of an MSC.

5.34   Secondly, as complaints were handled as disciplinary matters, patients would be required to present their complaint in person to the MSC and be challenged on their allegations by the practitioner or their representative. The burden of proving a case for disciplinary action rested with the patient. For any patient, this would have been a daunting prospect and even more so when the subject matter of the allegations was as intensely personal and distasteful as those concerning Ayling.

5.35   Thirdly, the system was reactive and did not allow for approaches to be made to patients to elicit their complaints and concerns. We recognise that the role of the FPC and FHSA until 1996 was to administer a complaints procedure which, despite its name, was in fact a disciplinary procedure over which it had very little or no authority for independent action. The handling of the Police case in 1991 is illustrative of this. Action could be taken by the FHSA if the complaint was treated as a matter for professional advice within the remit of the Medical Director but not as a complaint without the patient's personal involvement.

5.36   Within both the primary care and hospital settings, there was a perception amongst staff that a complaint required to be in writing to form the basis of an investigation. Whilst there was some justification for this in the GP setting, in the hospital and other service settings we believe this was caused by a confused interpretation of oral and informal complaints as set out in the 1976 complaints procedure, and not clarified until 1981. The consequence was that staff who heard from patients of their concerns about Ayling's manner and conduct felt that they could take no action unless these were described in writing, as evidenced by the response Val Dodds received when she spoke to her managers about the concerns about Ayling she had heard from patients attending family planning clinics.

5.37   Similarly, those who learned from hospital patients who wished to remain anonymous of concerns about Ayling believed that these complaints could not be investigated without knowing a name, and that the patient's wish for confidentiality and to remain outside a formal complaints procedure should be respected. Action could only be taken through other routes such as the expediency of Ayling's rolling contract, as was the case at the William Harvey Hospital in 1987 and Thanet Hospital in 1988. We have touched on the issue of patient confidentiality in handling complaints which patients were reluctant to put in writing in previous sections and the NHS Executive guidance of 1996 regarding the breach of confidentiality only where there is an overriding public interest, and we recognise the difficulty that the wish for anonymity presents in operating a process to resolve grievances that is fair and equitable. This is the dilemma which Dr Voysey very clearly described to the Inquiry over the anonymous complaint she received in 1988.

5.38   Until 1991, the exclusion of managers and external scrutiny from complaints handling meant that complaints were dealt with by clinicians as a matter of individual "technical" failure to be contained within the profession rather than drawing out wider implications. Thus the complaints made by Patient I and her husband in 1980 were directed by Mr Fullman at Kent & Canterbury Hospital towards the confidential, peer review of the "Three Wise Men" procedure, itself limited to evaluating whether there was any underlying health reason for the actions of the doctor referred to them, rather than to the complaints procedure operated by the hospital administrator. Similarly, Mr Patterson dealt with the complaint made by Patient D at Thanet Hospital in 1981 in a way that diminished the patient's experience to a clinical mishap.

5.39   Finally, we heard from GPs who were made aware by their patients of concerns about Ayling that they felt they could not act without breaching patient confidentiality.

Barriers to Making Complaints – Staff and Colleagues

5.40   The single most important barrier to staff such as nurses and midwives formally expressing their concerns about Ayling was the absence of any formal procedure for doing so. When they did so, the only route was to their immediate manager, as was the case for the nurses working in the Colposcopy Clinic at William Harvey Hospital, or to a consultant, as Penny Moore did at Thanet Hospital in 1980, or through informal collective action, such as the petition or letter the Inquiry heard was circulating amongst midwives in Thanet Hospital in the late 1970s. For nursing managers, there was no guidance as to how to handle the information they were given. Responses varied, as we heard, from attempts to observe Ayling's behaviour directly to denial and rejection on the basis that nothing could be done. Professional guidance to nurses and midwives did not provide clear guidance on what to do about concerns about a colleague or fellow-professional until 1992.

5.41   It was not until 1993 that formal guidance was given to the NHS on concerns at work and subsequently developed into the policies and procedures we have set out in Annex 8.

5.42   For medical colleagues, such as other GPs and doctors working in the family planning services, the only guidance was that from the GMC. As we have discussed previously, until 1995 this was ambiguous and until then, it suggested that reporting concerns about a fellow doctor should be tempered with caution about denigration and defamation. The consequence of this equivocation on decisive action was expressed very clearly to us by, for example, Dr Pickering in his evidence to the Inquiry.

The NHS Today

5.43   We outline in the next chapter of our Report the changes in the last decade to the importance the NHS now places on assuring high quality and safe patient care. This development has been matched by an equivalent growth in acknowledging patient experience as a valued contribution to improving health care. Complaints are now seen as a part of the wider "learning" for the NHS, and take their place alongside patient satisfaction surveys and clinical audit as a source of information to manage risk and improve service quality.

5.44   Generating confidence in the complaints system, that is, enabling patients to believe that their complaint will make a difference, requires patients to be given support in navigating an unfamiliar system, and an advocate where necessary. Until 2002, independent Community Health Councils provided this. With their demise, these functions have passed to the NHS for local implementation as part of a wider drive to promote public and patient involvement in health care [Involving Patients and the Public in Healthcare, DH, 2001]. The transition has not been smooth and the emergence of fully formed structures to provide support and advocacy for patients in their dealings with the health care system is not yet complete.

5.45   The two services established to assist and advise patients following the dissolution of CHCs are the Patient Advice and Liaison Services (PALS) and the Independent Complaints Advocacy Services (ICAS).

5.46   PALS are intended to provide users of the NHS in each NHS Trust with an identifiable person to whom they can readily turn if they have a problem or need information whilst using services. PALS staff act as independent facilitators to handle patient and family concerns with direct access to the Chief Executive, and are expected to be catalysts for service change and improvement. There is a linkage between PALS and clinical governance systems in Trusts.

5.47   An immediate issue which has surfaced in developing PALS has been the difficulty for PCTs of providing this service in GP surgeries within a limited resource of time and trained staff; within a hospital setting the visibility of PALS is more evident.

5.48   We heard that PALS officers are acting to support patients at the first stage of raising an informal concern. They might, for example, see that an issue was discussed by arranging a meeting with the clinicians concerned. In their role as supporters of patients, PALS officers might take independent clinical advice before such a meeting. However, if a formal complaint is submitted, PALS is expected to 'bow out', in order to avoid confusion. But it should refer patients to other sources of support available, such as ICAS.

5.49   A further difficulty has been that PALS were established in advance of ICAS. ICAS are intended to help individuals through the formal complaints system should they prefer not to work directly with those staff in NHS Trusts responsible for handling complaints. The intention behind ICAS is that patients should have access to advocates who will be able to support and befriend them when they face any difficulties within the NHS system and wish to complain. It is for patients to define and control the level and forms of support which would assist them. The help would be available to support patients through all forms of complaints processes – including regulators, such as the GMC, who do not form part of the NHS itself.

5.50   Access to ICAS may be by referral from PALS or other local or national mechanisms, including NHS Direct and local health websites.

5.51   The Inquiry heard that, although the intentions behind ICAS are to be applauded, it faces two major difficulties. The first is practical: the recurring problem of resourcing. We heard that ICAS has insufficient money. The second and more fundamental problem relates to the difficulty of separating 'health' from other social problems. We heard that patients who approach ICAS might well, in many cases, suffer from a wide range of social needs – housing problems, or social security benefits claims are examples. If so, the ICAS advocate would be expected to deal only with a small part of the whole. Each advocate would be torn between supporting the client with only a fragment of their life, or taking on wider issues than they were funded, trained or supervised to address. In these circumstances, we heard calls for the government to develop a cross-public sector approach to the development of advocacy services.

5.52   The third anxiety about the future of ICAS concerns the ability of advocates to reach those parts of the community who are most in need of help, but least likely to bring complaints or to access their services.[1]

Progress Thus Far

5.53   Mark Outhwaite commented:

> "The issue for me is that you could do as much as you like in terms of structural issues. I think there is a major cultural issue which needs to be addressed. It is clearly an incredibly difficult thing, particularly for a woman in this situation to raise an issue, and therefore – that is as much about having a receptive culture as it is about any form of organisational change. And so my caution would be, is that just the creation of PALS or an independent sort of conciliation and advisory service, or whatever it is called, is not a solution. It is part of a solution set, some of which routes its way back as far as doctors' training, approaches to clinical governance and a range of other things. It is part of the plan."

5.54   CHI has a particular commitment to ensure that the perceptions and views of patients, carers and service users are reflected in its work, and in any inspection it assesses how the NHS has succeeded in this objective.

5.55   In the acute sector, CHI has found that: "very few Trusts are routinely involving patients and relatives in the development of services and policies. There is a general shortage of information for patients on their care. What there is often not accessible. Many barriers still exist to patients and staff making complaints."[2]

---

1   In addition, in a recent announcement, John Reid spoke of introducing 'patient advisors' into the surgery:

"We need to recognise that not everyone has the same social capital. Some people know the system, some people are educated, some people are confident, and some are articulate. To make the choice meaningful you need to have patient advisers who will help people through the choices. You need to perhaps allow a day for them to go back and reflect. …We fully intend to be bringing in patient advisers to help those people who perhaps are less confident or know the system less well. We are trying to make sure that in every surgery we develop people who will be advising patients."

2   CHI website. CHI is not able to comment on the primary care sector, as it has not to date gathered a significant amount of good practice in primary care.

Reform of the 1996 Complaints Procedure

5.56   In 2003, further reforms of the 1996 procedures were announced[3]. Annex 10 provides an outline of the proposed new procedures. A review of the procedures in 1999 had found, in common with the Davies and Wilson reviews, that complainants wanted a system that:

- was simpler to use and easier to access
- resolved complaints quickly
- opened up the process, making it more independent where appropriate
- was more responsive to the outcome of complaints so effective improvements were made as a result.

5.57   The proposals in "Making Things Right" included:

- changing attitudes to complaints, by improving communication and 'customer care' in Trusts through enhanced training
- better and readier access for patients to information about treatment and care, through the development of a National Knowledge Service which will provide information reflecting best clinical practice
- gathering patient feedback systematically, through PALS, and through mechanisms such as patient comment cards and surveys
- integrating information from complaints into the wider system of quality assurance
- improving local resolution via a 'Good Practice Toolkit'
- promoting conciliation and other forms of alternative dispute resolution, through the development of national standards and accreditation for conciliation providers.
- establishing ICAS.
- making CHAI and the Commission for Social Care Inspection (CSCI) responsible for the Independent Review stage of the complaints procedure. This would place the review stage of the procedure in the hands of a demonstrably independent body.

5.58   Further, it was proposed that patients should be given the right to complain directly to their PCT – either informally through PALS or formally to the complaints manager – when they had concerns about a family health services practitioner but did not wish to raise these issues with the practice directly. PCTs would be responsible for seeing that the complaint was addressed or investigated formally.

5.59   The timetable for the introduction of these changes has been dictated by that of the primary legislation required to establish CHAI from April 2004. In addition, the Department of Health has stated that the complaints handling system would be considered further, in the light of the Chief Medical Officer's recommendations for reform to the system for dealing with clinical negligence claims in "Making Amends", published in June 2003.

3   DH February 2003: Making Things Right

5.60   "Making Amends" set out proposals for reforming the approach to clinical negligence in the NHS. The analysis of the weaknesses of existing systems included those of the 1996 complaints system. The central point was that both complaints systems and litigation structures were adding to the distress felt by patients when a serious medical accident occurred, and failed to provide the remedies which they wanted.

5.61   Proposals were set out for reform. Central was the suggestion that a NHS Redress Scheme should be set up to enable investigations when things went wrong, and to provide remedial treatment, rehabilitation and care where needed, as well as explanations and apologies; and financial compensation in certain circumstances.

5.62   "Making Amends" noted that harm to a patient could come to light in a number of ways: from an adverse incident, from a complaint or from a claim by a solicitor. In all cases, the proper response was an investigation of the incident; the provision of an explanation to the patient, and an apology if appropriate; some compensation; and the development and delivery of a remedial care package. The report envisaged that the Scheme would be administered by a renamed NHS Litigation Authority (NHSLA), performing functions such as the assessment of claims, the management of the financial compensation element, and monitoring the provision of care and rehabilitation packages at a local level.

5.63   Access to the Scheme would therefore follow upon a **local** investigation of an incident or complaint; or following an investigation by authorities such as CHAI or the Health Service Ombudsman – the Scheme's employees would not carry out the primary investigation. However, "Making Amends" noted the need to strengthen local investigations, noting that, despite the NHSLA guidance summarised above, claimants and patients were not receiving what they regarded as genuine apologies or full explanations in all cases.

5.64   Thus, it recommended that new standards should be developed for after-event or after-complaint management by local NHS providers. These would cover matters such as the need for a full and objective investigation of the facts of an incident, the need for a full and non-technical explanation, an apology if something had gone wrong, and a specification of the action being taken to prevent reoccurrence. 'Where a service improvement is being implemented, the patient or family should be invited back to the hospital to see or hear about it when implementation is complete.' Within each Trust, an individual at Board level should be identified to take overall responsibility for the investigation of and learning from adverse events, complaints and claims; and compliance with the standards would be subject to scrutiny by CHAI.

5.65   "Making Amends" repeated the recommendation made in 'Getting it Right', that NHS staff should receive enhanced training in communication in the context of complaints handling. It also proposed that a new 'duty of candour' should be introduced, by legislation, to require all healthcare professionals and managers to inform patients where they become aware of a possibly negligent act or omission. This would give statutory force to the provision in the GMC's "Code of Good Medical Practice for Doctors". Accompanying such a requirement would be provisions providing for exemption from disciplinary action by employers or professional regulatory bodies for those reporting adverse events – except where the healthcare professional had committed a crime or it would not be safe for him or her to continue to treat patients.

5.66   Finally, the report recommended that the rule which requires an investigation under the NHS complaints procedure to be stopped if the complainant starts a legal action should be dropped.

5.67   The report proposed that the Scheme be piloted and developed within the hospital community health services, initially. After evaluation, it would be possible to assess whether it should be extended to cover family health services. Thus, for the moment, the situation in which claims against general practitioners were handled by the medical defence organisations would remain in place, consistent with the contractual status of GPs within the NHS. Since GPs are not direct employees of the NHS, liability for their actions is not covered by the NHSLA but through individual insurance with one of the two commercial medical defence organisations.

Conclusion

5.68   The systems in operation during the period of the Inquiry's terms of reference for investigating complaints and concerns have twice been subject to detailed analysis, review and reform and await implementation of a third review.

5.69   We have described in considerable detail the current proposals to amend the NHS complaints and associated procedures because we support the intention underlying the current proposals to make the complaints process for patients easier, more responsive and evident in prompt remedial action for the individual and in systemic learning for the organisation – aspects which we found lacking in the contemporaneous handling of complaints and concerns about Ayling. However, since these have not yet been enacted, we cannot comment on their potential efficacy in dealing with complaints such as those relating to Ayling's manner and behaviour in a clinical setting. We would reiterate that the greatest barrier to formal complaints about which we heard during the Inquiry was the patients' lack of a benchmark by which to judge their experience, and that when complaints were made and investigated, each was treated individually and the information from these not connected either within or across organisations.

5.70   We therefore believe that in developing an integrated system from the proposals in "Making Things Right" and "Making Amends", particular attention must be paid to the development of those proposals which concern the context of a complaints procedure rather than the procedures itself. We deal in more detail with this in our final recommendations.

CHAPTER 6
THE NHS TODAY

Introduction

6.1   In the last five years the organisational changes in the NHS which are described in Annex 1 have been matched by a shift in emphasis towards assuring the quality of patient care and patient safety, and ensuring the patient's experience of care is built into the organisation of local health care. The focus of care has moved from the hierarchical and paternalistic model described to us during the time Ayling was in practice towards one of team working where the patient is seen as an informed partner. For example, the Inquiry heard that in the South Kent Hospitals Trust it is now the practice to conduct a 'debriefing' of a woman who has been admitted to the maternity unit. This provides an opportunity for comment, both positive and negative. It was not the practice at the time when Ayling was a clinical assistant in those hospitals.

6.2   The Inquiry is required to make recommendations, in the light of past events, that will result in improvements to current policies and procedures. To do so, we need to sketch out the main developments within the NHS since that date. This is not an exhaustive account: the focus is upon those systems that are relevant to the Ayling story. In looking at each one, we have tried to assess what difference it would have made to the events we have described. We are looking to see whether there are systems now in place within the NHS that would either prevent another Ayling from practising, or would make sure that action was taken quickly, when problems were identified.

6.3   Two key documents published in 2000 set out the framework for the new focus of the NHS: 'The NHS Plan' and 'An Organisation with a Memory'. The former set out an agenda for change in the NHS which would "redesign the NHS around the needs of the patient", and the latter a series of measures to develop a "modern NHS...constantly alert to opportunities to review and improve performance"[1]. Not only was there an explicit restatement of NHS values but a concern to ensure greater uniformity of good practice throughout the NHS, so that outcomes, practices and results for patients did not vary greatly across the country. Trusts whose performance was poor would receive special attention until standards rose; Trusts whose standards were good would be eligible for further investment in developing high quality services. An example of the expectations of Primary Care Trusts in the NHS of today and the way in which achievement of these is measured is given in Annex 11.

6.4   From these, we have drawn out a number of principles which seem pertinent to the establishment and development of procedures which today would ensure action was taken over the concerns and complaints about Ayling when they were first expressed. These are:

1   The NHS Plan (2000): A Plan for Investment, A Plan for Reform; Building a Safer NHS for Patients (2001): Implementing An Organisation with Memory – The Report of an Expert Group on Learning from Adverse Incidents, chaired by the Chief Medical Officer

- Monitoring and Accountability
- Quality Assurance and Good Practice
- Patient Safety
- Patient Empowerment and Involvement:
- Creating incentives for good performance and good outcomes.

6.5   We discuss these below, together with our assessment of their potential impact on events had they been in place when Ayling was in practice.

Monitoring and Accountability

6.6   The drive to establish quality assurance processes within NHS organisations has gathered pace over the last five years and is now embedded in a series of interlocking regulatory bodies with the responsibility to identify and address poor performance. These organisations can be described, generically, as public bodies for the regulation of health care and professional associations with public duties.

6.7   The National Institute for Clinical Excellence (NICE, established in 1999) has the responsibility to provide authoritative guidance to the NHS on best clinical practice, based on the appraisal and synthesis of research evidence.

6.8   The National Patient Safety Agency (NPSA, established in 2001) has the responsibility to gather information from the NHS on adverse incidents and 'near misses', learning lessons and ensuring these are fed back to health care providers and into the treatment that is organised and delivered.

6.9   The National Clinical Assessment Authority (NCAA, established in 2001) provides support for NHS bodies which have concerns about individual doctors, will take referrals, carry out targeted assessments and make recommendations to the referring organisation.

6.10   The Commission for Health Care Audit and Inspection (CHAI, established 2004), now known as the Health Care Commission took over the responsibilities of the Commission for Health Improvement (CHI, established in 1999) for undertaking clinical governance reviews, investigating instances of serious failure, advising the NHS on good practice, checking compliance with NICE guidelines and publishing NHS performance ratings, together with the part of the Audit Commission's responsibility for undertaking 'value for money' studies in the NHS.

6.11   Alongside these sits the General Medical Council (GMC, established in 1858) with four key functions: to promote good medical practice, to keep an up-to-date Register of qualified doctors, to promote high standards of medical education and to take action if it has doubts about whether a doctor should remain on the Register.

6.12   The GMC itself is subject to review by the Council for Regulation of Health Care Professionals (CRHP, established in 2003). The NHS Plan (2000) identified the need for an overarching regulatory body to co-ordinate the existing professional self-regulators.

6.13   CRHP covers a number of regulators, including the GMC, the Nursing and Midwifery Council and the Health Professions Council. It is expected to scrutinise regulators' performance, and publish an annual report upon this. It will seek to ensure that regulators work in a consistent manner, with good practice shared and used to generate improvements across all.

6.14   These bodies are formally committed to sharing information and have agreed between them Memoranda of Understanding, which set out which body takes what action in relation to information on poor performance.

6.15   A new NHS Modernisation Agency has been established to support the implementation of best practice: this will be instrumental in, for example, "developing organisational capacity and competence in PCTs and SHAs...and strengthening the management of performance of complaints handling" ("Making Things Right").

6.16   NHS Trusts are now subject to closer routine external scrutiny of their performance as well as the independent investigation of untoward events. This, taken together with the internal monitoring of service quality and individual clinical performance we describe below, might have identified particular problems and continuing concerns about Ayling in the hospital setting, and earlier and more positive action taken to remove Ayling from unsupervised clinical practice. However, the absence of contemporaneous records of problems and concerns which we identified during the Inquiry would have diminished the potential for such action. Furthermore, within the setting of Ayling's general practice, as a single-handed GP the major source of information about concerns would still be patients.

Quality Assurance

Clinical Governance

6.17   A new concept of clinical governance, which aimed to draw many 'quality initiatives' together, was launched in 1999.[2] A description of the place of clinical governance in the NHS today is given at Annex 12. Clinical governance is a systematic approach to quality assurance and improvement, defined as:

> "A framework through which NHS organisations are accountable for continuously improving the quality of their services and safeguarding high standards of care by creating an environment in which excellence in clinical care will flourish."

6.18   The basic components are 'a coherent approach to quality improvement, clear lines of accountability for clinical quality systems and effective processes for identifying and managing risk and addressing poor performance.'[3] The idea of clinical governance is to introduce a culture where health professionals routinely think: 'How could my care be better?'[4]

---

2   HSC 1999/065: 'Clinical Governance: Quality in the New NHS'

3   [DH website].

4   Roland, Baker: "Clinical Governance: A Practical guide for primary care teams." (1999) National Primary Care Research and Development Centre.

6.19   Clinical governance arrangements were underpinned by a new statutory 'duty of quality' placed on all health authorities and NHS Trusts by the Health Act 1999, s18. This required each to "put and keep in place arrangements for the purpose of monitoring and improving the quality of health care which it provides to individuals". The duty to set up clinical governance systems applies not only to hospital Trusts. Within the primary care setting, Primary Care Trusts are expected to support general practitioners to develop clinical governance systems within their practices.

6.20   Clinical governance is not of itself designed to deal with poorly performing doctors. The aim of clinical governance is to prevent poor performance in the first place by ensuring the development of professionals and offering support to those who need it.

6.21   Since beginning its work in 2000, CHI has published clinical governance review reports on most acute and specialist Trusts, most ambulance trusts and some mental health and Primary Care Trusts. A CHI clinical governance review assesses the Trust across seven components of performance:

• risk management
• clinical audit
• research and development
• patient involvement
• information management
• staff involvement
• education and training

6.22   Professor Malcolm Forsythe's view to the Inquiry was that:

"Clinical governance done properly is very good, but it has been a slow progress over many years to introduce it."

6.23   Speaking of its development in his own area of responsibility, where he is Chair of a PCT, he told the Inquiry:

"Clinical governance in my part of the world is in its infancy. It would be the simplest way I could put it. I mean, even the words "clinical governance" to some GPs in Kent say, "What is this? What is this phrase? Is it medical audit, what we used to do years back?", so there is an attitude problem there. It is slow. It is slow and we have just been – CHI, the Commission for Health Improvement has just done [an inspection] and it.. described our system of clinical governance as being all in place, but not much evidence of success."

6.24   Clinical governance systems are intended to assure that organisations learn and develop best practice. One element of such a programme is ensuring that staff too are learning and developing. At the level of individual healthcare professionals, this may be achieved through participation in continuing professional development (CPD), directed and guided by a process of annual appraisal.

Continuing Professional Development

6.25   Doctors are required to keep themselves up to date. The GMC's 'Good Medical Practice' (September 2001) states:

> "You must keep your knowledge and skills up to date throughout your working life. In particular, you should take part regularly in educational activities which maintain and further develop your competence and performance."

6.26   Nurses and midwives are subject to a similar professional duty to maintain their professional skills. It is supported by the requirement that, when renewing their registration (which they must do every three years), they must demonstrate that they have undertaken at least five days (35 hours) of learning in the previous three years.

Appraisal

6.27   In *Supporting Doctors, Protecting Patients* (1999), the Chief Medical Officer proposed that all doctors employed in or under contract to the NHS should undergo regular appraisal.

6.28   April 2001 saw the introduction of appraisal for NHS consultants, now rolled out to non-consultant career grade doctors, public health consultants, locum doctors and clinical academics. Appraisal for principals in general practice was introduced from April 2002. Participation in appraisal will be a contractual requirement under the new GMS contract. It is expected that this requirement will apply to non-principals as well. In this sector, the appraiser should be another GP, who has been properly trained in appraisal. It is for the PCT to ensure that an appraisal scheme is in place, that appropriate appraisers are available, and that developmental needs identified are met.

6.29   Setting up the system, with trained appraisers, has been a major exercise when coupled with other organisational changes,[5] and the appraisal system is still in its early stages.[6] Those working to develop and embed appraisal emphasise that it is a formative or educational process. It is a confidential process designed to support and develop. As the DH has stated, "It is about identifying development needs, not performance management. It is a positive process, to give GPs feedback on their past performance, to chart continuing progress and identify development needs." [DH website]. It is about 'underperformance' in the sense that all can generally be helped to perform better; but it is not about poor performance. The NHS 'cannot (and should not) rely on a formalised annual appraisal process to detect very deficient performance.'[7]

Revalidation of Doctors by the General Medical Council

6.30   Doctors will be required to be 'revalidated' or re-licensed every five years, if they are to continue practising. From April 2005 every doctor who wishes to practise will be required to hold a 'practising licence' which

5   See, e.g. Hasler J, 'Appraisal for general practitioners – what have we learned?' Clinical Governance Bulletin (May 2003).

6   BMA letter to MF, 6.3.03.

7   'Appraisal for GPs' (October 2001), ScHARR, Chapter 2 paragraph 26.

must be renewed every 5 years. The evidence to demonstrate continued fitness to practise will be presented to the GMC and reviewed by it. The GMC envisages that appraisal tools will be capable of feeding into the system for revalidation of doctors, when implemented.

6.31   The revalidation system is being designed to dovetail with the annual appraisal system, so as to prevent duplication of effort. It is proposed that the outcomes of the last five annual appraisals should be presented to the GMC and, if satisfactory, would provide the basis for continued revalidation. The GMC is currently developing the details of the revalidation process, and is working upon matters such as the verification checks that it would need to carry out, to be satisfied of the accuracy and completeness of the material presented to it. However, the GMC have stated that they feel that satisfactory participation in annual appraisal in a managed system should be sufficient to achieve revalidation. [GMC, 2003 – GMC Licensing and Revalidation Briefing]. There is a tension between this desire to streamline processes, and the 'formative' end of appraisal, and the need to secure 'high-trust vitality and honesty'.[8]

6.32   These are long-term changes, which could not be expected to produce a measurable effect within only a few years. There is a tension between a 'softly-softly' approach, designed to encourage participation, and a more robust and directive assessment process. There are good grounds to think it may help to encourage a more systematic approach to meeting continuing developmental needs, but identifying development needs is not the same as detecting bad medical practice. It is not the role of an appraiser to monitor patient experience.

Poorly Performing Doctors

6.33   The primary aim of the systems described above is to ensure that healthcare professionals are competent and well supported, and that their clinical skills develop every year. Thus, the aim is to prevent problems from occurring.

6.34   However, systems to deal with poor performance have also been further developed.

6.35   In the first place, guidance on appointments systems has been reviewed to ensure that fuller information is available about candidates prior to appointment.

Hospital Doctors

6.36   Since June 2000, all NHS employers are required to include in their medical staff post application forms a declaration that the applicant must complete stating whether he or she has been or is the subject of fitness to practice proceedings by a UK or an overseas regulatory body, or investigations or conviction by the Police. Since May 2002 these checks have been mandatory on all new NHS staff.

8   'Extending Appraisal to all GPs' (July 2003), ScHARR, p11.

GP Principals

6.37   In 2001, new regulations were published altering the application process for doctors seeking admission to the GMS list.[9] An applicant must supply details of, for instance, any criminal record, any involvement in NHS fraud investigations and the outcome, and past investigations by regulatory and licensing bodies (in the UK and abroad), where there has been an adverse finding. A doctor will be asked to give consent to the sharing of information between the Primary Care Trust and professional bodies. Primary Care Trusts are able to refuse to admit doctors to their lists when this seems justified on efficiency, fraud or suitability grounds. Furthermore, doctors already on the list will have to report adverse finding by regulatory and licensing bodies.

Non-principals

6.38   In December 2001, a 'supplementary list' was introduced. Non-principals (i.e. deputies, assistants, locums, salaried GMS doctors etc) working in general practice must register on the supplementary list of their 'local' PCT.[10] From June 2002, a principal using an organisation that supplies deputising services must obtain an undertaking from the organisation that it will provide a doctor from the medical list, the supplementary list or a named PMS practitioner only. Principals intending to engage deputies must ask for and take up references.

6.39   Secondly, specific new arrangements for dealing promptly with concerns about a doctor's conduct or performance have been introduced which provide for a clear set of actions to be taken in handling the concerns and steps to be taken to protect the public such as restrictions on practice or exclusion from work. Details of these arrangements are set out in Annex 13.

6.40   It seems unlikely that any of these mechanisms would have detected the issues surrounding Ayling's performance. However, they will help to make it more difficult for those doctors who have been subject to adverse findings by official bodies (e.g. regulatory authorities) to move into other areas of work without their past history being considered.

Poor Performance in Post

6.41   Following the publication in 1997 of a report commissioned by the DH, "Measures to assist GPs whose performance gives cause for concern", and the introduction of new performance procedures by the GMC, HAs established Poorly Performing Doctors' Committees. Although these had no statutory powers, membership of such panels included the HA Medical Director, and the LMC Chair and Secretary. The role of such committees was to protect patients, and to act on information received from a variety of formal and informal sources which suggested there were concerns about a GP's performance. These committees operated in a supportive

9   The NHS (General Medical Services) Amendment (No 4) Regulations 2001(SI 2001/3742).

10   A non-principal may be on one list only, but admission on that list allows him or her to practice in other areas. However, if he or she does no work within the area of the 'home' PCT for 12 months, they may be removed from that list.

manner towards GPs, encouraging remedial and educational models of reform where deficiencies in practice were identified.

6.42   Dr Snell, Medical Director of the East Kent HA, explained to the Inquiry:

"The Panel [the Poorly Performing Doctors Committee] had a number of options available to it. It could recommend no further action, make arrangements for re-training, education or support or render a GP to the GMC or other bodies…any recommendation to the GMC or other bodies would have to be ratified by the EKHA."

6.43   This system has continued with little change, although the expertise available to Trusts has been enhanced by the creation of the National Clinical Assessment Authority (NCAA).

6.44   When contacted, the first role of the NCAA may be that of providing expert advice to those who are working to address a concern about a doctor's performance and who may have had little if any previous experience of dealing with a 'problem' doctor. A doctor who has a concern about his or her own performance may also contact the NCAA for advice. The NCAA stresses that its task is to strengthen local performance arrangements, not to supplant them.

6.45   As for anonymous information, the NCAA states that:

"If we receive information from someone who does not wish to be named and we think that on the basis of the information supplied further steps may need to be taken, we may:

–   remind the caller (if they are a health care professional and/or work in the NHS) that they have a duty to act when they believe that patients are or may be seriously at risk

–   suggest they discuss their concern with the appropriate person in their place of work or with the PCT

–   suggest that they discuss the situation with their professional defence organisation or the independent charity Public Concern at Work

–   suggest that they provide information anonymously if they still feel unable to identify themselves

–   ask for enough information from the caller to enable us to contact the contracting organisation offering advice or inviting them to consider referring the case for an NCAA assessment

–   advise the caller to contact the GMC directly if the information provided suggests that there may be a very serious and imminent risk to patients. It is possible for the GMC to accept a case in certain circumstances even when the caller refuses to be identified".

(Source: GP Handbook, NCAA Handbook for Prototype Phase General Practice in England).

6.46   Where local procedures have not been successful in resolving an issue or where they are not appropriate, the NCAA itself may carry out an assessment. Any assessment requires the consent and the co-operation of both the referring organisation and the doctor concerned. The doctor must be kept fully informed about the process and be copied into any information sent by the referring organization. However, for GPs a failure to comply with a request for an NCAA assessment is a breach of the terms of service under the new NHS regulations introduced in December 2001 – so sanctions are available if co-operation is not forthcoming[11] and compliance with an NCAA assessment, when requested by a PCT, is now a condition of being on the medical list.

6.47   The purpose of an NCAA assessment is to clarify areas of concern and to make recommendations for how these may be addressed. The assessments are confidential to the employer or PCT, and the doctor concerned. Their purpose is formative (i.e. educational) and they are not designed to see whether a doctor is fit to practise – that is the role of the GMC. However, if the assessors do come across areas of practice that raise serious concerns about patient safety, the NCAA would advise the referring organisation to take action.

6.48   The NCAA can also provide advice and support to referring organisations on media handling, if there are public concerns about a doctor's performance.

6.49   The NCAA will not, itself, implement any recommendations. That is the job of the doctor concerned and the referring organisation, although it will seek to support both. The NCAA is an advisory body, and the NHS employer or PCT remains responsible for resolving the problem once the NCAA has produced its assessment.

6.50   If Ayling's colleagues or peers, such as the GPs working at the White House surgery, the LMC or hospital nurses and midwives, had been able to contact the NCAA about their concerns, it seems likely that they would have been reminded of their professional duty to act when they believe that patients are or may be at risk, and advised to discuss the matter with their employer or the PCT.

6.51   As Dr Padley observed to the Inquiry, the NCAA:

> "does offer a route to sweep up all the [cases] in which there is an impasse",

and its assessors can:

> " provide a body of evidence to address the issue of the doctor. I think the hardest thing is the basis question whether the doctor is having an unfortunate patch or whether they are systematically underperforming in some way".

6.52   But educational models for addressing poor performance are predicated on a willingness or ability by a doctor to acknowledge the need for further training or education. Poor performance derived from lack of insight, denial of a problem or misconduct amounting to a criminal offence cannot

11   The Inquiry heard that similar arguments would be used by hospital Trusts in disciplinary proceedings if the doctor had not been willing to co-operate.

be tackled through such systems. The existence of such systems may in fact delay the recognition of motivation beyond the influence of remedial action by the doctor's contracting organisation.

Power of Suspension

6.53   As employers, hospital and other NHS Trusts have always had formal powers of suspension. However, the DH seeks to discourage a 'suspension culture' in which the automatic response to a serious complaint is long-term suspension. Although it stresses that ensuring patient safety is paramount, it argues that suspension may not be needed to secure this end, and is costly for the NHS, and severely demoralising for the health professional. All Trusts are now expected to consult the NCAA before suspending a doctor and the NCAA will help to assess whether the suspension is genuinely required.

6.54   The same requirement to consult the NCAA is now placed on PCTs. However, in the general practice setting there have also been procedural changes to the method by which a general practitioner can be suspended.

6.55   In December 2001, the NHS Tribunal was abolished.[12] The power of removal and suspension of a doctor from the medical list was first vested in health authorities, and then taken over by Primary Care Trusts as they replaced health authorities.

6.56   Primary Care Trusts may remove doctors from their lists on the grounds of efficiency, fraud or suitability. They are also able to make continued inclusion on the list subject to specific conditions.[13]

6.57   Primary Care Trusts may suspend a doctor from their lists when they consider that this is necessary to protect the public or is otherwise in the public interest. This echoes the test applied by the GMC's Interim Orders Committee. There is no right of appeal against the PCT's decision, but the doctor may ask for it to be periodically reviewed by the PCT.

6.58   PCTs are required to make payments so as to ensure that the provision of general medical services is maintained for patients – i.e. to fund a locum if needed. They are also required to ensure, by making payments, that the practitioner's level of income is protected, so far as reasonably practical.[14] The Inquiry heard that with the introduction of the new GMS contract, under which payments are made to the practice rather than to the principal, this issue may become complex, if provisions in the partnership agreement impact adversely on the doctor's right to maintain his income.

6.59   The Inquiry heard examples of these powers of suspension being exercised by PCTs. So today, if a PCT was (like the East Kent Health Authority) persuaded that it was necessary to suspend a doctor facing

---

12   The Health and Social Care Act (Commencement No. 6) (England) Order 2001
        (SI 2001/3738). Tribunals will continue to deal with extant cases.

13   The NHS (General Medical Services) Amendment (No 4) Regulations
        2001(SI 2001/3742.

14   See Paragraph 46 of the Statement of Fees and Allowances paid to General Practitioners,
        as amended on 14 December 2001.

criminal charges, it would no longer be necessary to prepare a case for the NHS Tribunal. The PCT could take action itself. Of course, a hearing in which the arguments of the practitioner concerned were assessed would need to be held. Furthermore, the decision of the PCT could be challenged in the High Court (by way of an application for judicial review). In any such hearing, it would be possible for the practitioner to argue that, if the bail conditions did not prohibit practice, it was not necessary to suspend him. However, in such a challenge, the PCT would be able to present its own evidence on the suitability of the bail conditions, and could also point out that the practitioner's income would be secure during suspension.

6.60   In the case of Ayling, we believe that these powers would have been used to secure his suspension from practice until trial, although there are issues about whether a PCT could suspend a doctor for as long a period as a prosecution.

6.61   The Inquiry has been told that it is not routine for the Crown Prosecution Service (CPS) to consult regulatory organisations about conditions of bail, but that this was possible.

Sharing Information: Alert letters
6.62   In 1997, guidance was issued to formalise existing arrangements for circulating information about a doctor who was believed to pose a risk to patient safety, but who (for example) moved employer before disciplinary processes were instigated or completed. The system was further overhauled in late 2002, when further guidance was issued (HSC 2002/011).

6.63   When an employer considers that their employee or former employee may place patients or staff at serious risk, they should request the Regional Director of Public Health (RDPH) to issue an alert letter. Referral should also be made to the relevant regulatory body (e.g. the GMC) at the same time, as a matter of urgency. An alert letter notifies, on a confidential basis, employers within the UK healthcare sector, about the professional concerned. It is for the RDPH to decide whether or not to issue the letter, and also to monitor whether there is a continuing need for it to remain in force. Letters are designed to cover a situation of risk that exists before the relevant regulatory body has been able to take appropriate action. If, therefore, it has had a chance to act (by making an interim order for suspension, for example) or if the risk no longer continues (because there has been appropriate re-training, for example) then it should be rescinded.

6.64   The alert letter guidance is not mandatory for independent practitioners such as GPs. However, PCTs coming to hear of risks to patient safety would be required to invoke it. They are also required to make their alert letter database accessible to general practitioners, and to work with them, and other independent practitioners, to ensure that procedures for making appointments (permanent and temporary) are robust. In other words, general practitioners would be encouraged to check the database before appointing any staff.

6.65   It will be apparent that the efficacy of the system would depend, first, on the willingness of any employer to invoke it by contacting the RDPH and secondly, the existence of reasonable grounds of belief that there is a risk to issue a letter. The individual concerned must be notified of the existence of the letter and has a right of appeal. Thus, it seems unlikely that an individual whose term of employment ended when the evidence available was not strong enough for disciplinary or regulatory proceedings to be initiated would be the subject of a letter. Furthermore, once an individual has left an organisation, there would (we believe) be a tendency for the employer to bring any investigations to an end. If so, the necessary evidence might never be gathered. From what we heard in the course of the Inquiry, we believe this was the case with Ayling and the ending of his employment at the Kent and Canterbury, Thanet and William Harvey Hospitals.

6.66   The system does not work well for doctors outside a directly managed setting (locums, for instance, or GPs). The Inquiry heard the suggestion that alert letters should be registered on a GMC database and linked to the medical register.

Gathering and Sharing 'Soft' Information

6.67   A repeated theme during the course of the Inquiry was the need to capture 'soft' or informal information that fell short of a formal complaint. The Inquiry heard that, in practice, information might be gathered by a medical director or a manager, on a personal basis. If so, there would be few formal mechanisms for ensuring that such information remained available with a change in personnel. Any formal recording of 'soft' information would also be subject to the requirements of the Data Protection Act.

6.68   In its seminars, the Inquiry heard that the Data Protection Act 1998, coupled with the Human Rights Act 1998, has created a climate in which there is less sharing of information across organisations. Staff hide behind the Acts either deliberately or through ignorance, since the Data Protection Act does not prohibit the sharing of data in this context. But there is a need for better information for staff on this issue.

6.69   Additionally, there can also be a reluctance to accumulate information that may have to be disclosed to the person concerned, making it more difficult to develop a picture of an individual's activities.[15] There is a grey area about what a doctor needs to be told about employers sharing information about him. There is no accepted view across the system of where the balance should be struck between the needs of the professional and those of the public, with each constituent part making its own judgements. The

---

15   Regulatory bodies such as the GMC are able to refuse a request from a doctor to access the information held about him (or her) by the GMC during the course of an investigation. Under section 31 of the Data Protection Act, personal data which are processed for regulatory functions (one of which being 'to protect members of the public against... dishonesty, malpractice or other seriously improper conduct by, or the unfitness or incompetence of, persons authorised to carry on any profession or other activity') are exempt from the 'subject access' provisions to the extent that doing so would prejudice the carrying out of the regulatory functions. However, when a case is finished or for closed cases, this bar would no longer apply. As a result, there are fears that information will not be logged for fear of future potential disclosure.

DPA does not specify how long data may be kept for; it is up to each organisation to be able to justify what is 'longer than necessary'. The nature of the information held varies in weight and significance across organisations and it can be difficult to assess the real meaning of some data, especially where it is unverified. The timeliness of information may be an issue, as it may relate to some years ago and it is unclear what has happened since. People need to be clear about their responsibility to contribute to an information base, as well as their duties of confidentiality.

Patient Safety

6.70   'An Organisation with a Memory' argued that 'patient safety' needed to be prioritised within the NHS. The NHS should learn from serious failures in health care, or 'adverse events'. The report identified a need to develop not only better mechanisms for reporting, analysing and learning from error, but a more open and fair culture in which errors could be acknowledged and discussed. It argued for a major shift from a 'person-centred' or 'bad apple' approach, in which an individual is blamed for mistakes made, to a 'systems approach' in which the wider underlying causes of error are examined.

6.71   The development of this approach is being led by the new NPSA. A national system for the collection of anonymised data about 'adverse events' or 'near misses', modelled on the aviation industry, is being established by the NPSA.

6.72   The NPSA has developed a National Reporting and Learning System (NRLS) which will be rolled out across the NHS from November 2003.

6.73   The NPSA states:

> "Over time, the NRLS will enable NHS staff, patients and their carers in England and Wales to report any incident or prevented incident (near miss) that they are involved in or witness. The information they provide to the NPSA will be stored in an anonymous form and analysed to identify patterns and key underlying factors. This data will be cross-referenced with a number of other information sources to establish patient safety priorities, for which the NPSA will research and develop practical national solutions, together with a wide range of NHS staff and involving patients. These solutions will then be fed back to staff and organisations across the NHS to implement locally. The NPSA will work in partnership with NHS organisations to achieve this, and the NRLS has been designed to complement the vital reporting, learning and action that also takes place at a local level."

6.74   The system is intended to integrate with other national reporting systems. Currently at a national level, there are some 23 reporting systems in the NHS linked to patient safety, ranging from incidents resulting in avoidable death or disability to incidents associated with the use of medical devices and equipment, as well as matters of infection or communicable disease.

6.75   Further, it seems likely that the NPSA's reporting system will form part of the development of a standard approach to adverse incident reporting, as

Trusts and general practice seek to avoid setting up multiple and overlapping systems. At present, there is no national guidance governing adverse or critical incident reporting in the NHS in England. At local level, adverse incident reporting in the NHS is linked to risk management standards.[16] But new national guidance on adverse incidents reporting in the NHS, including guidance on what should be reported by SHAs to the Department of Health, is being developed by the Department of Health in collaboration with SHAs.

An 'Open and Fair' Culture

6.76   The NPSA's system forms a part of the wider campaign to create an 'open and fair' culture in which it is the failure to report an incident, rather than the reporting of an incident, that attracts criticism. The general idea which has gathered support is that if an adverse incident or 'near miss' has occurred, it should not lead to disciplinary action against a member of staff unless that staff member has acted recklessly or criminally; or he or she has failed to report it.

6.77   Thus, an 'open and fair culture' would not have prevented action being taken against Ayling – rather, it is thought, it would have encouraged staff to speak up about the activities which they had witnessed. However, there are tensions and conflicts created by the movement towards such a culture. The boundaries of criminal or civil liability for mistakes can be drawn narrowly or broadly. The desires of patients or members of the public, who may wish to see an individual held accountable for a mistake, may conflict with the 'systems' model, which may see that person as a casualty of an inadequate or flawed system.[17]

Staff Hierarchies

6.78   Increased openness and a willingness to query decisions has marched hand in hand with increased team-working. Professor Forsythe told the Inquiry that:

> "Team work has become greater and greater, and, of course, it was always our policy to avoid having single-handed consultants wherever possible, because you have no local peers. Even where you had single-handed consultants, we are trying to get them to buddy with another consultant. But the fact is that now healthcare is delivered by teams of people, and that is the most important feature of the reasons of change. And of course in primary care we have the same too."

16   These form one component of NHS Controls Assurance requirements (which are the subject of extant guidance).

17   See the case of Wayne Jowett, a young boy who died in 2001 after a cancer drug was wrongly injected into his spine. One of the doctors responsible, Dr Feda Mulhem, was prosecuted and eventually pleaded guilty to unlawful killing. Equally, an independent report by Professor Toft criticised staff and procedures at the hospital and highlighted design faults in syringes and drug packaging. The design of the phials used is being changed so that they can no longer be fitted to spinal injection kits.

6.79 Thus a family planning nurse told the Inquiry, when she spoke of concerns raised in the early 1990s:

> "At the time of these incidents, nurses did not have the type of relationship with doctors that they often do now. Now all matters are likely to be discussed as a team. Then it was much more a case of the doctors and nurses working as separate professional groups."

6.80 One particular feature of the Ayling story that the Inquiry noted was the level of knowledge about Ayling's clinical practices that generated anxiety amongst both hospital and community nurses and midwives. But the culture of the time mitigated against open discussion of this. We believe that today this silence would be broken, not only through the cultural shift away from professional hierarchies but also through processes we discuss below for raising concerns about patient safety.

Admissions of Mistakes

6.81 By 2001, the GMC's Code of Good Medical Practice for Doctors stated:

> "If a patient under your care has suffered harm, through misadventure or for any other reason, you should act immediately to matters right, if that is possible. You must explain fully and promptly to the patient what has happened and the likely long and short-term effects. When appropriate, you should offer an apology."

6.82 Furthermore, the NHS's 'insurers' too began to encourage the medical profession to admit errors without fear that this would lead to penalty under the terms of any indemnity. By a circular sent in February 2002, the NHSLA stated that it would not decline indemnity or take any point against a member on the basis of an apology, explanation or expression of sympathy made in good faith. Rather, it acknowledged the importance of expressions of regret following adverse outcomes, and the desire which patients had for explanations of what had gone wrong, and what had been learnt for the future.

6.83 In June 2003, the Chief Medical Officer issued a consultation document "Making Amends" which proposed reforms to the way matters of clinical negligence were handled by the NHS and in particular the introduction by legislation of a duty of 'candour' under which all healthcare professionals and managers must inform patients when they become aware of possibly negligent acts or omissions.

6.84 We consider that had the events at Thanet Hospital in 1977 (Patient B) occurred today, formal systems to review such a tragic event would have been much stronger. The likely outcome would have been a documented investigation and report, an acknowledgement that something untoward had occurred, an explanation offered to the parents and the educational needs of the practitioner identified. This would be a significant improvement on the silence which followed the death of a child in 1977.

6.85 Equally, we consider that there would be a fair prospect that at least some of the incidents which distressed nursing staff in the family planning clinics would have been documented today as untoward or adverse incidents. Although we do not underestimate the difficulties faced by nurses in criticising doctors, in these cases they would have been reporting violations of formal service protocols on chaperoning rather than their personal disquiet.

Procedures for Raising Concerns

6.86   The first NHS guidance on procedures for staff to raise concerns about patient safety or NHS services was published in 1993 (see Annex 7). Since that date, there has been increasing recognition of:

> "…the need for the hospital *[or other NHS organisation]* to create an open and non-punitive environment in which it is safe for healthcare professionals to report adverse events, safe to admit error, safe to admit when things have almost gone wrong and safe to explore the reasons why." [BRI Report, page 359, para 17].

6.87   In July 1999, the Public Disclosure at Work Act came into force. The Act encourages people to raise concerns about malpractice in the workplace, and provides protection against victimisation if this follows concerns being raised.

6.88   New NHS guidance was issued to ensure that the key features of the Act were reflected in local policies and procedures.[18] The guidance required that all NHS Trusts and Health Authorities were required to:

- designate a senior manager to deal with employees' concerns and protect whistleblowers;
- put in place local policies and procedures that complied with minimum standards;
- issue guidance to all staff so that they know how to speak up against malpractice.

6.89   Inevitably, the Inquiry heard a range of views as to how much, if at all, things had changed. Whilst Julie Miller, a midwife in Canterbury and Thanet AHA, spoke of doctors being "the Gods of the hospital" twenty years ago, whom she would not have challenged, she felt now that:

> "The whole culture of the NHS is changing. It possibly isn't quite there yet, but it's certainly getting there, so that there is a lot more respect between the medical staff and the nursing staff now, and opinions on both sides are now valued. If you've got any – if you had any cause for concern, then you can – you would feel – I would feel happy to go to the consultants or to the lead consultants and speak about the problem."

6.90   To Professor Malcolm Forsythe:

> "People are willing to put their heads above the parapet, but there still is not that culture of openness. There is still a huge defensiveness on the part of professionals about being criticised, which affects people's willingness to be open and you have to try and deal with both those aspects, because if you raise a problem and all you get is antagonism

---

18   HSC 1999/198: 'The Public Interest Disclosure Act 1998: *Whistleblowing in the NHS*' 27 August 1999.

and then revenge, if you see that happening somewhere else in your organisation you are going to be pretty loath to do it yourself. So things are better, but they are not as good as they should be."

6.91 In May 2003, Public Concern at Work and Unison published the results of a joint survey of 2000 NHS staff, to establish their experience of attempts to report concerns. They reported that the key findings were that:

- 90% had blown the whistle when they had a concern about patient safety
- 50% did not even know if their Trust had a whistleblowing policy
- 33% say their Trust would want them to blow the whistle even if it resulted in bad publicity
- 30% say their Trust would not want to be told there was a major problem and
- 25% say the culture is improving

6.92 Of those who had blown the whistle on a patient safety concern:

- One-third said they suffered some personal comeback
- One-half said their concern was dealt with reasonably

6.93 Where a whistleblowing policy was used, no staff reported reprisals and two in three said the concern was reasonably dealt with.

6.94 However, as Professor Malcolm Forsythe commented to the Inquiry:

"…in my experience GPs are not telling PCTs and Trusts who the poor consultants are; they just don't refer their own patients to those consultants."

6.95 Equally, consultants would not report who the poor GPs were.

"Within GP practices, I believe that there is still a tendency to keep conduct or performance problems in house perhaps because of a fear of the practice being affected adversely if the problem came out into the open."

6.96 These findings suggest that, whilst substantial improvement is still needed, NHS staff are increasingly willing to speak up for patient safety, even at some personal risk. However across much of the NHS it seems that this welcome change is in spite of, not because of, management action or encouragement. We therefore believe that were colleagues today having to decide how to report their concerns about Ayling, it would take considerable courage on their part to use a whistleblowing policy, especially in light of the reported accounts we heard of Ayling's aggressive denial of questionable conduct and practice.

Patient Empowerment and Involvement

6.97 Government policy stresses the need to ensure that the public is involved in decision-making about health and the provision of health services and has charged the Commission for Patient and Public Involvement in Health (CPPIH, established 2003) with leading this agenda. It is a successor to Community Health Councils, whose demise was strongly contested.

6.98   Its remit is to ensure that the public is involved in decision making about health and health services. Under its leadership, a Patient and Public Involvement Forum (PPIF) will be set up for every NHS Trust and Primary Care Trust (PCT) in England. They will be made up of local people. The intention is that the forum members should play an active role in health related decision making within their communities.

6.99   Through the PPIFs, CPPIH also has the responsibility to commission and set quality standards for Independent Complaints Advocacy Services (ICAS) and to monitor the effectiveness of local Patient Advice and Liaison Services (PALS).

6.100   PALS are not independent of their host Trust and its officers are expected to use their knowledge of their employing organisation to help find speedy solutions to the issues brought to them by patients, carers, their family and friends or members of the public. They can take forward issues, even if patients who raise them do not wish to do so personally or wish to remain anonymous. Thus PALS are expected to be an 'early warning' system for Trusts and a key source of information of information and feedback.

6.101   The establishment of ICAS and PALS potentially offers a source of advice and support which was lacking for patients such as those who were concerned but unsure about the motivation for Ayling's actions and who had no-one with whom they could discuss this. But patient consent would still be needed for an individual concern to be pursued, and there is no guidance as to when PALS officers might have a duty to follow up concerns. Therefore it seems likely that this would be left to local discretion. The introduction of PALS should not mean that other staff within an organisation transfer their responsibility to respond directly to concerns raised with them to PALS.

6.102   Moreover, as Mark Outhwaite commented to the Inquiry:

> "The issue for me is that you could do as much as you like in terms of structural issues. I think there is a major cultural issue which needs to be addressed. It is clearly an incredibly difficult thing, particularly for a woman in this situation to raise an issue, and therefore – that is as much about having a receptive culture as it is about any form of organisational change. And so my caution would be, is that just the creation of PALS or an independent sort of conciliation and advisory service, or whatever it is called, is not a solution. It is part of a solution set, some of which routes its way back as far as doctors' training, approaches to clinical governance and a range of other things. It is part of the plan."

6.103   As we have noted above, CHI has a particular commitment to ensure that the perceptions and views of patients, carers and service users are reflected in its work, and in any inspection it assesses how the NHS has succeeded in this objective.

6.104 In the acute sector, CHI has found that: "very few Trusts are routinely involving patients and relatives in the development of services and policies. There is a general shortage of information for patients on their care. What there is is often not accessible. Many barriers still exist to patients and staff making complaints."[19]

Rewarding Good Performance

Personal Medical Services (PMS)

6.105 The NHS (Primary Care) Act 1997 opened the door to a new method of providing general medical services. Instead of general practitioners operating as independent contractors, it enabled health authorities, and then Primary Care Trusts, to employ doctors directly, using their own locally developed contracts. The aim was to create flexible solutions to local needs – enabling Health Authorities and subsequently PCTs to recruit doctors to work in both geographical and clinical areas that are poorly served by 'traditional' models. Such doctors are then subject to the scrutiny of performance brought about by accountability to an employer but directly remunerated without the complexity of the fees and allowances model of the national GP contract.

New GP Contract

6.106 A new contract governing the provision of general medical services (GMS) by general practitioners has been negotiated and accepted by general practitioners (see Annex 14). Existing practices transferred to the new contract in April 2004. The main features of the new contract are as follows:

- each contract will be between the PCT and the practice, rather than the individual general practitioner. This global sum will give practices new flexibility to appoint salaried staff, including doctors.
- all practices will be required to provide essential services. Practices will have a preferential right to provide additional services (e.g. cervical screening, contraceptive advice, maternity services) and will normally do so. Both will be funded through a global sum to practices.
- in addition, PCTs may commission enhanced services, as they think appropriate. These would include essential or additional services delivered to a higher standard or services such as those provided by nurses or GPs with special interests. There will be no obligation on any GP practice to provide enhanced services.
- from April 2004, PCTs are responsible for commissioning out-of-hours care; they may contract with existing practices to supply the service.
- a quality framework will reward practices' achievements in organising and delivering services. There will be four 'domains' or areas within this framework:
  - the clinical domain (management of CHD, strokes, mental health and other specified medical conditions);
  - the organisational domain (management of records, patient information, education and training, practice management and medicines management);

19   CHI website. CHI is not able to comment on the primary care sector, as it has not to date gathered a significant amount of good practice in primary care.

- the additional services domain;
- the patient experience domain.

- the inclusion of the patient experience in the key service indicators provides an opportunity for practices to obtain systematic feedback from patients about the services which they provide, to include these within their service development plans and to engage patients in these plans.

- the contract will incorporate systems to ensure the appraisal of doctors recently established (see above) and will ensure proper funding of appraisal within each PCT. The fixed retirement age of 70 will be abolished, as each GP will instead be subject to appraisal and revalidation.

- the new contract "will encourage an expanded role for practice management in primary care, supported by the development of practice management competencies.... Practices will receive funding for practice management through the global sum. In some cases it will not be cost-effective for every practice to have its own practice manager."[20]

- about two-thirds of the increased investment will be spent on rewards for higher quality.

- there will be a new obligation to give a warning to a patient before removal from a practice list, and to give reasons for any removal.

6.107   The Inquiry heard that Ayling was a single-handed practitioner who, for sometime, employed his wife as his practice manager. Thus his clinical isolation was, in our view, compounded by his organisational isolation. The move away from an individual GP contract to a practice–based contract would not impact greatly on a single-handed practitioner as such. However, the elements of appraisal, active engagement of patients and the expanded role for practice management under the closer scrutiny of a PCT may lead to an earlier and more open identification of questionable activity by a single-handed GP.

6.108   As Professor Forsythe observed to the Inquiry:

> "I think that they [practice managers] are beginning to feel part of the organisation [the local PCT]. In a sense, currently in general practice the practice manager, potentially is a very isolated person."

Conclusion

6.109   The impact of the Government's plans and investment in health services has dramatically altered the landscape of the NHS. At an organisational level, it is almost unrecognisable as the NHS in which Ayling practised. The emphases on patient safety, remedial action for poor clinical performance, closer scrutiny of untoward events and empowering patients in the management of services are greatly welcomed.

6.110   For individual patients, however, we believe it is too early to conclude that should they encounter another Ayling, particularly in the general practice setting, improved systems are yet fully developed which would enable their concerns to be heard and acted upon.

20   RCGP Briefing on New GMS Contract, February 2003.

6.111 Our recommendations, therefore, are directed towards strengthening what is now in place rather than offering new or alternative proposals for action that is specifically directed to the individual elements of the Ayling story. Identification of criminal activity lies outside the boundaries of the NHS, but we do believe that, should there be a repetition of the complaints and concerns surrounding Ayling in his years of practice, the potential exists for earlier identification of these and more assertive action to be taken.

LIST OF ANNEXES

ANNEX 1
CHANGES IN CLINICAL PRACTICE – OBSTETRICS AND GYNAECOLOGY IN HOSPITAL AND COMMUNITY SETTINGS

Introduction

The very sensitive nature of the field of medicine dealing with women's diseases and reproduction demands of those who practise it, tact, courtesy and consideration for the patient. The Inquiry covers the period from 1971–2000. During those three decades, clinical practices changed. In general terms, sensitivity to the need to justify intimate personal examinations increased, whilst modern diagnostic equipment, especially ultrasound scanning, created alternative ways of gathering necessary information. The shift has been gradual. The pace of change has varied, not only from practice area to practice area, but from practitioner to practitioner.

This account of changes in clinical practice has been written with the advice and input of the three clinical experts appointed to assist the Inquiry. They are Mr Peter Bowen-Simpkins, Mr Jonathan Lane and Dr Michael Jeffries. Further details of their background and expertise are to be found at Appendix 5. The Inquiry is grateful to them for their work in ensuring that its understanding of clinical practice and procedures has been accurate and full.

Pelvic Examination

In gynaecological clinics in the 1970s, diagnosis of the cause of a complaint was through a process of detection. The first step was to take an accurate history. An extensive physical examination followed. Jeffcoate, for example, advised that "A full general examination is as important in gynaecology as in any other branch of medicine and more important than in some." [1] Such examinations could include examination of the heart, lungs and breasts (since "In all women who have not previously been pregnant, and in many who have, the breast changes constitute one of the earliest and most reliable signs of pregnancy"), before abdomen and pelvic examination. The last should be to confirm a diagnosis already made or suspected from the history or symptoms, but it should not be omitted and might need to be repeated from time to time when an illness was long-lasting, for the situation might change. Jeffcoate added 'Attempts to put the patient at ease by the use of familiar terms such as "my dear" or "mother" are doomed to failure.'

Equally, in family planning clinics in the 1970s it was standard practice to carry out pelvic examination and to take a cervical smear on an opportunistic basis (except in patients with no sexual experience). The standard texts of the day indicated that this was good practice. [2]

This position can be contrasted with standard good practice accepted by the late 1990s. Short draft guidance on intimate examinations was produced by the GMC in 1996. This was reviewed by a Working Party of the Royal College of Obstetricians and Gynaecologists (RCOG), which published more detailed recommendations in September 1997 (revised in 2002).

1   T.N.A. Jeffcoate, *Principles of Gynaecology*, Third Edition (1967), London, Butterworths.

2   See for example, Barnes J: *Essentials of Family Planning*, p. 16, Blackwell Scientific Publications, 1976.

RCOG discussed pelvic examinations in the gynaecological patient and advised that: 'Pelvic examination should not be considered an automatic and inevitable part of every gynaecological examination.' It was necessary to consider what information could be gained from such an examination as opposed to other sources, such as ultrasound. It noted that "the predictive value of 'routine' bimanual pelvic examination as a screening test in asymptomatic women is very poor." Also influential in this shift of emphasis was 1998 NHS Cancer Screening Programme guidance on clinical management of cervical smear taking. Routine pelvic examinations and smears are considered unhelpful unless there are clinical indicators such as family history or relevant symptoms.

The RCOG guidance noted that no remarks of a personal nature should be made during the examination even if they might be clinically relevant. They should await the point when the patient had dressed once more. For example, no comments about body weight should be made whilst a woman was undressed, despite its possible relevance to gynaecological problems. An exception might properly be made if examining a woman with dyspareunia, when sexual problems could be discussed during the examination. If so, it should be made clear to the patient that any questions asked were entirely technical, relating to the site and quality of the pain, and that the woman's feelings and sexual response were not being discussed.

Cultural attitudes vary toward intimate examinations in gynaecology. In North America, patients are more likely to perceive them as an essential part of every gynaecological assessment, especially in the private sector, often with a transvaginal pelvic ultrasound scan at the same time.

Wearing of Gloves in Performing Intimate Examinations
It has been considered mandatory practice for many years to wear gloves in performing pelvic examinations (especially on the examining hand), and all standard texts in obstetrics and gynaecology reflected this. Most gynaecologists would now wear gloves on both hands, and discard them after each patient. Today, gloves comprise a thin latex rubber or vinyl membrane, though in earlier years they would have been of thin low-grade polythene film or thicker rubber material. Examination of the rest of the body is usually undertaken without gloves, though practice can vary between countries.

Breast Examination
Breast examination may be performed either as a screening procedure, on an 'opportunistic' basis, or as a diagnostic examination of a woman with relevant symptoms.

Just as it was standard practice to carry out routine pelvic examinations in the 1970s, it was also standard practice in antenatal settings to carry out breast examination on the same basis. In the 1970s, some standard texts in obstetrics and gynaecology recommended routine breast examination in the antenatal setting, and a midwife often carried this out.[3] For gynaecological patients, clinical practice varied in the 1970s in relation to routine examination of the breasts at first visit to a hospital.

3   e.g. T.N.A. Jeffcoate, *Principles of Gynaecology*, Third Edition (1967), London, Butterworths. Other standard texts in obstetrics and gynaecology, such as those by Dewhurst, Wilson Clyne, and Guillebaud, did not refer to routine breast examination.

Today, in the UK and the Irish Republic, pelvic examination and breast examination are carried out only if there are clinical indicators to do so. Routine examination of the breasts in young women, particularly those seeking contraception, would be considered most unusual unless the patient herself requested it. The incidence of malignant conditions of the breasts in young women is so rare that it would not be justified in normal circumstances.

In guidance published in September 1997, RCOG noted that the American practice was to include breast examination within gynaecological practice, and noted that "Among obstetricians and gynaecologists in the UK practice varies." It advised that, although many women expect breast examination to be part of any gynaecological examination, there is no evidence that mortality from breast cancer can be reduced by any screening procedure in women under the age of 50. Obviously, breast examination is essential when women have reported the presence of a relevant symptom.

Contraceptive Advice

As noted above, in Family Planning Clinics in the 1970s it was common practice to perform both a pelvic examination and breast examination on patients seeking contraceptive advice. The standard texts of the day reflected this. For example:

> "The *breasts* should always be examined. The *blood pressure* should be recorded and an examination made of the *heart*. Examination of the *abdomen* follows to detect any abnormal masses, tenderness, or enlargement of any viscus.
>
> *Pelvic examination.* Since a cervical smear will be taken from most women at the time of first examination it is usual to begin the examination by passing a vaginal speculum to expose the cervix. [...] A bimanual examination is now made."[4]

Family Planning Association guidelines issued to clinic staff in 1974 stated:

> "History, examination and discussion with the patient precede the final choice of method. A gynaecological examination should be carried out at the first visit unless: the patient is menstruating and objects to being examined (or) the patient chooses a method such as the Sheath for which examination is not required."[5,6]

During the period of the Inquiry, the Family Planning Association issued several patient advice leaflets which referred to the possible need for examination by a nurse or doctor.

The Inquiry heard that from the early years, data sheets produced by the manufacturers of some[7] oral contraceptive pills stated that physical examinations should be part of the routine check made when prescribing oral contraceptives.

---

4   Barnes J: *Essentials of Family Planning*, p. 16, Blackwell Scientific Publications, 1976.

5   Family Planning Association Medical Department: *Family Planning Association Clinic Handbook*, p. 2, 27 November 1974.

6   Similar advice is contained in the booklet: Ramaswamy S, Smith T: *Practical Contraception*, Pitman Medical Publishing, 1976.

7   In other cases, such as the data sheet on Ovran produced in 1972 by Wyeth Limited, no statement of this kind was included.

For example, data sheets produced by Schering Chemicals Limited in 1974 stated:

> "A gynaecological examination (including breast examination) should precede the prescribing of any oral contraceptive. During treatment such examinations should be repeated every six months (WHO recommendation, 1968), together with checks on blood pressure."[8]

More recently, in 1999, the drug manufacturers Schering Health Care and Wyeth Laboratories stated:

> "Examination of the pelvic organs, breast and blood-pressure should precede the prescribing of any combined oral contraceptive and should be repeated regularly." [9]

However, the value of such examinations, particularly when set against their deterrent effect, was increasingly questioned. A 1980 pamphlet by a leading family planning doctor stated specifically that internal examinations were unnecessary.[10] In guidance published in September 1997, RCOG advised that "the low productivity of pelvic examination in the asymptomatic young woman prior to commencing use of the oral contraceptive pill makes it very difficult to justify such an examination which may deter uptake of contraception in vulnerable young women." The study cited in support dated back to 1975.

A local general practitioner gave evidence to the Inquiry that when he trained as a GP (qualifying in the late 1980s), the advice he had received was that the data sheet examinations were not necessary or appropriate. However, he also noted that he had observed, as a student, that there were practices in Kent where the policy was to adhere to the data sheet guidelines. Their justification was that if anything were to be missed, and if (for example) a form of cancer became apparent, then they would be liable for malpractice. However, by 1996, he considered that there was a consensus amongst GPs not to adopt this practice.

The Community Nursing Services Manager for South East Kent[11] told the Inquiry how practice developed in the Young Persons family planning clinic. Speaking of the early 1990s, she said:

> "… we were very concerned to ensure that we had the confidence of young people and that they would not be deterred from attending the clinic. We had learned as a result of a questionnaire filled in by the clients that they loathed having to have vaginal examinations. We therefore thought that it was very important that these should not be carried out as a matter of routine, that the question of carrying out such an examination should be broached very carefully by the doctor and the reason for the examination should be explained very carefully." (Susan Sullivan, para 9)

8   Association of the British Pharmaceutical Industry, *ABPI Data Sheet Compendium: Data sheets for Anovlar 21, Gynovlar 21, Minovlar, Minovlar EB, Eugynon 30 and Eugynon 50*, pp 621 and 623, 1974.

9   Association of British Pharmaceutical Industries: *Compendium of Data Sheets 1999 – 2000*, pp.1452 and 1748.

10   Guillebaud J: *The Pill*, 1980.

11   From 1992–1998.

The contents of the RCOG guidance published in September 1997 have been noted above. The guidance added that it was 'essential' that teenagers were made aware that prescription of the oral contraceptive pill was not conditional upon undergoing a pelvic examination.

Equally, breast examination in a family planning context is carried out only if there is a history of breast problems, when consent is taken as implied. Today, all standard texts in obstetrics and gynaecology implicitly reflect this guidance.

Diagnosis of Pregnancy: the GP Surgery

The Inquiry was told that before the development of reliable pregnancy tests and the widespread use of ultrasound scanning, it was common practice to undertake pelvic examinations of pregnant women at the first visit to a medical practitioner, in the first twelve weeks of their pregnancy. This was to ascertain the size of the uterus, to compare it to the gestational age of the pregnancy, based on the last menstrual period. A relatively accurate idea of the estimated date of delivery could be gained.

Reliable laboratory pregnancy tests, which simply necessitated the delivery of a urine sample to a local hospital laboratory, were widely available by the mid 1970s, and use of ultrasound scanning was standard practice in hospital settings by the late 1980s. This meant that, by then, except in cases of confinement at home or in a general practice obstetric unit, it was not common practice for general practitioners to carry out pelvic examinations in the general practice surgery.[12]

The Inquiry was shown examples of the 'co-operation card' or medical notes held by women during pregnancy in the 1980s. The 'boxes' recording the 'first visit' or examination, which might be performed by the woman's GP, made provision for both pelvic and breast examinations to be carried out. The same remained the case in notes current in the early 1990s. Notes current by the mid-1990s provided for examinations of the heart and lungs, examination of breasts, but instead of pelvic examination, there was simply a comment as regards the need for a cervical smear, if not up to date by the time of pregnancy. By 1999, the notes referred only to 'general physical examination', 'if required'.

However, almost inevitably, the format of the notes tended to lag behind clinical practice, as it developed. We were told that, whilst it is still common practice in many countries to undertake a breast and pelvic examination in early pregnancy and prior to prescribing the oral contraceptive pill, in the UK a pelvic examination is currently only done in most units when there is a specific problem or clinical indication such as the need to take an overdue cervical smear. A large number of general practices would not be in the habit of performing the breast and pelvic examinations that the clinical notes suggested might still occur or be permissible.

This shift occurred mainly as a result of developments in abdominal and pelvic ultrasound technology and the ready availability of reliable pregnancy tests. With increasing use of ultrasound through the 1980s the practice of vaginal examination was largely discontinued. Equally, pregnancy tests meant that an

12   Nor was it standard practice in hospital settings to conduct a pelvic examination earlier in
       pregnancy. The Inquiry was told that in hospital settings, vaginal examinations would
       sometimes be carried out in late pregnancy, if there were indications, in order to ascertain
       the capacity of the pelvis, or to assess the state of the cervix. A 'stretch and sweep'
       procedure would sometimes be recommended at the end of a pregnancy.

examination was no longer needed to diagnose pregnancy, and might be regarded as more intrusive than the alternative of a urine test. Thus, the Inquiry heard that by 1986, the practice of Dr Sarkhel, Consultant Physician in Sexual Health, was not to perform a vaginal examination when prescribing the emergency contraceptive pill. Whilst Ayling apparently did, stating that he did so in order to exclude the possibility of a pre-existing pregnancy, Dr Sarkhel's evidence was that he regarded the examination as unnecessary because a pregnancy test could perform the same function.

The Ante-Natal Clinic
The usual practice is for women to be referred, by their GP, to a hospital consultant and seen in a hospital ante-natal clinic in the first, or early into the second, three months of pregnancy.

The Inquiry heard that, up to the mid 1980s, a vaginal examination was often made at the patient's first attendance at the antenatal clinic to confirm the pregnancy and its duration (see above), to determine the position of the uterus and to exclude other abnormalities, such as ovarian cysts. The bony pelvis might also be examined. However, by that time and increasingly into the early 1990s, most patients attending hospital antenatal clinics would be examined by ultrasound. More and more frequently, an ultrasound scan would be done in the second trimester, at any time from 16 weeks through to 20 weeks (although ideally now it is done at 20 weeks gestation). If an ultrasound were done, it would not be necessary to examine the patient vaginally as well, especially as some women miscarry in early pregnancy and might blame vaginal examination for this misfortune.

In guidance published in September 1997, RCOG discussed vaginal examination. It advised that there was no scientific evidence to support the use of "routine" vaginal examination at the first antenatal visit. It noted that "routine" vaginal examination later in pregnancy is practised widely in some European countries. "There is no evidence that it reduces the risk of pre-term labour or has any effect on pregnancy outcome." [1995].

The Inquiry was told that since the introduction of the transvaginal scanning probe, vaginal examinations in early pregnancy have virtually ceased except in circumstances where a miscarriage or ectopic pregnancy is suspected.

Breast examination was an integral part of all booking visits at an antenatal clinic until the mid to late 1980s. It was commonly carried out on all pregnant women in the antenatal booking clinic, for two reasons. This was first to establish that the nipples were well developed and suitable for breastfeeding and, secondly, to exclude any obvious breast disease. The practice continued into the 1990s when it was largely abandoned. Community midwives undertook advice about breast-feeding.

In 1997, RCOG advised: 'There is no evidence to support routine breast examination in the asymptomatic pregnant woman. Antenatal interventions for the management of inverted and non-protractile nipples are of no value." [ref 27, 1997].

Labour and Delivery

The Inquiry was advised that in the early 1970s obstetric intervention reached new heights. Induction of labour was commonplace in some units, reaching 30% of all patients. The delivery methods, apart from normal vaginal delivery, were predominantly with forceps. The vacuum extractor (as described below) was seldom used. The Caesarean section rate was around 10–12%.

Obstetric forceps have been in use since the late 17th century. Obstetric forceps consist of two blades, a shank, which locks as a joint, and handles. They are somewhat akin to a pair of scissors. However, the lock is not fixed and the two blades can easily disassemble. The blades have two curves, namely a cephalic curve designed to fit around the baby's head and a pelvic curve, designed to fit into the pelvis and, more particularly, the birth canal. The normal presentation of a baby's head when full dilatation has occurred is for the occiput (the back of the head) to be uppermost so that the baby is facing towards the mother's anus. The two blades are applied separately and then are locked together. Traction is then applied with maternal effort and her contraction, and the baby is thus delivered. These are so called mid-cavity forceps and the most commonly employed.

Occasionally, a baby presents in the transverse position. In this circumstance the head lies to one side, facing one or other of the mother's hips. In this position the infant cannot be delivered vaginally and rotation of the head, to the occiput anterior position, has to be performed. If this is not possible then a Caesarean section needs to be undertaken. When the head is in the transverse position it can either be rotated manually to the occiput anterior position and then the mid cavity forceps applied, or Kiellands forceps can be used.

Kielland's forceps are unique. They do not have a pelvic curve and they have a sliding shank so that one blade can slide up or down on the other. This is so that the baby's head, which is often tilted to one side or the other in the transverse position, can be corrected. The advantage of the Kiellands forceps is that they can be rotated through as much as 180° as there is no pelvic curve. They are sometimes known as straight or rotational forceps. They require considerably more expertise, both to apply and to perform the rotation. The morbidity associated with the procedure is considerably higher than that with mid cavity forceps. Damage can occur to the baby, in terms of brain trauma, or to the mother, particularly in terms of large vaginal tears. Very good analgesia is required for their use. In the 1970s many obstetricians were expert at using rotational forceps although from 1975 onwards their use declined steadily.

Although vacuum extraction (the Ventouse) had been introduced in the late 1960s, it did not regain any great popularity until the 1980s. This particular form of obstetric instrument consists of a metal cup which fitted over the occiput of the baby's head. A vacuum is rapidly developed with a pump and the cup is thus firmly attached to the baby's scalp. This gives an excellent method of both flexing the baby's head and applying pressure with maternal contractions and effort. It is relatively atraumatic to the mother but may lead to minor problems with the baby. It has become increasingly commonplace and is now more commonly used than forceps. The disadvantage is that with firm traction the cup, occasionally, pulled off and re-application is difficult. In these cases attempts to use forceps would often then take place.

Since the 1990s much greater reliance has been placed on Caesarean section as the procedure itself has an increasingly lower morbidity and anaesthesia has become much simpler with the use of spinal and epidural analgesia.

In the 1970s, and until relatively recently, decisions about mode of delivery were made by consultants in the antenatal clinic. Active involvement on the labour ward was usually only undertaken in circumstances where the doctor on call (usually a registrar) contacted the consultant because of difficulties. It would be unusual for the consultant to be actively involved at the birth.

Cervical Smear Tests

Cervical screening began in Britain in the mid-1960s, and by the mid 1980s many women were having regular smear tests. The NHS Cervical Screening Programme was set up in 1988. A woman could choose whether to have her smear taken at her GP surgery by the GP or practice nurse, or at a community clinic such as a family planning or well-woman clinic.[13]

A leaflet published in 1994 by RCOG noted that all women between 20 and 64 who had ever had sexual intercourse should have regular cervical smear tests. It suggested that, whilst many trained GPs performed smears themselves, many had an experienced practice nurse to perform the procedure, and patients 'can have the smear taken by someone of the same or opposite sex according to your preference'.

In guidance published in September 1997, RCOG advised that there was no justification for taking cervical smears in teenagers. The NHS Cervical Screening Programme[14] recommended that calls for routine cervical cytology should be initiated after a woman's twentieth birthday and before her twenty-fifth birthday.[15]

Colposcopy

Colposcopy is indicated when a patient has two or more mildly abnormal (low grade) cervical smears, or after one moderately/severe (high grade) smear. In many private health systems (US and Germany) colposcopy is offered following a single low-grade cervical smear. The majority view in the UK has been that such a philosophy may lead to over-treatment in many young women of childbearing age. However, new guidelines on colposcopy developed by the NHS Cervical Screening Programme – in press – will recommend, as best practice, that colposcopy be carried out after a single mildly abnormal smear.

Colposcopy is almost always now carried out in an outpatient specialist hospital setting. With the patient's legs supported on rests, the cervix is examined through a low power microscope sited outside the genital tract. It allows the doctor an enlarged three-dimensional view of the cervix. Visualisation of the cervix may be assisted by painting the cervix with a dilute acetic acid ('vinegar'), and sometimes with an iodine solution. Cervical dysplasia becomes temporarily whiter than the adjacent healthy skin when acetic acid is applied to it, and, unlike healthy skin, it does not stain brown with iodine. Abnormal areas identified can be sampled by

13   See, for example, *Cervical Screening – A Pocket Guide*, NHS Cervical Screening Programme, November 1996.

14   Duncan, I (ed.): NHS Cervical Screening Programme, Publication No. 8, December 1997, p. 6.

15   Guidance issued by the National Institute for Clinical Excellence guidance in 2003 now recommends that cervical screening be deferred until the twenty fifth birthday.

small, directed punch biopsies. These small pieces of the tissue are sent to the laboratory for examination and confirmation of the diagnosis. The patient can return at a later date for treatment if required. Alternatively some patients can be managed on a "see and treat" single visit basis using a diathermy loop to excise the pre-cancerous area under local anaesthetic (LLETZ).

When Ayling started practising as a colposcopist in 1984, colposcopy was in its early days (in the UK) and there was no formalised training. Interested practitioners would usually attend a course in basic colposcopy and then receive supervised practical training from a more experienced practitioner.

In January 1996, 'Standards and Quality in Colposcopy' was published by the NHS Cervical Screening Programme. It noted that, at the time, only a few commissioners were likely to have defined a set of minimum standards for the colposcopy service within the screening programme. It hoped that these guidelines would provide an opportunity for review, and setting a clear service specification.

In April 1998, the British Society for Colposcopy and Cervical Pathology's (BSCCP's) scheme for accreditation was introduced. The Society established a register of practising colposcopists certified by the Society. It noted that, in the UK, colposcopy was predominantly carried out as part of the NHS Cervical Screening Programme; 'in this context colposcopy should only be performed by either BSCCP certified colposcopists or trainee colposcopists under supervision.'

For staff that were already in practice in April 1998, a 'grandfather clause' existed. This enabled them to apply for certification on the basis of their existing practices. Applicants were required to submit a short CV, and an audit of their personal colposcopic practice for a continuous 6-month period. Each colposcopist was required to see a minimum of 50 new colposcopy patients per annum: 'A Colposcopist who fails to see more than 50 new colposcopy patients per year will not be granted certification." The accreditation scheme came into effect in 2000, the date by which all practising colposcopists had to be accredited.

HSG (96) 31 – *A National Framework for the Provision of Secondary Care within General Practice* – stipulated that, from 1 April 1996, provision of secondary care services by GPs required Health Authority approval. For gynaecology procedures, the guidance specified that "links with specialists at a local provider unit to ensure back-up facilities will be necessary." Re-approval at least every 5 years was recommended, informed by regular clinical audit and peer review.

Today, due to the practical difficulties involved, only a handful of GPs in England are known to provide a specialist colposcopy service in the primary care setting. Under current quality assurance arrangements, NHS GPs providing a colposcopy service are visited and assessed every 3 years against the colposcopy standards developed by the NHS Cervical Screening Programme.

Chaperones
The Inquiry heard that within the hospital setting it was normal practice throughout the 1970s and subsequently, for a female chaperone to be present whenever a male doctor examined a patient. Thus, Mr John Brace, Consultant in Obstetrics and Gynaecology at the North Middlesex Hospital from 1959–1984,

stated: "Another rule of the department was that a male doctor would not examine a patient without being chaperoned by a female member of staff".[16]

In guidance published in September 1997, RCOG advised that:

> 'A chaperone should be offered to all patients undergoing intimate examinations in Gynaecology and Obstetrics irrespective of the gender of the gynaecologist. If the patient prefers to be examined without a chaperone this request should be honoured and recorded in the notes.'

It advised that 'No remarks of a personal nature should be made during pelvic examination' and that 'Throughout the examination the doctor should remain alert to verbal and non-verbal indications of distress from the patient. Any request that the examination be discontinued should be respected.'

RCOG's Working Party (2002) recommended that a 'chaperone should be available to assist with gynaecological examinations irrespective of the gender of the gynaecologist.' Ideally, that person should be a professional; but it noted that others, including receptionists, secretaries and family members could be acceptable when small or charitably funded clinics faced funding difficulties. Thus, pelvic examinations should 'normally' be performed in the presence of a female chaperone, preferably unrelated to the patient.

Chaperones in General Practice

Whilst the practice of ensuring male doctors in the hospital setting were chaperoned was well established, there was, and remains, considerable variation in practice amongst general practitioners. The RCOG guidelines noted that 'In a survey of general practitioners in the UK, Speelman et al found that 75% of female and 21% of male general practitioners never use a chaperone when performing intimate examinations on patients of the opposite sex. None of the female doctors and 16% of the males always offer a chaperone in these circumstances.' The study cited was published in 1993. In its Seminars, the Inquiry heard further evidence of considerable variations of practice amongst general practitioners, in the use of chaperones in their practice.

In April 1995, in the 'MDU News', the Medical Defence Union advised its members that it was advisable to have a chaperone present whilst examining female patients. It advised that this was a matter for the discretion of individual doctors but the circumstances that posed problems included examining the torso of female patients without proper explanation. The 1996 GMC guidance on intimate examinations suggested that 'whenever possible', doctors should offer a chaperone or invite the patient to bring a relative or a friend.

In later guidance (2002), the RCOG noted that the MPS would take the view that a family member would not fulfil their criteria for a chaperone, as they defined this as 'someone with nothing to gain by misrepresenting the facts.'

Also in 2002, the RCN produced a leaflet: "Chaperoning: The role of the nurse and the rights of patients", to provide guidance for nursing staff. It argued that 'all patients should have the right, if they wish, to have a chaperone present irrespective of organisational constraints.' Patients should be offered a chaperone and any refusal noted on the medical record. "When the chaperone is a nurse or

---

16   Inquiry Statement paragraph 8.

other member of the health care team, they can act as advocate for the patient, helping to explain what will happen during the examination or procedure, and the reasons why." It noted that a chaperone could be a reassuring presence.

Nurses and other health care professionals were also advised that they should consider being accompanied by a chaperone when undertaking intimate procedures, to avoid misunderstandings and, in rare cases, false accusations of abuse. The suggestion that a chaperone should act as a support to the patient, or as her advocate, is only one of a number of roles that the chaperone was expected to fill. Other roles would include that of helper for the doctor (assisting in procedures); as a protection for both patient and doctor; and as a witness. These roles are not necessarily compatible with one another.

GLOSSARY
Cervical Smear Test
A sample of cells is taken from the cervix and smeared onto a microscope slide to identify abnormal cells.

Colposcopy
Examination of the cervix through low power microscope sited outside the genital tract. It allows the doctor an enlarged three-dimensional view of the cervix.

D & C
Dilatation of the cervix and curettage of the uterine cavity. During the 1970–1980 period the most commonly performed minor gynaecological operation under general anaesthetic. Indications – mostly menstrual disorders and postmenopausal bleeding (to exclude cancer of the uterine body). Main risk is perforation of the uterus by the exploratory instruments (1–2%).

Now largely replaced by hysteroscopy, which allows visual entry and examination of the uterine cavity using a fine telescope with a videocamera. The perforation rate is lower, the complication more likely to be recognised and the procedure may be done with either local or general anaesthetic.

Laparotomy
The general term to describe any open abdominal surgical procedure. Usually used on consent forms where the diagnosis (and treatment) is uncertain prior to surgery. Often follows on from a diagnostic laparoscopy if minimal access surgery is not feasible – e.g. ectopic pregnancy in a fallopian tube. Most gynaecologists use a transverse suprapubic ('bikini') incision for cosmetic reasons. During closure of the abdominal wall a plastic tube drain may be left in place to prevent a wound haematoma (collection of blood). This is removed after 2–3 days by the ward nursing staff.

Pelvic, Bimanual or Internal Examinations
This refers to a form of examination of the female pelvis where one hand of the examiner – usually the left – is placed on the lower abdomen of the patient, and the forefinger and middle finger of the right hand together are inserted into the vagina. The structures between the two hands, mainly the womb and ovaries, can then be felt and their size, position and mobility ascertained.

Trimesters
The blocks of three months into which pregnancies are conventionally divided.

ANNEX 2
ORGANISATION OF THE NHS IN EAST KENT 1971 – 2002

1971–1974

On the foundation of the NHS in 1948, community health services, family practitioner and hospital services were organized in three separate structures. Community health services such as health visiting remained the responsibility of local government. The administration of family practitioner contracts (those GPs, dentists, pharmacists and opticians who contracted to provide services to the NHS) became the responsibility of Family Practitioner Committees (FPCs). Hospital services, with the exception of "teaching" hospitals, were grouped geographically under Regional Hospital Boards, and each had their own Hospital Management Committee (HMC):

In Kent, the administration of family practitioner contracts was organised on a countywide basis through the Kent FPC. Hospital services were organised through the SE Metropolitan Regional Hospital Board, which had the responsibility for service planning and development, appointing and holding the contracts of consultant medical staff in the hospital groups in their area and for medical staff training. In East Kent, the Thanet Hospital (which had two wings, one in Margate and the other in Ramsgate) and the Kent & Canterbury Hospital were the responsibility of the Isle of Thanet and Canterbury Group HMC.

1974–1982

This structure remained in place until 1974. The first major restructuring of the NHS in that year was predicated on setting up organisations based on natural geographical areas and populations to be served by more integrated health services. Regional Health Authorities (RHAs) were established, each with a number of Area Health Authorities (AHAs), to which Family Practitioner Committees became responsible. In each Area Health Authority there were a number of District Health Authorities (DHAs), which became responsible not only for the hospital(s) in their geographical district but also for community health services, transferred to the NHS from local government. Hospitals were identified as District General Hospitals (DGHs). The RHAs retained the responsibility for medical training and staffing, service strategy, hospital building programmes and the allocation of resources to the AHAs. Management of AHAs and DHAs was exercised through teams of appointed administrators, doctors, nurses and finance officers and at District level, representatives nominated by the hospital consultants and local GPs. The teams were expected to work through consensus agreement. This reorganisation also brought into existence Community Health Councils, coterminous with DHAs, which were charged with the responsibility to represent patient interests in the planning and delivery of health care in their District.

In East Kent, the SE Thames Regional Health Authority succeeded the former SE Metropolitan Hospital Board. The Kent FPC became accountable to the newly established Kent AHA. Within the Kent AHA, the Canterbury and Thanet District Health Authority and SE Kent District Health Authority were created. The Canterbury and Thanet DHA took over responsibility from the former Thanet and Canterbury Group HMC for the hospitals in the group. The Thanet General

Hospital and the Kent & Canterbury Hospital each became a DGH but were managed as before as a single entity. The South East Kent DHA became responsible for the William Harvey Hospital in Ashford as well as the Buckland Hospital in Dover, the Royal Victoria Hospital in Folkestone, and the Victoria Hospital in Deal.

1982–1984
In 1982, a further reorganisation took place, which was designed to decentralize policy and planning. This abolished the AHA tier of management, leaving DHAs responsible directly to RHAs and re-established FPCs as separately managed bodies accountable to the Department of Health. Consultant medical staff contracts were transferred from the RHA to the new DHAs. Hospitals and community health services were organised into individual administrative units.

In Canterbury and Thanet DHA, the administration of the Kent & Canterbury and Thanet General Hospitals was separated into two units. The hospitals in South East Kent DHA were also organized into two units – the Ashford Unit (which included the William Harvey Hospital) and the Channel Ports Unit, which included the Dover, Deal and Folkestone hospitals.

1984–1990
In 1984/5, the principle of general management was introduced into the NHS. In each RHA, DHA, FPC, hospital and health service unit a General Manager (GM) was appointed, with operational, financial and professional accountability to the next level of management for the performance of their organisation. Efforts were made to appoint doctors to these posts, as well as those with experience of public service management outside the NHS. GMs were expected to exercise a strong leadership role in their organisations in contrast to the consensus management of the past decade.

Of the GM appointments in east Kent, a surgeon was appointed to the Ashford Unit and an anaesthetist to the Thanet General Hospital Unit. The new GM of the Canterbury and Thanet DHA was a former admiral in the Royal Navy.

1990–2002
In 1990, the NHS was radically re-structured to create the "purchaser – provider" split, under which DHAs became the purchasers and commissioners of health care services provided by hospitals and other health services units, which in turn became autonomous NHS Trusts, with a Chief Executive and a Medical Director. Trust status was granted in annual "waves" from 1990/91 onwards. FPCs were renamed Family Health Services Authorities (FHSAs), to be managed by a Chief Executive, working with a new appointment of Medical Director. FHSAs were expected to move from a largely administrative function to a more managerial role in relation to GPs and issues of differing quality of care between practices.

In April 1994, the William Harvey Hospital, together with the Dover, Deal and Folkestone Hospitals, became the South Kent Hospitals NHS Trust. In this same year, the Canterbury and Thanet and South East Kent DHAs merged to form the East Kent District Health Authority.

In 1996, FHSAs as independent authorities were abolished and their responsibilities amalgamated into those of DHAs. The responsibilities of the Kent

FHSA were transferred to the re-formed East and West Kent DHAs. In 1996, the Kent and Canterbury Hospitals NHS Trust was established, as was the Thanet Healthcare NHS Trust.

In 1999, the three hospital Trusts (Kent & Canterbury Hospital, South Kent Hospitals and Thanet Healthcare) merged to become the East Kent Hospitals NHS Trust.

2002–

In 2002, further reforms of the NHS established Strategic Health Authorities (StHAs) and Primary Care Trusts (PCTs). StHAs are directly accountable to the Department of Health for monitoring the performance of all the NHS Trusts in their area, and for the overall framework of health care planning and policy for the population in their area. Primary Care Trusts largely emerged from Primary Care Groups (PCGs), which had been set up by DHAs in 2000 on the abolition of "fundholding". PCGs consisted of all GPs in a geographical area working together to manage a significant amount of the DHA's purchasing budget. PCTs inherited the full purchasing and commissioning responsibilities of the former DHAs, together with responsibility for the family practitioner services.

In Kent, the Kent and Medway SHA was established as a Kent-wide body, and in East Kent four PCTS were created: Ashford, Canterbury & Coastal, Shepway and Thanet & Dover.

ANNEX 3
CLINICAL ASSISTANTS IN THE NHS

What is a clinical assistant?

1.   Clinical assistants are career grade doctors employed on permanent contracts in hospital and community health services, who are not consultants or doctors in training. A clinical assistant does not require specialist accreditation, and works under the supervision of a consultant.

2.   The clinical assistant grade for doctors has existed in the NHS since its inception in 1946. The term is not found in the hospital medical staff terms and conditions of service, but is covered by the appointments procedure specified at paragraph 94, and by the NHS General Whitley Council agreements.

3.   Today, the majority of clinical assistants are employed on national terms and conditions of service, working on average two sessions per week.[1] General practitioners often undertake clinical assistant sessions in specialties that interest them. The clinical assistant pay scale overlaps with the pay scales for other hospital non-consultant career grades (NCCGs).

4.   Other non-consultant career grade (NCCG) doctors include Associate Specialists, Staff Grade doctors (from 1989), Hospital Practitioners (from 1979),[2] Senior Community Medical Officers and Community Medical Officers, and their many equivalents working on local NHS Trust contracts. An Audit Commission report on medical staffing in August 2002 found the Associate Specialist and Staff grades to be the fastest growing categories of hospital doctor.

How many clinical assistants are there in the NHS?

5.   The Department of Health collects annual statistics on all staff employed in the NHS in England.[3] The numbers of staff in the category *'clinical assistant'* have fallen steadily over the past decade,[4] from 7,084 (1,809 whole time equivalents) in 1992 to 3,942 (1,183 whole-time equivalents) in 2002.[5] The average annual percentage decrease between 1992 and 2002 was –5.7 per cent, between 1997 and 2002 was –7.3%, and between 2001 and 2002 was –12.3 per cent. The percentage of women has increased slightly from 33% in 1992, to 40% in 2002. The percentage of all clinical assistants who qualified in the United Kingdom was 74% in 2002, and the large majority work on part-time contracts.

1   PriceWaterhouseCoopers survey for the Pay Review Body, 2002

2   The hospital practitioner grade was introduced in 1979 for general practitioners with at least 2 years' full time hospital experience in a relevant specialty, or with a relevant specialist diploma and five years' experience as a clinical assistant.

3   Department of Health annual medical workforce census of NHS staff

4   The Department of Health is not able to supply statistics on numbers of clinical assistants prior to 1992

5   *Hospital, Public Health Medicine and Community Health Services Medical and Dental Staff in England 1992–2002*, Department of Health Statistical Bulletin, June 2003

6.   Since introduction of the Staff Grade in 1989, numbers in this grade have grown steadily to 5,088 in non-dental specialties in England in 2002.

Arrangements for appraisal of clinical assistants

7.   Following agreement with the British Medical Association on a national appraisal scheme, the Department of Health introduced annual appraisal for all non-consultant career grade doctors in October 2002.[6,7] Clinical assistant posts fall within the scope of the new arrangements. The appraisal process is the vehicle through which the General Medical Council's proposed revalidation requirements (i.e. five-yearly demonstration of fitness to practise) will be delivered for non-consultant career grade doctors. Employers must ensure that the requirement to participate in appraisal is a contractual requirement for all new employees.

8   The content of the national appraisal scheme – which relies on standard documentation to ensure consistency – covers clinical performance, teaching and research, and personal and organisational effectiveness. The appraiser will usually be the Clinical Director, lead clinician or named consultant, with the option of a specialty or sub-specialty review by those with relevant expertise and knowledge.

9   The guidance states that where serious concerns are identified during an appraisal, they should be dealt with in accordance with the agreed employer procedures – which may include the Chief Executive informing the Trust Board in a closed session – and the appraisal temporarily suspended until the identified problems are resolved. Both appraiser and appraisee are reminded of the "need to recognise that as registered medical or dental practitioners they must protect patients when they believe that a colleague's health, conduct or performance is a threat to patients." (GMC *Good Medical Practice* para 26, *GDC Maintaining Standards* para 2.4).

Modernising medical careers

10   The government outlined its intention to modernise NHS non-consultant career grades in February 2003:

>   "We intend to align the reform of (the NCCGs) closely with new training structures so that existing difficulties for doctors who wish to re-enter training are removed. New arrangements will have clear pathways back into training and better support for the continuing professional development of non-consultant career grades. This work will be linked with new provisions to allow more of their skills and experience to be assessed, recognised and used to help their careers. It will also reflect the work done on competency-based assessment."[8]

6   Advance Letter (MD) 05/02

7   The Code of Practice relating to the appointment and employment of HCHS locum doctors, issued in 1997, requires written assessment reports/references on locum doctors, including clinical assistants, at the end of each locum episode.

8   From the government's response to the consultation on SHO modernisation *Unfinished Business*, 25 February 2003.

11   In July 2003, following a review exercise, the Department of Health published a consultation document on modernising medical careers for non-consultant career grade doctors, including full-time hospital clinical assistants.[9] This drew attention to the following problems:

- "The grades are not seen as existing in their own right.
- The routes into the grade and the qualifications for entry are poorly defined.
- Support for continuing professional development (CPD) and further training in the NCCGs is inconsistent across the NHS.
- There is no clear structure for enabling recognised career progress.
- The nature of the work undertaken by NCCGs varies widely and there is little scope to recognise formally the significant competencies often deployed by them."

12   The following recommendations were put forward for consultation:

- "Entry to a career grade post should only be available to those who have met clear educational standards and can demonstrate specialty-specific competencies.
- The existing NCCG grades should be integrated into a single, simplified structure with no more than two recognised levels of practice.
- A system of limited accreditation of competencies is required through which NCCGs with formally recognised skills can work independently at the appropriate level.
- The medical Royal Colleges in working with the Department of Health and the Postgraduate Medical Education and Training board to establish competency-based assessment for trainees should seek to identify linked competencies for NCCGs.
- Local employers, Workforce Development Confederations (WDCs) on behalf of Strategic Health Authorities and postgraduate deans should ensure that resources and infrastructures are available for the CPD needs of NCCGs.
- Postgraduate Deans should support the education and development of NCCGs.
- All NCCGs whether employed on local or on national terms and conditions of service should be appraised annually and have a personal development plan (PDP).
- Workforce planners, both nationally and locally, should in co-operation with postgraduate deans ensure that a meaningful number of training slots for senior entrants are available in specialist training programmes.
- A new career structure for NCCGs should be seen as an integrated part of a new, modernised structure for medical careers.
- The new structure should no longer be called the non-consultant career grades.
- A new career structure and competencies will need new pay and terms and conditions of service which are appropriate for it.

---

9   *Choice and Opportunity: Modernising medical careers for non-consultant career grade doctors*, Department of Health, July 2003

- Special, formal arrangements will be required to place existing NCCGs at fair and appropriate points in the new structure.
- Further scoping work is required to determine the size and makeup of the current NCCG workforce.
- Further work will be undertaken to establish how the principles of the other recommendations may be given effect in the dental specialities."

13   Under the General and Specialist Medical Practice (Education, Training and Qualifications) Order 2003, a new Postgraduate Medical Education and Training Board (PMETB) replaces the Specialist Training Authority as the competent authority for assessment of eligibility for specialist registration. One aim of the Order is to broaden access to the GMC's specialist register by allowing training and qualifications to be assessed wherever obtained and medical experience to be taken into account.

ANNEX 4
THE "THREE WISE MEN"

1   Special professional panels (generally referred to as the "Three Wise Men") were set up by District Health Authorities under circular HC(82)13: 'Prevention of Harm to Patients Resulting from Physical or Mental Disability of Hospital or Community Medical or Dental Staff'. The procedure had been first conceived under HM(60)45: "Prevention of Harm to Patients Resulting from Physical or Mental Disability of Hospital Medical or Dental Staff". It was reviewed in 1982 following structural changes to the NHS.

2   The "Three Wise Men" procedure was separate from employment-based NHS disciplinary and suspension procedures. The purpose of the process was to provide a method by which the health of consultants and other practitioners could be reviewed by their peers, where concerns about a doctor's competence were suspected to be health-related. However, the procedure could be used "in cases where it is possible that disciplinary action could arise but where there is reason to suspect disability."[1]

3   Under HM(60)45, each hospital or group of hospitals was advised to appoint "a small sub-committee of the Medical Staff Committee consisting of members of the senior medical staff who would receive and take appropriate action on any report of incapacity of failure of responsibility, including addiction." The sub-committee, appointed by annual election, would comprise three or four members who would be known and readily accessible to all members of the medical staff. It was responsible to the Medical Staff Committee, who determined its terms of reference, but it did not have a duty to report back to the Medical Staff Committee.

4   The "Three Wise Men" would make confidential inquiries into cases brought to their attention, and where necessary, would bring serious cases to the notice of the hospital authorities to decide on any action to be taken. In so doing, the "Three Wise Men" could claim the protection of qualified privilege against any action for defamation.

5   Under HC(82)13 the procedure was modified, and extended to include general practitioners in connection with health authority appointments held in hospitals or community clinics:

- It was recommended under HC(82)13 that each District Health Authority set up a standing Special Professional Panel of senior medical/dental staff. When a case was presented, a small sub-committee drawn from this panel was organised to receive and take action on any report of incapacity due to physical/mental disability. The sub-committee was not required to report back to the Panel.
- The membership of the Panel was laid out in the guidance, along with the suggested composition of a sub-committee. For hospital doctors, the sub-committee would comprise of three consultants. Where the

---

1   HC(82)13, at paragraph 15.

subject of inquiry was also a GP, a member of the Local Medical Committee would be added.

- Health authorities were asked to make arrangements to protect the confidentiality of all communications made under the procedure unless disclosure was ordered by due legal process.

- A case would be relayed in the first instance to a Panel member, who would then inform the Chairman of the Panel. The Chairman would then convene a sub-committee of three members selected from the Panel.

- The sub-committee was not obliged to prove that the practitioner was a risk to patients through ill-health but, if it decided that there was a risk, it was required to inform the Regional Medical Officer and the Medical Officer of the employing authority.

- It was then the duty of the Medical Officer of the authority to decide on the basis of that report whether a further investigation and/or action needed to be taken.

6   In the 1990s this responsibility was not transferred to NHS Trusts, and the process has fallen into disuse in most parts of the country.

7   For community-based general practitioners, a similar system existed based on Local Medical Committees. For example, where a Family Practitioner Committee was concerned about a doctor's incapacity to carry out the obligations of his terms of service due to physical or mental disability, a doctor would be required to supply a medical report to the Local Medical Committee. In removing a doctor's name from the medical list, at least a third of members of any FPC sub-committee would be doctors from a panel nominated by the Local Medical Committee.[2]

8   In 1994, Liam Donaldson (then Regional Director of Public Health in Northern and Yorkshire Region, now Chief Medical Officer in the Department of Health in England) commented on the effectiveness of the "Three Wise Men" procedure in hospitals in the following terms:

    "The "Three Wise Men" procedure, in which a panel of consultants in a hospital has the power to intervene when patients are at risk of harm because of a doctor's illness, is often criticised as ineffective and not widely known. This is partially justified. The panel invariably operates in secret. ... Experience suggests, however, that the mechanism can work well: many examples exist of sick doctors who have been identified by it, treated and successfully returned to work without anyone in the hospital being aware of the problem. The same is true of the work of members of local medical committees on behalf of sick general practitioners."[3]

9   The British Medical Association's Consultants and Specialists Committee and the Department of Health are now developing a new framework for discipline and suspension, for Trusts in England to use in drawing up their own detailed procedures for responding to concerns about the practice of doctors and dentists. The proposed new framework will replace existing

2   SI 1974/160

3   *Sick doctors*, Editorial, British Medical Journal, 309, 557-558, 1994 (3 September)

guidance on discipline, suspensions, and the "Three Wise Men" procedures. It will also replace the 'paragraph 190' right of appeal to the Secretary of State against termination of appointment.[4]

10   A BMA/DH joint statement of agreed principles, issued on 9 September 2003, stated that:

> "The framework is intended to address the 'suspension culture' in the NHS by introducing new arrangements for restrictions on practice and exclusions from work. The focus of the framework is to help doctors and dentists. Exclusion will be regarded as a last resort and no practitioner should be excluded from work other than through these new arrangements." (para 1)

11   Under the framework, Trusts will be required to develop a co-ordinated approach to handling concerns, to quickly establish the facts, ascertain the extent of any risk or validity of any concern, and take immediate appropriate action. Investigation into concerns about a doctor's practice will be handled by appropriately trained individuals locally, and the advice of the National Clinical Assessment Authority (NCAA) will always be sought on options to resolve the matter. Disciplinary procedures will be regarded as a last resort.

---

4   Paragraph 190 of the 'old' terms and conditions of service for hospital medical and dental staff. In October 2003, consultants in England voted in favour of accepting the new consultants' contract.

ANNEX 5
THE REGULATORY FRAMEWORK FOR VOCATIONAL TRAINING QUALIFICATIONS IN GENERAL PRACTICE

The following notes are extracted from the websites of the Royal College of General Practitioners (www.jcptgp.org.uk/certification/framework.asp) and the Department of Health (www.doh.gov.uk/medicaltrainingintheUK/about.htm).

1979: The National Health Service (Vocational Training) Regulations

1   The length and content of vocational training for general practice in the United Kingdom is determined by parliamentary regulations. The National Health Service (Vocational Training) Regulations 1979 came into operation in England and Wales on 16 February 1980.[1] These regulations made vocational training mandatory for doctors entering the profession as principals after 15 February 1981.

2   The Regulations, inter alia, prescribe the medical experience which, under section 31 of the National Health Service Act 1977, a medical practitioner is required to have acquired before being included in a Health Authority's list of practitioners undertaking to provide general medical services. The prescribed experience specified by the Regulations is set out at **Annex A**.

3   The Joint Committee on Postgraduate Training for General Practice[2] is appointed to administer the regulations for the whole of the United Kingdom, and must abide by them in considering applications for certificates from doctors who have completed the training.

1986: European legislation and freedom of movement

4   In 1986 the first phase of European law came into force which gave doctors rights of free movement in Europe. This laid down certain minimum requirements for the training of general practitioners including the length and content of the training period. Each member country was required to introduce a package of training conforming to these requirements by 1 January 1990.

5   The second phase, which made specific training mandatory for all who wished to work in general practice, took effect from 1 January 1995. The arrangements are enshrined in law under Title IV, Council Directive 93/16/EEC of 5 April 1993 to facilitate the free movement of doctors and the mutual recognition of their diplomas, certificates and other evidence of formal qualifications. This is often shortened to the 'European Directive' or the 'Medical Directive'.

6   Under the terms of Council Directive 93/16/EEC, each Member State must appoint a Competent Authority or Authorities. The Competent Authority has two main functions: first to supervise the training for

---

1   Corresponding regulations came into operation on the same day in Scotland and Northern Ireland.

2   There are plans to replace both the Joint Committee and the parallel body for hospital doctors with a new single body, the Postgraduate Medical Education and Training Board.

general practice within that Member State, to issue certificates to doctors who complete the training programme satisfactorily, and to issue certificates of Acquired Rights to those doctors who are eligible for this. Secondly, it is responsible for the verification of certificates or diplomas issued under Council Directive 93/16/EEC presented by doctors entering the Member State. Host Member States are required by the Directive to recognise certificates or diplomas issued under 93/16/EEC by other Member States.

7   For the purposes of general practice, these responsibilities are divided between two Competent Authorities in the United Kingdom. The Joint Committee on Postgraduate Training for General Practice is the Competent Authority with responsibility for the supervision of training and the issue of certificates. The General Medical Council has responsibility for the recognition of certificates presented by doctors entering the UK from Europe to practise medicine.

1994: European Requirements and amending Regulations in the UK

8   The Vocational Training Regulations of 1979 were amended and supplemented in England, Wales and Scotland by the Vocational Training for General Medical Practice (European Requirements) Regulations 1994, which came into force on 1 January 1995.[3] The 1994 amendments brought important changes for doctors working as locums and assistants in general practice.

9   From 1981 to 1994, vocational training in the United Kingdom was mandatory only for those doctors who wished to enter the profession as principals in general practice. Locums and assistants were not affected and could practise simply on the basis of their full registration with the General Medical Council. Since 1 January 1995, all doctors working in general practice in the National Health Service (other than as GP Registrars), have been required to possess a certificate of prescribed or equivalent experience issued by the Joint Committee, or an exemption from the need to have the experience referred to in the Vocational Training Regulations, or an Acquired Right. In other words, the Regulations now require specific training for all who wish to work as general practitioners within the NHS, unless the doctor holds a legal exemption or an Acquired Right.

1997: NHS Vocational Training for General Medical Practice Regulations

10   In 1997 most of the regulations and their amendments mentioned above were revoked and replaced by The National Health Service (Vocational Training for General Medical Practice) Regulations 1997. These regulations came into force on 30 January 1998 and give effect to some of the long-term aims of the Joint Committee and the profession.[4] For the first time since 1979 amendments were made to the prescribed training programme, the arrangements for final or Summative Assessment of doctors completing the programme, and the approval of training posts. The revised list of prescribed medical experience specified by the

---

3   Corresponding regulations were again made in Northern Ireland.

4   Corresponding regulations came into operation on the same day in Scotland and Northern Ireland.

Regulations, and the competencies to be tested by summative assessment, are set out in **Annex B**.

11   Some of the 1994 Regulations remain extant today in so far as they refer to the Medical Directive, the Competent Authority, assistants and deputies and acquired rights. All doctors working in general practice today, whether as a principal, assistant, locum or deputy, must possess a certificate of prescribed or equivalent experience issued by the Joint Committee on Postgraduate Training for General Practice, or a legal exemption, or an acquired right to practise. The only exceptions are doctors who are training in general practice (GP Registrars) and those working outside the National Health Service, in private practice.

Eligibility to Practise

12   In order to be eligible to practise as a general practitioner principal in the National Health Service, doctors must satisfy one of the criteria listed below:

a.   Doctors who possess a Certificate of Prescribed Experience or a Certificate of Equivalent Experience issued by the Joint Committee on Postgraduate Training for General Practice.

b.   Doctors who possess a Certificate of Specific Training in General Medical Practice awarded in one of the member states of the European Economic Area (EEA) other than the UK.

c.   Doctors who possess a Certificate of Acquired Rights awarded in one of the Member States of the European Economic Area (EEA) other than the UK.

d.   Doctors who were principals in NHS general practice on 15 February 1981.

e.   Doctors who were on 15 February 1981 serving in the Defence Medical Services in a capacity which could be regarded as equivalent to that of a principal in general practice in the NHS, and are in possession of a statement from the Director General of Medical Services confirming this.

f.   Doctors who were principals in NHS general practice before 15 February 1981 and returned to the Medical List of a Health Authority or Health Board as a principal general practitioner in the NHS before 15 February 1990.

g.   Doctors who hold a recognised primary medical qualification awarded in one of the member states of the European Economic Area (EEA) other than the UK entitling them to be fully registered under section 3 of the Medical Act 1983, and who were established in the United Kingdom on 31 December 1994.

h.   Doctors who wish to practise as principals for the provision of limited medical services and were included in the Medical List of a Health Authority or Health Board as providing such limited services on 31 December 1994.

13   Doctors may be employed as locums, deputies or assistants in general practice if they fulfil one of the criteria a) to g) listed above. The only other doctors who may be employed as locums/deputies/assistants are those who were employed in these capacities, in NHS general practice, on either 10 days in the four year period ending 31 December 1994, or, on 40 days in the ten year period ending 31 December 1994. Doctors in this group hold Acquired Rights and may practise as locums and assistants but not as principals.

ANNEX A
EXTRACT FROM THE NATIONAL HEALTH SERVICE (VOCATIONAL TRAINING) REGULATIONS 1979[5]

Prescribed experience[6]

5. – (1) "Subject to the provisions of regulations 7(4) and 8(3), the medical experience needed to satisfy paragraph (a) of section 31 (2) of the Act is –

(a)   before 16th August 1982 the satisfactory completion of a period or periods of training amounting to at least 12 months whole-time employment or its equivalent as a trainee general practitioner;

(b)   on and after 16th August 1982 the satisfactory completion of a period or periods of training amounting to at least 3 years whole-time employment or its equivalent, of which –

    (i)   at least 12 months whole-time employment or its equivalent shall be training as a trainee general practitioner, and

    (ii)   the remainder shall be training as a practitioner in educationally approved posts and shall include not less than 6 months whole-time employment or its equivalent in each of two of the following specialities –

>   General Medicine,
>   Geriatric Medicine,
>   Paediatrics,
>   Psychiatry,
>   One of Accident and Emergency Medicine or General Surgery,
>   Any one of Obstetrics or Gynaecology, or Obstetrics and Gynaecology

(2) The medical experience prescribed in paragraph (1) shall be acquired within not more than 7 years immediately preceding the date of application for a certificate of prescribed experience."

5   SI 1979 / 1644

6   After 15 February 1981, doctors applying to be included on the Medical List had to produce a vocational training certificate of prescribed (or equivalent) experience issued by the Joint Committee on Postgraduate Training for General Practice, or a statement of exemption. The Medical Practices Committee had the power to refuse an application if a doctor was not suitably experienced, and a health authority could not include a doctor on the Medical List unless the MPC had granted the application.

ANNEX B
EXTRACT FROM THE NATIONAL HEALTH SERVICE (VOCATIONAL TRAINING FOR GENERAL MEDICAL PRACTICE) REGULATIONS 1997:[7]

Prescribed medical experience:

"6. – (1) Subject to regulation 12(9), the medical experience prescribed for the purposes of section 31(2)(a) of the Act is the satisfactory completion of a period or periods of training amounting to at least three years employment, and meeting the other requirements of this regulation.

(2) The reference in paragraph (1) to three years employment, and the references in paragraphs (3) and (4) to other periods of employment, are to periods of whole-time employment; but, subject to paragraph (8), the requirements of this regulation may be satisfied by periods of part-time employment of equivalent duration.

(3) The training shall include a period or periods amounting to at least 12 months employment as a General Practice (GP) Registrar with a practitioner who falls within regulation 7(1).

(4) The remainder of the training -

(a)   shall be spent as a practitioner in posts falling within regulation 8; and

(b)   shall include a period or periods amounting to not less than 6 months nor more than 12 months employment in each of two specialties mentioned in different paragraphs below -

      (i)   General Medicine;

      (ii)   Geriatric Medicine;

      (iii)   Paediatrics;

      (iv)   Psychiatry;

      (v)   One of -
          Accident and Emergency Medicine; or
          General Surgery; or
          Accident and Emergency Medicine together with either General Surgery or Orthopaedic Surgery;

      (vi)   One of -
          Obstetrics; or
          Gynaecology; or
          Obstetrics and Gynaecology.

(5) Where training is spent in employment in specialties which are not mentioned in sub-paragraph (b) of paragraph (4), not more than six months employment in any one such specialty may be taken into account in calculating, for the purposes of paragraph (1), the period or periods of training undertaken.

7   SI 1997/2817

(6) The Joint Committee shall supervise the training and shall in particular secure that it complies with the requirements of article 31(1) of the Medical Directive, or (in the case of part-time training) article 31(1) as appropriately modified together with article 34 (the text of articles 30, 31(1) and 34 as they had effect on the date these Regulations were made is reproduced in Schedule 1).

(7) The prescribed experience must be acquired within the period of seven years ending on the day on which a person makes an application for a certificate of prescribed experience under regulation 10.

(8) In relation to periods of part-time employment -

(a)   in computing any period of training which began on or before 31st December 1994 there shall be disregarded any period of part-time employment during which the duties of the person employed occupied less than half of the time usually occupied by the duties of persons employed whole-time in similar employment; and

(b)   in computing any period of training which began after 31st December 1994 there shall be disregarded any period of part-time employment during which the duties of the person employed, taken week by week, occupied less than 60 per cent of the time usually occupied by the duties of persons employed whole-time in similar employment;

and in relation to any period of training which began after 31st December 1994 employment which is not whole-time shall not be regarded as equivalent to whole-time employment unless it includes at least two periods of whole-time employment, each lasting not less than one week, one such period falling within paragraph (3) and one within paragraph (4).

(9) For the purposes of this regulation, a "month" includes a period which begins on the first Wednesday of the month (whether or not that is the first day of the month) and ends on the last day of the month.

Competencies to be tested by summative assessment:[8]
"The competencies to be tested by summative assessment are:

* factual medical knowledge which is sufficient to enable the practitioner to perform the duties of a general practitioner;
* the ability to apply factual medical knowledge to the management of problems presented by patients in general practice;
* effective communication, both orally and in writing;
* the ability to consult satisfactorily with general practice patients;
* the ability to review and critically analyze the practitioner's own working practices and manage any necessary changes appropriately;
* clinical skills; and
* the ability to synthesize all of the above competencies and apply them appropriately in a general practice setting."

8   SI 1997/2817 at Regulation 9 (2).

ANNEX 6
GP DEPUTISING CO-OPERATIVES

1   In 1974, the statutory responsibility of NHS general practitioners to arrange the provision of out-of-hours care (i.e. at night, weekends, bank and public holidays when the surgery is closed) for their patients was set out in the Terms of Service for doctors, at Schedule 1 of the 1974 General Medical Services Regulations.[1] Out-of-hours care would usually be delivered by the patient's own general practitioner or practice partners, by other GPs in the locality on a formal or informal rota system, or by a commercially-run GP deputising service.

2   Formal regulation of deputising services was introduced gradually. In 1984, Family Practitioner Committees (FPCs) were required to monitor the use and quality of deputising services by GPs, and were given the power to terminate unsatisfactory deputising arrangements. The monitoring of these deputising services was usually discharged by the appointment of a doctor at the FPC to act as deputising services liaison officer.

3   Over the years a number of changes were made to the GPs' Terms of Service to reflect changing policies and practices. Major changes were made to the Terms of Service following the introduction of a new GP contract in 1990. This reinforced the GP's responsibility for the care of his patients at all times, including responsibility for any deputy, and set out in more detail requirements on a GP's availability to patients, including provisions for doctors working less than full-time. These changes, together with the various other amendments to the Terms of Service since 1974, were consolidated in the NHS (General Medical Services) Regulations 1992 at Schedules 2, 12 and 13.[2]

4   SI 1992/635 provided that "a doctor shall be under no obligation to give treatment personally to a patient provided that reasonable steps are taken to ensure the continuity of the patient's treatment". It stipulated that a GP was responsible for the acts and omissions of any doctor acting as his deputy, any deputising service while acting on his behalf, and any person employed by, or acting on behalf of, him or such a deputy or deputising service. In the case of doctors acting as deputy to another doctor whose name is also included in the Medical List, the deputy was responsible for his own acts and omissions.[3] The regulations further required that GPs must inform the Family Health Services Authority (FHSA) of any arrangement for engaging a deputy on a regular basis, and obtain the FHSA's consent before entering into such an arrangement.

---

1   SI 1974/160.

2   SI 1992/635.

3   Recent changes in the regulations have allowed GPs and personal medical services providers fully to transfer (rather than delegate) responsibility for out-of-hours care to a PCT-accredited provider.

5   The first GP co-operative was established in Bolton in 1977. A GP co-operative is a group of locally based general practitioners who come together to provide out-of-hours services on a non-profit making basis. In effect, a GP co-operative delivers an extended deputising rota system in its locality. It provides services in competition with commercial deputising services, which are privately owned and managed. By taking control locally of service quality and costs, the purpose is to deliver a more responsive and cost-effective service. In many areas, GP co-operatives have become a focus for wider social, professional and educational contact between GPs.

6   Further GP co-operatives were set up in the North of England, followed by a several in the South East.[4] In 1993, 31 co-operatives operated in England and Wales. By 1997, the National Association of GP co-operatives had 261 members, co-operatives varying in size, sophistication and number and location of emergency centres. Over the past 10 years, the pattern of provision of out-of-hours care has changed significantly, with most GPs working in co-operatives and with other NHS providers having been developed, notably NHS Direct and Walk-In Centres.

        Today, two thirds of all general practitioners in the UK are part of a GP deputising co-operative, and over 300 such co-operatives exist across the UK.

7   The key features of GP co-operatives typically include the following:

        •   GP co-operatives tend to be companies limited by guarantee, with each member GP being liable for £1. All members have an equal share in ownership and an equal vote. There is no share capital. Any surplus cash flow is owned by members, and usually redistributed in the form of increased payments to members for work done.
        •   GP co-operatives are governed by a board, management committee or Council whose members (unpaid) are elected by member GPs.
        •   GP members appointed as medical managers of the co-operative are usually paid for their work at a sessional rate linked to the NHS hospital practitioner grade.
        •   GP co-operatives often have a manager who is accountable to the Board for the smooth running of the organisation.
        •   In most cases, out-of-hours work is undertaken by GP co-operative members. Exceptionally, a co-op may use doctors who are not members.

8   In the early 1990s, the National Association of GP Co-operatives (NAGPC)[5] – a body representing the majority of GP deputising co-operatives at national level – was set up. The NAGPC started as a pressure group to influence government policy and resourcing in relation to out-of-hours provision. It now exists to encourage and support the

4   The Association of South East Kent and East Sussex Doctors on Call Ltd (SEADOC), of which Clifford Ayling was a member, was established in August 1992.

5   The NAGPC is a company limited by guarantee that has a chairman and council members elected from and by the membership. Council members are elected on a regional basis for a two-year period. Each subscribing GP co-operative has one vote at the annual general meeting. Subscriptions cost £1·00 per month per GP.

development of GP co-operatives, and represent its members. It provides practical guidance on setting up and running co-operatives, and holds an annual conference. Its current guidance states: "Although the level of complaints is generally very low, all patient complaints should be recorded and investigated fully."

9   In 1995, the Department of Health established a £45 million Out-of-Hours Development Fund and reformed the fee structure for out-of-hours services. The purpose was to help develop and maintain GP out-of-hours services, by allowing GP co-operatives to bid for funds to offset operating costs.

10   In 1999, the GPs Terms of Service were changed to give GPs the right to decide whether and where patients should be seen.[6] All practitioners in general medical practice, including those providing restricted services or with limited lists (but excluding those who were relieved of the responsibility to provide out-of-hours services under **paragraph 18(2) of the terms of service**) are eligible, at the discretion of the Health Authority, to receive direct reimbursement of certain expenses which they incur to maintain or improve out-of-hours services.

11   In March 2000, John Denham, Minister of State in the Department of Health, commissioned an independent review of out-of-hours medical care services in England. Led by Dr David Carson, its remit was to consider all aspects of out-of-hours provision, focusing on quality, accountability, accessibility, integration, consistency of response, and value for money. The review report, *Raising Standards for Patients: New Partnerships in Out-of-Hours Care*, published in October 2000, recommended the introduction of an accreditation scheme, and integration of out-of-hours services with NHS Direct (the nurse-led telephone advice service), and other out-of-hours services such as district nurse services, 24-hour pharmacy services, and social services emergency duty services. The review proposals were accepted by the government and are being implemented.

12   In June 2002, the Department of Health published quality standards in the delivery of out-of-hours services, which specified in relation to complaints handling that:

• "All out-of-hours providers will comply with the NHS complaints procedure.
• All providers will monitor and audit complaints in relation to individual staff.
• All providers will always investigate and review all significant events and all reports on such events must include clear recommendations; all reports will be submitted to the PCT responsible for the area in which the event took place.
• All providers must demonstrate that they are continuously monitoring patient satisfaction and taking appropriate action on the results of that monitoring."[7]

6   National Health Service (General Medical Services) Regulations 1999.

7   *Quality Standards in the Delivery of GP Out-Of-Hours Services*, Department of Health, June 2002, at pages 3-4.

13   From 1 October 2002, accreditation of organised out-of-hours providers became the responsibility of Primary Care Trusts. All organised providers of out-of-hours services are required to submit a quarterly report to their Primary Care Trust on the manner in which they have delivered their service measured against the benchmark of specified quality standards.[8] All organised providers of out-of-hours services (i.e. GP co-operatives or commercial deputising services) are to be accredited by 31 March 2004 and thereafter will be subject to re-accreditation once every three years, or sooner if there are grounds. The accreditation system and quality standards are currently being reviewed in order to streamline and reduce bureaucracy.

14   In June 2003, the BMA announced that general practitioners had voted to accept the new general medical services contract negotiated between them and the NHS Confederation. The new contract allows GPs a choice as to whether they provide out-of-hours care to their patients. This does not prevent practices continuing to provide routine surgeries in the evening or at weekends where they choose to do so in response to patient need. Practices will have to apply for PCT approval if they wish to provide out-of-hours care directly to their patients.

15   On 4 March 2004, the Health Minister John Hutton announced a new £30 million incentive scheme that will reward Primary Care Trusts for providing high quality out-of-hours healthcare for patients. Under the new scheme, Strategic Health Authorities will be responsible for assessing whether a PCT has qualified for payments.

16   From April 2004, PCTs will become responsible for planning the delivery of out-of-hours care to their population, and for commissioning out-of-hours care. They may contract with existing practices to supply the service. There will be flexibility to develop innovative models of working using a combination of service providers including the GPs themselves, but also NHS Direct, NHS walk-in centres, GP co-operatives, practice partnerships, paramedics, GPs/primary care nurses in A&E departments and deputising services. GP co-operatives, where they continue to exist, will be expected to design, implement and manage new methods of delivering a high quality service. Strategic Health Authorities have overall responsibility for performance management of the changes, and for helping Primary Care Trusts work together where an out-of-hours provider covers more than one PCT area.

8   *The roles and responsibilities of those engaged in the delivery of GP out-of-hours services*, Department of Health, June 2002. The quality standards for out-of-hours accreditation were developed by the Department of Health in conjunction with the Royal College of General Practitioners. All GP co-operatives are required to have complaints procedures accredited with the Health Authority.

ANNEX 7
NURSE REGISTRATION, QUALIFICATIONS, AND CLINICAL GRADING AS AT 1998

1   In 1998, the High Court ordered that Ayling's examinations of female patients should be chaperoned by a 'qualified nurse'. Ayling appointed as a nurse chaperone an enrolled nurse, at clinical grade B. This note provides summary background briefing on nurse registration, qualifications and clinical grading in 1998.

Nurse registration:

2   'Qualified' nurses were those who met the competencies specified, for the purpose of nurse registration, in The Nurses, Midwives and Health Visitors Rules Approval Order 1983.[1] The Rules do not describe the role of the nurse at either level of registration but state the competencies to be achieved or outcomes established *at the point of registration* (known as threshold standards.) The Rules provide for two levels of registered nurse.

3   The competencies required for the purpose of registration are set out at Rules 18 (1) and 18 (2), which are reproduced in full at **Annex A**. The competencies set out at Rule 18 (1) became known as Level 1, and those at Rule 18 (2) as Level 2. Nurses with Level 2 competencies (referred to as second level nurses) would undertake nursing care under the supervision of nurses with Level 1 competencies (referred to as first level nurses).

4   The United Kingdom Central Council for Nursing, Midwifery and Health Visiting (UKCC)[2] maintained a register of nurses, comprising several parts that included:

•   Part 1 – first level nurses trained in general nursing;
•   Part 2 – second level nurses trained in general nursing (England and Wales);
•   Part 12 – first level nurses trained in adult nursing (Project 2000 – see para 7 below).

5   All registered nurses were required to work in accordance with the standards set out in the UKCC's Code of Professional Conduct. This made it clear that all registered nurses were accountable for their practice.

Nurse qualifications:

6   'Registered nurses' were qualified nurses who had undertaken a 3 year course of training and were eligible for registration under Part 1 of the UKCC register. Enrolled nurses were qualified nurses who had completed a 2 year, less theoretical, course of training and were eligible for registration under Part 2 of the UKCC register. In other words, enrolled nurses were 'second level nurses' for the purpose of registration.

---

1   SI 873/1983

2   The United Kingdom Council for Nursing, Midwifery and Health Visiting (UKCC) was abolished in 2002. Its statutory functions were taken over by the Nursing and Midwifery Council (NMC) in April 2002.

7   In May 1986, the UKCC published *Project 2000 – A New Preparation for Practice*. This proposed that, for the purpose of registration, there should be only one level of trained nurse by the year 2000. Enrolled nurse training would cease, and existing enrolled nurses would be given the opportunity to convert to Level 1 registration through 'conversion' training programmes. Conversion would not be a condition of continued registration. The government agreed the proposals in 1989, and enrolled nurse training was subsequently phased out.[3] By the mid 1990s, Project 2000 pre-registration nurse education programmes based in the higher education sector were widely implemented.

8   In October 1997, the UKCC published *Enrolled Nursing – An Agenda for Action*. This followed concerns that employers were limiting the practice of second level nurses and were deploying them as healthcare assistants. In July 1998, in response to concerns about shortages of qualified nurses, the DH's Chief Nursing Officer asked NHS employers to consider ways to encourage back into NHS employment enrolled nurses who had let their registration lapse, and would like to return to work. The Chief Nursing Officer stated:

> "The UKCC's Code of Conduct and Scope of Professional Practice make it clear that while all nurses must acknowledge the limits of their competence they can develop their practice to the benefit of patients beyond the level reached to achieve registration. Many enrolled nurses have acquired additional knowledge, skills and competencies beyond those required at the point of their registration, which should be fully taken into account when considering opportunities for employment."[4]

9   Currently, the following statement on the competence of the enrolled nurse is published on the website of the Nursing and Midwifery Council:

> "Rule 18(2) of The Nurses, Midwives and Health Visitor Rules Approval Order No. 873 1983 sets out a list of competencies that an enrolled nurse is required to have met prior to registration. It is recognised, however, that enrolled nurses who have undertaken further professional development, additional professional experience and/or have completed post-registration education courses will expand their knowledge and competence over time."[5]

Nurse clinical grading and pay:

10   A new clinical grading structure, providing for 9 new pay scales (A–I), was introduced in the NHS from April 1988.[6] The definitions of Scales B and D are set out at **Annex B** attached.

---

3   See Davies C and Beach A: *Interpreting Professional Self-Regulation – a History of the United Kingdom Central Council for Nursing, Midwifery and Health Visiting*, Routledge, 2000.

4   HSC 1998/137, *Enrolled Nursing – An Agenda for Action*, 31 July 1998

5   Nursing and Midwifery Council, 2003

6   Advance Letter (NM) 1/88

11   For pay code purposes, it was made clear that second level (enrolled) nurses should be assigned to the minimum point on Scale D (NP 26), and first level (registered) nurses to a higher point on Scale D (NP 31).[7] In 1998, Scale B pay started at £9,675, and Scale D pay at £12,630. (As independent contractors to the NHS, general practitioners could determine the pay grade of the staff they employed.)

12   In 1998, the DH published *'Agenda for Change – Modernising the NHS Pay System'*. This proposed a new national pay framework with local flexibilities that would apply to all directly employed NHS staff (except doctors and dentists and most senior managers). It stated:

> "For **nurses and midwives**, there will be a new modern career structure, replacing current clinical grades. There will be three broad flexible ranges – qualified nurses, a higher range of expert nurses and clinical managers and above that nurse consultants. There would be a clear minimum pay threshold for each of these, reviewed nationally. Locally pay rates and pay progression within each range would depend on assessment of particular responsibilities and professional competencies needed in the job and satisfactory performance. Qualified nurses will be supported by vocationally qualified staff – who may, under our new approach to lifelong learning, develop their skills progressively to complete professional training."

13   Subject to successful pilot ('early implementation') schemes, the new NHS pay and grading system will be implemented across the NHS from October 2004.

Nurse chaperones:

14   No qualification is needed for appointment as a nurse chaperone, and in hospital settings it is common practice for nurses in the healthcare assistant grade (Scales A–C) to be used as chaperones. Healthcare assistants could be vocationally qualified (NVQs). Where registered nurses are appointed as nurse chaperones, it would be usual to appoint second level nurses.[8]

---

7   Advance Letter (NM) 1/98 at Appendix 2, Part 2, Section 1.

8   Janice Gosby, Nursing and Midwifery Council, personal communication.

ANNEX A
THE NURSES, MIDWIVES AND HEALTH VISITORS RULES
APPROVAL ORDER 1983[9]

Rule 18 (1):

"Courses leading to a qualification the successful completion of which shall enable an application to be made for admission to Part 1, 3, 5, or 8 of the register shall provide opportunities to enable the student to accept responsibility for her personal professional development and to acquire the competencies required to:

a. advise on the promotion of health and the prevention of illness;

b. recognise situations that may be detrimental to the health and well-being of the individual;

c. carry out those activities involved when conducting the comprehensive assessment of a person's nursing requirements;

d. recognise the significance of the observations made and use these to develop an initial nursing assessment;

e. devise a plan of nursing care based on the assessment with the co-operation of the patient, to the extent that this is possible, taking into account the medical prescription;

f. implement the planned programme of nursing care and where appropriate teach and co-ordinate other members of the caring team who may be responsible for implementing specific aspects of the nursing care;

g. review the effectiveness of the nursing care provided, and where appropriate, initiate any action that may be required;

h. work in a team with other nurses, and with medical and para-medical staff and social workers;

i. undertake the management of he care of a group of patients over a period of time and organise the appropriate support services;

related to the care of the particular types of patient with whom, she is likely to come into contact when registered in that Part of the register for which the student intends to qualify."

Rule 18 (2):

"Courses leading to a qualification the successful completion of which shall enable an application to be made for admission to Part 2, 4, 6, or 7 of the register shall be designed to prepare the student to undertake nursing care under the direction of a person registered in Part 1, 3, 5, or 8 of the register and provide opportunities for the student to develop the competencies required to:

a. assist in carrying out comprehensive observation of the patient and help in assessing her care requirements;

b. develop skills to enable her to assist in the implementation of nursing care under the direction of a person registered in Part 1, 3, 5 or 8 of the register;

c. accept delegated nursing tasks;

9   SI 873/1983

d.   assist in reviewing the effectiveness of the care provided;

e.   work in a team with other nurses, and with medical and para-medical staff and social workers;

f.   related to the care of the particular type of patient with whom she is likely come into contact when registered in that Part of the register for which student intends to qualify."

ANNEX B
CLINICAL GRADING DEFINITIONS FOR NURSES – SCALES B AND D:[10]

Scale B:

"2.11 Scale B applies to posts in which the post-holder carries out assigned tasks involving direct care in support of a registered nurse, midwife or health visitor and:

a.   regularly works without supervision for all or most of the shift;

or

b.   leads a team of staff at Scale A.

No statutory nursing or midwifery qualifications are required for posts at this level."

Scale D:

"2.13 Scale D applies to posts in which the post-holder is responsible for the assessment of care needs and development of programmes of care, and/or the implementation and evaluation of these programmes. The postholder is expected to carry out all relevant forms of care without direct supervision and may be required to demonstrate procedures to and supervise qualified and/or unqualified staff.

The post-holder is required to have:

(i)   first level registration;

or

(ii)   second level registration, plus a recognised post-basic certificate, or to have an equivalent level of skill acquired through experience;

or

(iii)   second level registration and to supervise the work of other staff."

---

10   Extract from Advance Letter (NM) 1/88, issued by the Department of Health on 13 May 1988, and still extant in 1998.

ANNEX 8
POLICY GUIDANCE RELATING TO 'WHISTLEBLOWING'
IN THE NHS

1   The Department of Health issued guidance relating to whistleblowing in
        the NHS for the first time in June 1993, under cover of EL(93)51.[1] This
        stated that: "An important principle of this guidance is that it should be for
        local management in consultation with all staff and local staff
        representatives to implement it in a way that is appropriate to local
        circumstances. They will wish to consider how best to promote a culture of
        openness and dialogue which at the same time upholds patient
        confidentiality, does not unreasonably undermine confidence in the
        service and meets the obligations of staff to their employer."

2   NHS Trusts were encouraged to develop internal whistleblowing policies
        and procedures at local level for handling staff concerns about health care
        (separate from the statutory complaints procedure or established
        grievance procedures), and to identify designated officers outside the line
        management chain to whom staff could take concerns. At the same time,
        warnings were given of the risks of making outside disclosures.

3   In September 1993, following criticism of the guidance at a Select
        Committee hearing on Public Expenditure, the NHS Chief Executive
        issued a letter to all Trusts clarifying that the guidance did "not prevent
        staff from seeking the advice and guidance of their MP, as a constitutional
        right, at any time."[2]

4   Reports by the Audit Commission[3] and the Nolan Committee on
        Standards in Public Life[4] highlighted that implementation of the guidance
        was patchy. On 25 September 1997, the Minister of State for Health (Alan
        Milburn) wrote to Chairs of NHS Trusts and Health Authorities to urge
        them to incorporate the 1993 guidance into local employment policies and
        practices, and ensure that NHS staff were "able to raise their concerns
        about health care matters in a responsible way without fear of
        victimisation."[5] The letter also set out plans for greater openness and legal
        protection for whistleblowers.

5   On 2 July 1999, the 1998 Public Interest Disclosure Act came into force.
        The Act gives significant statutory protection to employees who disclose
        information reasonably and responsibly in the public interest and are
        victimised as a result. Gagging clauses in employment contracts and

1   EL(93)51, *Guidance for staff on relations with the public and the media*, Department of
        Health, June 1993.

2   Dear Colleague letter to NHS Trusts from Sir Duncan Nicol, NHS Chief Executive,
        entitled *Guidance for staff on relations with the public and the media* – EL (93)51, 7
        September 1993

3   *Ensuring Probity in the NHS*, Audit Commission, 1994.

4   First and second reports of the Committee on Standards in Public Life, 1995 and 1996.

5   'Dear Colleague' letter to Chairs of NHS Trusts and Health Authorities on *Freedom of
        Speech in the NHS*, from the Minister of State for Health, Alan Milburn, 25 September
        1997.

severance agreements which conflict with the protection afforded by the Act would be void.

6   On 27 August 1999, the NHS Executive issued new guidance on whistleblowing in the NHS.[6] This appended a summary of the main provisions of the 1998 Public Interest Disclosure Act, and enclosed a resource pack produced by Public Concern at Work to provide practical guidance on developing and promoting a whistleblowing policy. NHS Trusts and Health Authorities were asked to review their local policies on whistleblowing, and update as necessary to ensure that they complied with the new statutory protection for employees. In particular, they were expected to:

• Designate a senior manager to deal with employees' concerns and protect whistleblowers;
• make clear that NHS Trusts and Health Authorities should have in place local policies and procedures and set out minimum requirements;
• issue guidance to all staff so they know how to speak up against malpractice;
• provide whistleblowers with adequate protection against victimisation; and
• prohibit "gagging" clauses in contracts.

7   Whistleblowing policies and procedures in the NHS overlap with, and are intended to work in conjunction with, NHS policies and procedures in relation to employment, clinical governance, patient safety, discipline and complaints. They also overlap with professional codes of conduct and accountability. For example, the General Medical Council advises doctors that:

"If you have grounds to believe that a doctor or other healthcare professional may be putting patients at risk, you must give an honest explanation of your concerns to an appropriate person from the employing authority, such as the medical director, nursing director or chief executive, or the director of public health, or an officer of your local medical committee, following any procedures set by the employer. If there are no appropriate local systems, or local systems cannot resolve the problem, and you remain concerned about the safety of patients, you should inform the relevant regulatory body. If you are not sure what to do, discuss your concerns with an impartial colleague or contact your defence body, a professional organisation or the GMC for advice."[7]

6   HSC(99)198, *The Public Interest Disclosure Act 1998: Whistleblowing in the NHS*, NHS Executive, 27 August 1999.

7   *Good Medical Practice*, Third Edition, General Medical Council, May 2001.

ANNEX 9
THE CODE OF PROFESSIONAL ACCOUNTABILITY FOR NURSES AND MIDWIVES

Nurses have been regulated under statutory self-regulation since the Nurses Registration Act of 1919. The General Nursing Councils (GNCs) were set up under the Act to maintain discipline within the profession and to keep a register of those who were fit to practice.

Prior to the 1902 Midwives Act, anyone could practice as a midwife but have, since that date and following the first Midwives Registration Act, been regulated. Under the Act, the Central Midwives' Board was established consisting of four doctors. The Board was responsible for issuing midwives' certificates, laying down the conditions of admission to a new roll of midwives (also set up under the Act), regulating and restricting the practice of midwives and setting examinations. In addition to the Board, the Act made local councils the 'local supervising authority' over midwives, and they were responsible for investigating allegations against midwives in their local area. (please see pages 4 and 5 – Supervisors of Midwives).

Today, the Code of Professional Conduct for Nurses, Midwives and Health Visitors, published by the Nursing and Midwifery Council (NMC)[1] is 'a statement of principles' which outlines the procedures for accountability and practice which all registered Nurses, Midwives and Health Visitors must adhere to. Its purpose is to "inform the professions of the standard of professional conduct required of them in the exercise of their professional accountability and practice" and to "inform the public, other professions and employers of the standard of professional conduct that they can expect as a registered practitioner".

The overall purpose of the Code of Professional Conduct is to:

- inform the professions of the standard of professional conduct required of them in the exercise of their professional accountability and practice
- inform the public, other professions and employers of the standard of professional conduct that they can expect of a registered practitioner.

The core principles stated in the Code are:

- as a registered nurse, midwife or health visitor, you are personally accountable for your practice. In caring for patients and clients you must:
- respect the patient or client as an individual
- obtain consent before you give any treatment or care
- protect confidential information
- co-operate with others in the team
- maintain your professional knowledge and competence
- be trustworthy
- act to identify and minimise risk to patients and clients.

1   Source – Nursing and Midwifery Council Code of professional conduct – effective from 1 June 2002 and available at www.nmc-uk.org

The code also states that as a registered nurse, midwife or health visitor, you must:

- protect and support the health of individual patients and clients
- protect and support the health of the wider community
- act in such a way that justifies the trust and confidence the public have in you
- uphold and enhance the good reputation of the professions
- you are personally accountable for your practice meaning that you are answerable for your actions and omissions, regardless of advice or directions from another professional
- you have a duty of care to your patients and clients, who are entitled to receive safe and competent care
- you must act to identify and minimise the risk to patients and clients
- you must act quickly to protect patients and clients from risk if you have good reason to believe that you or a colleague, from your own or another profession, may not be fit to practise for reasons of conduct, health or competence. You should be aware of the terms of the legislation that offer protection for people who raise concerns about health and safety issues, and
- where you cannot remedy circumstances in the environment of care that could jeopardise standards of practice, you must report them to a senior person with sufficient authority to manage them and also, in the case of midwifery, the supervisor of midwives. This must be supported by a written record.

The following chronology, from 1970, relates to the Code of Practice for nursing and midwifery.

1970 – Briggs Committee established to consider quality and nature of nurse training. They recommended a unified central council with national boards for each of the 4 countries of the United Kingdom.

1979 – Nurses, Midwives and Health Visitors Act – states that "There shall be a corporate body known as the United Kingdom Central Council for Nursing, Midwifery and Health Visiting" (UKCC). Its responsibilities under the act were to:

- Set standards for education, practice and conduct
- maintain a register of qualified nurses, midwives and health visitors
- provide guidance to registrants
- handle professional misconduct complaints and allegations of unfitness to practice due to ill health.

1983 – The Nurses, Midwives and Health Visitors Rules Approval Order.

1992 – Nurses, Midwives and Health Visitors Act reforms the powers of UKCC as follows:

- UKCC becomes the directly elected body and the national Boards became smaller, executive bodies appointed by the respective Secretaries of State
- All professional conduct functions transferred to UKCC

1993 – Nurses, Midwives and Health Visitors (Professional Conduct) Rules 1993 Approval Order

1997 – The Nurses, Midwives and Health Visitors Act – consolidation of 1979 Act which established the UKCC and 1992 Act which reformed their powers and composition. A review of this Act finds that the relationship between the UKCC and the National Boards 'could be improved'

1998 – Nurses, Midwives and Health Visitors (Professional Conduct) (Amendment) Rules 1998 Approval Order

1999 – The Government approves proposals to replace UKCC and the four National Boards with a Nursing and Midwifery Council as listed in Health Service Circular HSC1999/030. The recommendations include "the appointment of a Director of Nursing Regulation and a director of Midwifery Regulation" and "the new council to have ultimate control of the regulatory process and ownership of setting and monitoring standards"

1999 – The Government publishes "Making a Difference" which sets out their strategy for nursing, midwifery and health visiting in England. In June 2000 the NHS Executive publishes an update to this paper titled "Integrated Working in Primary Care".

July 2001 – a consultation by the UKCC reviews its Codes, and the three documents are merged.

April 2002 – UKCC ceases to exist and its functions are taken over by the NMC, as are the functions of the English National Board. The Boards for the other 3 countries are replaced with new bodies.

1 June 2002 – the new 'Code of Professional Conduct' comes into effect, published by the NMC (formerly UKCC). The document is similar to the old Code in most respects, but introduces a specific requirement to help student nurses and midwives to develop their competence and includes indemnity insurance. The new code merges the former UKCC's 'Code of Professional Conduct' and two associated publications, 'The scope of professional practice' and 'Guidelines for professional practice'.

UKCC Publications[2]
A number of UKCC publications are still available on the subject of regulation and accountability. These include circulars, Registrar's letters, consultation documents, press releases, explanatory leaflets, research reports, guidelines, standards and position statements. The items produced were often a culmination of a consultation process. The following list gives some examples of the publications.

- July 1983 – Handbook of Midwives Rules
- November 1984 – Code of Professional Conduct for Nurses, Midwives and Health Visitor
- March 1989 – Exercising Accountability
- April 1993 – Standards for Records and Record Keeping

2   Source – Interpreting Professional Self-Regulation – Authors Celia Davies and Abigail Beach

- August 1993 – Complaints about Professional Conduct
- July 1997 – Protecting the Public
- June 1998 – Making a Complaint
- December 1998 – Midwives Rules and Code of Practice

Supervisors of Midwives

Background

The Nurses, Midwives and Health Visitors Act 1997[3] makes provision for the supervision of midwives by local supervising authorities (LSAs). The former United Kingdom Central Council for Nursing, Midwifery and Health Visiting (UKCC) (now The Nursing and Midwifery Council, NMC) recommended that a practising midwife who is professionally experienced in the supervision of midwives should undertake the function within the LSA.

The Midwives code of practice states, "you [a midwife] should contact your supervisor of midwives on all matters as required by the midwives rules. You and your supervisor of midwives, through your respective roles, should work towards a common aim of providing the best possible care for mothers and babies. You and your supervisor have a mutual responsibility for effective communication between yourselves in order that any problems can be shared and resolved. Your supervisor of midwives should give you support as a colleague, counsellor and advisor. This should be developed in order to promote a positive working relationship which is conducive to maintaining and improving standards of practice and care. Supervisors of midwives should ensure that effective communications exist between themselves, LSAs, those engaged in determining health service policy and medical staff in order that relevant issues are appropriately addressed and resolved."

Statutory Supervision of Midwives – Local Supervising Authorities (LSA) Standards for England[4]

"Effective supervision enables the development of midwifery leadership which creates a practice environment where midwives assume their professional accountability for high quality, evidence-based midwifery care." (ENB 1999 Advice and Guidance for Local Supervising Authorities and Supervisors of Midwives)

LSA are charged to "lead the development of standards and audit of supervision throughout the LSA which can serve as a basis for local frameworks." (ENB 1999 Advice and Guidance for Local Supervising Authorities and Supervisors of Midwives)

Responsible midwifery officers worked together to produce these standards to ensure an equitable approach to statutory supervision of midwives throughout England.

The focus is on a proactive model of supervision for all midwives who may work in a variety of settings providing midwifery care. These standards aim to give guidance to all concerned with the supervision of midwives and represent the minimum standard to be achieved.

3   Source – Midwives rules and code of practice – 1998

4   Source – www.midwife.org.uk/national_standards/Intro.htm

"Central to the quality of supervision is the relationship between the midwife and her supervisor and the trust which it engenders." (ENB 1999 Advice and Guidance for Local Supervising Authorities and Supervisors of Midwives).

Supervisors of midwives will strive to ensure that midwives have a positive relationship with their supervisor that: facilitates safe and autonomous practice and promotes accountability; is based on an honest and open dialogue; promotes trust and an assurance of confidentiality; enables midwives to meet with their supervisor of midwives at least once a year to help them to evaluate their practice and identify areas of development; enables the supervisor to act as the midwife's advocate when required.

An audit of the standards for statutory supervision of midwives should take place annually. It is envisaged that the audit process will be undertaken internally through an evidence-based approach and the results included in the annual report submitted to the LSA. Verification of evidence, provided by the individual supervisory teams, will be undertaken on a random basis by the Responsible Midwifery Officer or designated alternate.

Evidence derived from the use of this audit approach will inform strategic development of the LSA function. Involvement of all Supervisors of midwives in the audit process will provide greater opportunities for extending the sharing of good practice.

Evaluation of the Impact of the Supervision of Midwives on Midwifery Practice and on the Quality of Midwifery Care[5]

The above study was commissioned by the English National Board for Nursing, Midwifery and Health Visiting (ENB) and supported by the UKCC to examine the impact of statutory supervision upon midwives and their practice. Data was collected across the country and six very different sites were chosen for in-depth study.

Extracts from the main findings

- The vast majority of the midwives interviewed wanted to retain supervision.
- Most midwives interviewed lacked knowledge of supervision. This limited the extent to which they could make best use of it.
- Confidentiality in supervision was seen as essential by midwives. Where confidence was betrayed, trust was destroyed and this was likely to undermine the midwife's professional confidence. The issue of confidentiality in supervision is, however, complex.
- Midwives interviewed sought many different types of support from supervision. The longing to be heard and to have someone with whom to off-load to was the overwhelming support need.
- Approachability was valued highly in a supervisor. Many midwives also wanted their supervisor to exercise 'clout' within their organisation and to influence the quality of midwifery care at the level of policy.
- On some sites, the philosophy of general management in the Trust served to undermine the supervision of midwives.

5   Source – English National Board Research Highlights May 1998

ANNEX 10
REFORMING THE NHS COMPLAINTS PROCEDURE:
CONSULTATION ON DRAFT REGULATIONS

1   On   17 December 2003, the Department of Health launched a consultation on the draft regulatory framework – *The National Health Service (Complaints) Regulations 2004* – that will underpin a reformed NHS complaints procedure. The draft regulations, together with a covering letter, are published on the Department of Health's website at www.doh.gov.uk/makingthingsright/. The consultation period will run from 1 January to 31 March 2004.

2   Proposals for a reformed NHS complaints procedure recently received Parliamentary approval as part of the Health and Social Care (Community Health and Standards) Act 2003. The reforms meet the commitment made in the NHS Plan to change the NHS complaints procedure in the light of an independent evaluation study, and subsequent comments on its recommendations. *NHS Complaints Reform: Making Things Right*, published by the Department of Health in March 2003, set out reforms designed to make the NHS complaints system more accessible, responsive, independent and more closely linked to work to improve services.

3   The draft regulations, which would come into effect on 1 June 2004, provide for the following:

- All services provided by NHS bodies are covered by the NHS complaints procedure. Independent sector organisations providing care under NHS arrangements will be required, through their contracts, to operate a comparable complaints process.
- The Commission for Healthcare Audit and Inspection (CHAI) will undertake independent review of complaints referred to them where the complainant is dissatisfied with local resolution. This could involve consideration of the complaint by an independent panel of three lay people.
- Changes in the procedure for making complaints about primary care services bring time limits and reporting arrangements into line with those for other parts of the NHS.
- It is recognised that complaints may be raised with any member of staff and resolved on the spot.
- The time limit for making a complaint is extended from 6 months to one year. Complaints should be acknowledged within 2 working days and responded to within 25 working days. A complaint that is not resolved within 6 months may be referred to CHAI.
- Complex complaints that involve care provided by more than one body or events that are subject to more than one type of investigation, are recognised as needing careful assessment and response. There must be agreement between the bodies involved as to which of them should take the lead in handling and considering the complaint.

- A new duty is placed on NHS organisations and primary care practitioners to co-operate in receiving and investigating complaints, and in providing a co-ordinated response where appropriate. Provision is made for joint action by CHAI and the Commission for Social Care Inspection (CSCI).
- Subject to a complainant's agreement, a complaint may be referred straight to an independent body.
- NHS organisations and primary care practitioners must designate a Board member or similarly senior person to ensure that complainants receive full consideration and response, and that action is taken as a result of the findings of investigations.
- Each NHS body and primary care provider (and CHAI) must ensure that there is effective publicity and information on its complaints arrangements, and that its NHS staff are appropriately informed and trained in their operation.
- Regular reports must be provided on the numbers of complaints received, the substance of those complaints, and the action taken as a result.

4.   Comprehensive supporting draft guidance on the new procedure will be circulated for comment in early 2004. 'Sister' draft regulations about responding to social care complaints will also be published for consultation early in 2004.

ANNEX 11
QUALITY AND PERFORMANCE INDICATORS IN PRIMARY CARE

Introduction:

1   The Commission for Health Improvement (CHI), as the independent regulator of the NHS, has a statutory responsibility to carry out clinical governance reviews of all NHS bodies in England and Wales, and to publish overall ('star') ratings of NHS Trust performance against key targets and indicators.[1] The Government is responsible for setting priorities for the NHS, which in turn determines the indicators relating to key targets.

2   The two principal purposes of measuring NHS performance are to ensure accountability to the public and Parliament for the quality of service delivered in return for ever increasing levels of investment; and to enable NHS clinicians and managers to undertake meaningful benchmarking – comparing their performance results and methods against those of their peers – so that they can identify scope for improvement and share knowledge of best practice. The ratings and indicators are intended to provide people working in the NHS and the public with accessible and easy to understand information about the performance of local health services.[2]

3   Performance ratings for NHS Trusts in England covering the year ending March 2003 are the first to be produced and published by CHI. (In previous years, performance ratings were published by the Department of Health.) This year is also the first in which primary care trusts (and mental health Trusts) received full star ratings.

Performance ratings of NHS Primary Care Trusts:

4   In July 2003, the Commission for Health Improvement (CHI) published, for the first time, full performance ('star') ratings of all Primary Care Trusts in England. This followed publication, in March 2003, of the indicator lists for primary care. Key targets are the most significant factors in determining overall performance ratings. The ratings methodology for NHS Primary Care Trusts is similar to that for Acute Trusts, but indicators are grouped under unique headings that reflect Primary Care Trust responsibilities in public health improvement, and as providers of primary care and commissioners of primary and secondary care services.

---

1   Subject to the enactment of the Health and Social Care (Community Health and Standards) Bill, this responsibility will pass to the new Commission for Healthcare Audit and Inspection (CHAI) with effect from April 2004. Health Authorities also use performance indicators to measure the performance of local health services, including primary care organisations.

2   Further information on CHI reports and the development of Primary Care Trust indicators can be found at Annex C.

5   In a recent review, for CHI, of studies of patients' experience of general
        practice care, Coulter et al noted:

> '... there is no consensus on what is important to measure.
> Nevertheless, it seems clear that interpersonal communications and
> clinical competence feature highly in patients' minds as important
> factors affecting the quality of their experience, while access and
> organizational issues are also important, albeit slightly less so.'[3]

**Key targets and indicators for rating Primary Care Trust performance,
2002/03:**

6   CHI assessed the performance of NHS Primary Care Trusts during
        2002/03 against a limited number of key targets and a larger number and
        range of indicators. The NHS performance assessment framework for
        Primary Care Trusts highlights four areas of performance that are of
        interest to patients and the public, and relate to their core functions:

- key targets (i.e. the most significant areas of performance in the NHS
  Plan)
- access to quality services
- improving health
- service provision

7   The **key targets** for Primary Care Trusts in 2002/03 are listed in full at
        Annex A. The targets focus on access to care, numbers of patients on
        waiting lists, health promotion, and financial management. Performance
        against targets is assessed in terms of whether the target has been
        achieved, whether there has been some degree of underachievement or
        whether the target was significantly underachieved.

8   The **performance indicators for Primary Care Trusts** in 2002/03 are
        listed in full at **Annex B**. Indicators are constructed using routine
        statistical and survey sources, including the Primary Care Survey. The
        broader range of indicators make up a 'balanced scorecard' to refine the
        judgement on ratings. This balanced scorecard approach allows a broad
        range of areas to be measured within a single methodology. Trusts with
        high performance ratings therefore have to do well against a rounded set of
        indicators.

'Patients complaints procedures' as a quality indicator:

9   Within the service provision group of indicators, is the indicator 'patient
        complaints procedures'. This indicator refers to the percentage of written
        complaints for which a local resolution was completed within 20 working
        days. The data source is the DH statistical return on patient's complaints
        (K041A). The rationale for this indicator is described in the following terms:

> 'This indicator provides a vital insight into how well the NHS is
> performing in meeting targets set for the local resolution stage of the
> NHS complaints procedure. It is a key objective of the complaints
> procedure that complainants' concerns are resolved as quickly as
> possible.'[4]

3   Coulter A, Davis L-J, and Fitzpatrick R: *Patient and Public Perspectives on Health Care
        Performance*, Commission for Health Improvement, 2002.

4   Commission for Health Improvement, 2003

10   Patient transfers from GP lists are not included in the current list of NHS performance indicators for Primary Care Trusts.

ANNEX A
KEY TARGETS FOR ASSESSING THE PERFORMANCE OF PRIMARY CARE TRUSTS, 2002/03:

- access to a GP: percentage of patients who can be offered an appointment to see a GP within two working days.
- access to a primary care professional: percentage of patients offered an appointment to see a primary care professional within one working day.
- number of inpatients waiting longer than the standard: number of patients who were waiting more than 15 months throughout the year, or more than 12 months at end of March 2003, for an inpatient admission.
- number of outpatients waiting longer than the standard: number of patients who were waiting more than 26 weeks throughout the year, or more than 21 weeks at end of March 2003, for an outpatient appointment.
- total time in A&E: total time in A&E: percentage of patients waiting less than 4 hours in A&E from arrival to admission, transfer or discharge.
- single telephone access – implementation plans: appropriate implementation plan in place for local out-of-hours providers which will make available single telephone access to primary care out-of-hours services through NHS Direct by December 2004.
- four week smoking quitters: percentage of smokers who had quit at four week follow-up with the NHS smoking cessation services (performance against plan).
- Improving Working Lives: achievement of Improving Working Lives (IWL) Standard 'practice' or 'pledge' status (dependent on formation date of the organisation) by the end of Q4 2002/03.
- financial management: achievement of the financial position shown in the 2002/03 Plan without the need of unplanned financial support.

ANNEX B
PERFORMANCE INDICATORS FOR NHS PRIMARY CARE TRUSTS, 2002/03:

The broader range of indicators make up a 'balanced scorecard' to refine the judgement on ratings. This balanced scorecard approach allows a broad range of areas to be measured within a single methodology. Trusts with high performance ratings therefore have to do well against a rounded set of indicators. The indicators have been chosen to provide a balance across focus areas of access to quality services, improving health and service provision, outlined below:

1. Access to quality services:
- emergency readmission to hospital following treatment for a fractured hip
- substance misuse: percentage of GP practices in a shared care scheme
- sexual health: access to services for early unintended pregnancy
- level of 24 hour access to specialist mental health services

- A&E emergency admission waits (12 hours)
- twelve month heart operation waits
- delayed transfers of care
- access to NHS dentistry
- PCT survey – access and waiting
- PCT survey – better information, more choice
- PCT survey – building closer relationships
- PCT survey – clean, comfortable, friendly place to be
- PCT survey – safe, high quality, coordinated care
- prescribing of atypical antipsychotics

2. Improving health:
- death rates from circulatory diseases, aged under 75 (change in rate)
- death rates from accidents, all ages (change in rate)
- death rates from cancer, aged under 75 (change in rate)
- breast cancer screening
- cervical screening
- flu vaccinations
- teenage pregnancy: conceptions below age 18 (change in rate)
- diabetes services baseline assessment
- CHD audit
- suicide audit

3. Service provision:
- emergency admissions (change in rate)
- emergency admission to hospital for children with lower respiratory tract (LRT) infections (change in rate)
- primary care management – acute conditions (change in rate)
- primary care management – chronic conditions (change in rate)
- community equipment
- patient complaints procedure
- prescribing of antibacterial drugs
- prescribing rates for drugs acting on benzodiazepine receptors
- staff opinion survey
- GP appraisal
- sickness absence rate
- fire, health & safety
- generic prescribing

ANNEX C
CHI REPORTS ON PRIMARY CARE TRUST PERFORMANCE:

Each report summarises Trust performance against a set of published indicators and explains how the indicators were used to allocate the Trust's performance rating. It highlights areas in which the Trust has achieved high standards of performance, as well as identifying areas where performance has not been so good. Individual general practice surgeries are not separately identified in the report.

The main body of this report summarises the Trust's performance against the indicators in each of these four areas. For each area the report shows:

- how the Trust's performance compares to the national average

- which indicators the Trust has performed well on
- which, if any, indicators the Trust has performed poorly on

The NHS performance ratings system places performance into one of four categories ranging from three stars, performance at the highest level, to a rating of zero stars, reflecting poorest levels of performance. The star rating applies across the whole organisation, not to individual services. In using the report to investigate aspects of local performance, users are encouraged to refer also to other relevant local performance assessments provided by CHI, the NHS Modernisation Agency, or contained within audit letters.

The indicators do not necessarily reveal exactly why a Trust has done well, or in some cases not so well, in certain areas of performance. They highlight certain areas so that, following benchmarking and other local investigations, Trusts can share examples of best practice that are seen to be effective, and change any instances of poor practice that are unacceptable.

Primary Care Trusts (PCTs) issue a patient prospectus to every household within the PCT area, which should incorporate performance information for local health providers, including star ratings and performance indicators which contribute to them.

Strategic Health Authorities are expected to consider summary reports for all their constituent trusts and use these results to inform strategic planning and performance development initiatives. The performance ratings and indicators for different types of NHS Trusts are intended to provide an opportunity to identify and plan ways of addressing issues which cross organisational boundaries, and those internal to a particular organisation.

Development of Primary Care Trust indicators:
CHI is the independent regulator of NHS performance. The Government is responsible for setting priorities, which in turn determine the indicators relating to key targets. Other indicators have this year been designed by CHI and the Department of Health to reflect a wide range of performance issues, following consultation with the service and other stakeholders. PCTs are relatively new organisations and still in the early stages of development. As they develop their capacity, the commissioning agenda, and their roles as providers it will be possible to gather new levels of information and create new indicators. CHI works with PCTs and professional bodies, to ensure that future indicators are available to reflect these organisational developments.

ANNEX 12
CLINICAL GOVERNANCE IN THE NHS

Clinical governance policy and implementation:

1   Clinical governance (which is underpinned by a statutory duty of quality) was introduced in the NHS in 1999. The government's consultation paper, *A First Class Service*, defined clinical governance as *'a framework through which NHS organisations are accountable for continuously improving the quality of their services and safeguarding high standards of care by creating an environment in which excellence in clinical care will flourish.'*[1]

2   The purpose of clinical governance is to ensure that patients receive the highest quality of NHS care possible. The components of clinical governance, as set out in *A First Class Service*, are reproduced at **Annex A**. They cover the organisation's systems and processes for monitoring and improving services, including:

- patient and public involvement
- clinical audit
- risk management
- education, training and continuing personal and professional development
- clinical effectiveness programmes
- staffing and staff management
- use of information to support clinical governance and health care delivery

3   Effective clinical governance should therefore ensure:

- continuous improvement of patient services and care;
- a patient-centred approach that includes treating patients courteously, involving them in decisions about their care and keeping them informed;
- a commitment to quality, which ensures that health professionals are up to date in their practices and properly supervised where necessary;
- a reduction of the risk from clinical errors and adverse events as well as a commitment to learn from mistakes and share that learning with others.[2]

---

1   *A First Class Service: Quality in the New NHS*, Department of Health, 1998.

2   In 1998, the current Chief Medical Officer commented on clinical governance and complaints in the following terms: 'Changes to the NHS complaints procedures in 1996 reduced the fragmentation and inconsistency of previous arrangements as well as introducing more openness and lay participation. The health service has yet to develop a simple way to allow the important, generalisable lessons to be extracted from the extensive analysis, information gathering, and independent judgment which now underpin the handling of complaints. ... Clinical governance has the opportunity to address this weakness – requiring organisational as well as individual learning.' G Scally and L J Donaldson: *Clinical governance and the drive for quality improvement in the new NHS in England*, British Medical Journal, 1998, 317, (4 July).

4   The Department of Health issued guidance on implementing clinical governance across the NHS in HSC 1999/065. All NHS organisations are expected to complete and implement an annual clinical governance development plan, and to report on clinical governance within their Annual Reports. Implementation is supported by the Clinical Governance Support Team (CGST) which is a part of the Department of Health's Modernisation Agency.

5   Following the publication of "Shifting the Balance of Power" the NHS requested clarification on roles and responsibilities of new organisations. New guidance on clinical governance and performance management reporting processes, issued in November 2002 to all Chief Executives, identifies the functions for StHAs, NHS Trusts and new organisations. The framework aligns reporting processes with those for the Commission for Health Improvement clinical governance reviews. To ensure that clinical governance plans to improve the quality and safety of patient care are embedded within Local Delivery Plans, clinical governance reporting processes have been aligned with the new planning cycle.

CHI clinical governance reviews:

6   NHS bodies' progress in implementing clinical governance is assessed externally by the Commission for Health Improvement (CHI), in addition to existing internal management mechanisms. CHI has driven forward a rolling programme of clinical governance reviews of NHS Trusts. Clinical governance reviews of Primary Care Trusts were introduced in 2003 following pilot development work, and a guide was published in March 2003. It is not determined whether the new Commission for Healthcare Audit and Inspection (CHAI) will continue clinical governance reviews in their current form.

7   In partnership with the NHS Clinical Governance Support Team in England and the Clinical Effectiveness Support Unit (CESU) in Wales, CHI has developed a systematic framework for assessing clinical governance in NHS organisations so that judgements made in reports of reviews are reliable, fair and consistent. CHI's model for clinical governance assumes that effective clinical governance depends upon a culture of continuous learning, innovation and development and will improve patient experience of care and treatment in the NHS:

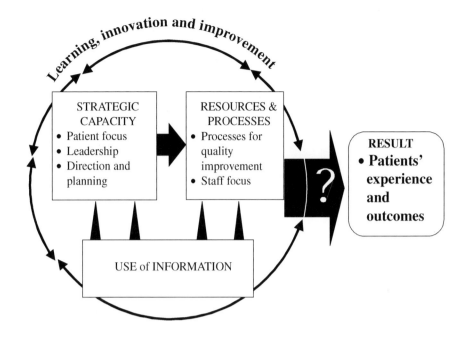

8   CHI uses the information it accumulates from reviews to help determine which aspects of clinical governance are the most important for improving patients' experience and outcomes.[3] CHI's clinical governance model has the following components:

Clinical governance area	Clinical governance components
(1) Strategic capacity	(Under development – dimensions may include partnership working, leadership, direction and planning, and patient involvement)
(2) Resources and processes **Processes for quality improvement:** **Staff focus:**	i. Patient and public involvement ii. Clinical audit iii. Risk management iv. Clinical effectiveness programmes v. Staffing and staff management vi. Education, training and continuing personal and vii. Professional development
(3) Use of information	Use of information to support clinical governance and health care delivery

3   CHI is working to identify the dimensions of patient experience and outcomes. It looks at the environment, privacy and dignity, clinical effectiveness and outcomes, access and organisation of care.

9   CHI's review teams assess how well clinical governance is working throughout a PCT by making enquiries about each of the seven components at corporate and directorate levels and in clinical teams. This involves collecting information systematically about **review issues** that have been defined for each component. To help with analysis and reporting the review issues are grouped into themes:

- accountability and structures
- strategies and plans
- application of policies, strategies and plans
- quality improvements and learning
- resources and training for staff

10   In PCT reviews, the review team additionally considers evidence on the PCT's capacity to implement clinical governance, on the basis of:

- its strategic capacity
- securing service delivery (commissioning)
- health improvement and protection, and
- patient experience and outcomes

11   On the basis of the evidence collected, each clinical governance component is assessed against a four-point scale, ranging from little or no progress, to excellence. In primary care settings, CHI is currently piloting a new approach to gathering the views of patients, service users, carers and the public, which involves writing directly to patients who have used community health services to invite them to stakeholder meetings. They are also seeking to use the results of the Department of Health's 2002 national survey of GP patients.

DH/Cabinet Office report – July 2003:

12   In July 2003, the Department of Health and the Cabinet Office's Regulatory Impact Unit jointly published a report on reducing burdens in healthcare inspection and monitoring.[4] Among 55 agreed actions listed, the report stated that DH will review the risk management standards for the NHS. In partnership with stakeholders, DH will develop a single set of standards on risk management for the NHS, with a single body responsible for co-coordinating inspection. This will remove overlap and disparity in risk management requirements and allow risk managers and front-line staff to concentrate on improving systems.

13   There will be a single NHS Litigation Authority (NHSLA) risk management standard for PCTs. Pilot assessments against a single set of combined Clinical Negligence Scheme for Trusts (CNST) and Risk Pooling Scheme for Trusts (RPST) standards, assessed at a single visit, took place in around 30 volunteer PCTs during May and June 2003. Subject to successful evaluation, all PCTs will be assessed against the Level 1 requirements of the new standard. This will streamline future NHSLA reviews for PCTs.

---

4   *Making a Difference: Reducing Burdens in Healthcare Inspection and Monitoring*, Department of Health and Cabinet Office, July 2003

National Audit Office report – September 2003:

14 In September 2003, the National Audit Office published a report reviewing improvements achieved through clinical governance.[5] The report's overall conclusions were as follows:

> "Our examination has confirmed that, while each component predated the formal introduction of clinical governance, since 1999 the machinery – the structures and organisational arrangements to make it happen – has been put in place. Virtually all Trusts have the necessary foundations, although the components are not fully embedded within all clinical directorates.
>
> The initiative has had many beneficial impacts. Clinical quality issues are now more mainstream; there is greater or more explicit accountability of both clinicians and managers for clinical performance; and there has been a change in professional cultures towards more open, transparent and collaborative ways of working. Moreover there is evidence of improvements in practice and patients care, though Trusts lack robust means of assessing this and overall progress.
>
> However, our research and the outcome of the Commission for Health Improvement's reviews indicate that progress in implementing clinical governance is patchy, varying between Trusts, within Trusts and between the components of clinical governance. There is, not surprisingly, scope for improvement in: the support provided to trusts, putting in place overall structures and processes; communications between boards and clinical teams; developing a coherent approach to quality; and improving processes for managing risk and poor performance. There is also a need to improve the way that lessons are learnt both within and between Trusts; and to put those lessons into practice. Overall, the key features of those organisations that have been better at improving the quality of care are quality of leadership, commitment of staff and willingness to consider doing things differently."[6]

15 In relation to patients' complaints, the report noted:

> "Properly accountable and learning NHS organisations need to have complaints systems that are accessible to patients; and to learn lessons from complaints and take action to avoid recurrences. Trusts see patients' complaints as a good source for lessons; 90 per cent rated their systems as fairly effective, or better, at leading to changes in clinical practice and patient care. Trust board members and senior managers confirmed that complaints provide useful information, but were less optimistic about the extent to which reviews led to improvements in quality."[7]

5　The main sources of evidence were a census of acute, mental health and ambulance Trusts, and a survey of Trust board members and senior managers in a sample of Trusts. Primary Care Trusts were not included.

6　*Achieving Improvements Through Clinical Governance: A Progress Report on Implementation by NHS Trusts*, National Audit Office, September 2003, page 3.

7　*Achieving Improvements Through Clinical Governance: A Progress Report on Implementation by NHS Trusts*, National Audit Office, September 2003, page 29.

ANNEX A
MAIN COMPONENTS OF CLINICAL GOVERNANCE[8]

1 Clear lines of responsibility and accountability for the overall quality of clinical care through:

- The NHS Trust Chief Executive carries the ultimate responsibility for assuring the quality of services provided by the Trust.
- A designated senior clinician responsible for ensuring that systems for clinical governance are in place and monitoring their continued effectiveness.
- Formal arrangements for NHS Trust and Primary Care Trust boards to discharge their responsibilities for clinical quality, through a clinical governance committee.
- Regular reports to NHS boards on the quality of clinical care given the same importance as monthly financial reports.
- An annual report on clinical governance.

2 A comprehensive programme of quality improvement activities which includes:

- Full participation by all hospital doctors in audit programmes, including specialty and sub-specialty national audit programmes endorsed by the Commission for Health Improvement.
- Full participation in the current four National Confidential Inquiries.
- Evidence-based practice is supported and applied routinely in everyday practice.
- Ensuring the clinical standards of National Service Frameworks and National Institute for Clinical Excellence recommendations are implemented.
- Workforce planning and development (i.e. recruitment and retention of appropriately trained workforce) is fully integrated within the NHS organisation's service planning.
- Continuing professional development: programmes aimed at meeting the development needs of individual health professionals and the service needs of the organisation are in place and supported locally.
- Appropriate safeguards to govern access to and storage of confidential patient information as recommended in the Caldicott Report on the *Review of Patient-Identifiable Information*.
- Effective monitoring of clinical care with high quality systems for clinical record keeping and the collection of relevant information.
- Processes for assuring the quality of clinical care are in place and integrated with the quality programme for the organisation as a whole.
- Participation in well-designed, relevant research and development activity is encouraged and supported as something which can contribute to the development of an 'evaluation culture'.

---

8   Extract from *A First Class Service: Quality in the New NHS*, Department of Health, 1998

3   Clear policies aimed at managing risks:

- Controls Assurance, which promotes self-assessment to identify and manage risks.
- Clinical risk systematically assessed with programmes in place to reduce risk.

4   Procedures for all professional groups to identify and remedy poor performance, for example:

- Critical incident reporting ensures that adverse events are identified, openly investigated, lessons are learnt and promptly applied.
- Complaints procedures, accessible to patients and their families and fair to staff. Lessons are learnt and recurrence of similar problems avoided.
- Professional performance procedures, which take effect at an early stage before patients are harmed and which help the individual to improve their performance whenever possible, are in place and understood by all staff.
- Staff are supported in their duty to report any concerns about colleagues' professional conduct and performance, with clear statements from the board on what is expected of all staff. Clear procedures for reporting concerns so that early action can be taken to remedy the situation.

ANNEX 13
'MAINTAINING HIGH PROFESSIONAL STANDARDS IN THE MODERN NHS: A FRAMEWORK FOR THE INITIAL HANDLING OF CONCERNS ABOUT DOCTORS AND DENTISTS IN THE NHS'

1   On 29 December 2003, under cover of circular HSC 2003/12, the Department of Health published a new national framework that replaces existing guidance[1] on the suspension of doctors and dentists in the NHS in England. The document contains the *Restriction of Practice and Exclusion from Work Directions 2003*, which came into force on 5 January 2004, and which require NHS bodies to make changes in their procedures to bring them into line with the principles of the framework.

2   The framework relates to: (i) the initial handling and investigation of concerns about the conduct and performance of doctors or dentists employed in the NHS, and (ii) the actions to be considered in protecting the public, such as restrictions on practice or exclusion from work.[2] The framework has been developed jointly by the Department of Health, the NHS Confederation, the British Medical Association and the British Dental Association, and constitutes the first two parts of a wider national framework for handling concerns about the conduct and performance of medical and dental employees. It follows concern about the way in which complaints about, and disciplinary action against, doctors and dentists have been handled in the NHS and particularly about the use of suspension in such cases.[3]

3   The new approach set out in the framework builds on the four key elements of appraisal and revalidation, the advisory and assessment services of the National Clinical Assessment Authority (NCAA), tackling the blame culture, and abandoning the 'suspension culture'. It fully integrates the work of the NCAA in providing advice to NHS employers on handling of cases.

4   The new framework provides in particular for:

- an immediate exclusion from work of not more than two weeks;
- any further exclusion limited to four-week periods which must be subject to active review;
- improved case management;
- quick but thorough investigation;
- the appointment of a Board member to oversee exclusion and subsequent action;

---

1   HSG (94) 49

2   The term **exclusion** from work is used in the framework to replace suspension, so as to avoid confusion with the action taken by the General Medical Council (GMC) or General Dental Council (GDC) to suspend a practitioner from their Register pending or following a hearing of the case.

3   See for example: Chapter 6 of *Supporting Doctors, Protecting Patients*, Department of Health, 1999; and *The Management of Suspensions of Clinical Staff in NHS Hospital and Ambulance Trusts in England*, National Audit Office, 6 November 2003.

- a programme for return to work where the doctor or dentist is not referred to disciplinary or capability procedures.

5   The new framework concerns initial handling of concerns about performance or conduct, and the actions to be taken in response to such concerns. Local conduct procedures will apply to where concerns relate to the conduct of a doctor. Subject to further joint discussions with the BMA and BDA, the Department of Health proposes to publish a new national disciplinary framework focusing on matters of clinical performance and capability. This will cover:

- conduct hearings and dismissal;
- procedures for dealing with issues of capability;
- handling concerns about a practitioner's health.

6   The new Directions require NHS Trusts and Primary Care Trusts to notify Strategic Health Authorities of the action they have taken to comply with the framework by 1 April 2004. Strategic Health Authorities are required to provide a report on local implementation of the framework to the Secretary of State by 30 September 2004.

ANNEX A
SOME KEY FEATURES OF THE NEW FRAMEWORK FOR INITIAL HANDLING OF CONCERNS ABOUT DOCTORS AND DENTISTS IN THE NHS

1   All NHS bodies must have procedures for handling serious concerns[4] about an individual's conduct and capability based on the new framework, and for handling less serious problems through informal resolution. Concerns about the capability of doctors and dentists in training should be considered as training matters, and the Postgraduate Dean should be involved at the outset.

2   The duty to protect patients is paramount. Where serious concerns are raised, the employer must urgently consider the need to place temporary restrictions on practice, to refer to the regulatory body, and/or to request the issue of an alert letter.

Initial handling of concerns:
3   All serious concerns must be registered with the Chief Executive, who must appoint a case manager. The Chairman of the Board must appoint a non-executive member to oversee the case. The Medical Director will act as the case manager in cases involving clinical directors and consultants, and is responsible for appointing a case investigator.

4   The case manager must: clarify what has happened and the nature of the problem or concern; discuss with the NCAA the way forward; consider the need for restriction of practice or exclusion from work; if a formal approach under the conduct or capability procedures is required, appoint

---

4   Serious concerns arise where the practitioner's action have adversely affected patient care, or could do so.

225

an investigator; if the case can be progressed by mutual agreement, consider whether an NCAA assessment would help clarify the underlying factors that led to the concerns and assist with identifying the solution.

5   The case investigator must: formally involve a member of the medical or dental staff where a question of clinical judgment is raised during the investigation process; safeguard confidentiality; ensure collection of sufficient written and oral evidence; ensure that a written record of the investigation is maintained; assist the designated Board member in reviewing the case; complete the investigation within 4 weeks of appointment, and submit their report to the case manager within a further 5 days.

6   An investigation report must provide sufficient information to enable the case manager to decide whether it would be appropriate to: refer to a conduct panel, the NHS's occupational health service, the NCAA, the GMC or GDC, or a capability panel; institute restrictions on practice or exclusion from work; or take no further action.

Exclusion from work:
7   Exclusion from work must be used only as an interim, precautionary measure while action to resolve a problem is considered. Formal exclusion must only be used where there is a need to protect the interests of patients or other staff pending the outcome of a full investigation of allegations of misconduct, concerns about serious dysfunctions in the operation of a clinical service, or concerns about lack of capability or poor performance of sufficient seriousness; or where the presence of the practitioner in the workplace is likely to hinder the investigation.

8   Alternative approaches to safeguarding patient safety must also be considered. These include supervision of normal contractual clinical duties, restricting the range of clinical duties that a practitioner may carry out, restricting the activities that a practitioner may engage in, or agreement to sickness leave.

9   The Chief Executive will have overall responsibility for managing the exclusion procedures. The NCAA must be notified before formal exclusion, and involved as appropriate. Exclusion can be up to 4 weeks at a time, following an initial 'immediate' exclusion of up to 2 weeks. A designated non-executive Board member will be responsible for monitoring the case. There is a right to return to work where no review is carried out. If there is no referral to disciplinary procedures or performance assessment, there must be a programme for return to work. The NCAA must be involved following 3 periods of exclusion, and the Strategic Health Authority notified about action taken. The maximum limit on exclusion will normally be 6 months, except where criminal investigation is involved. The Strategic Health Authority will receive monthly statistical summaries submitted to Boards, and collate these into a report for the Department of Health.

10   Exclusion from work will usually be on full pay, and the practitioner must remain available to work for their employer during their normal contracted hours. Exclusion will not automatically involve a bar from work premises.

11   Where there is a concern that a doctor or dentist may be a danger to patients, the employer has an obligation to inform other organisations, including private sector organisations, of any restrictions of practice or exclusion, and to provide a summary of the reasons. Where an NHS employer has placed restrictions on practice, the practitioner should agree not to undertake any work in that area of practice with any other employer. Where the case manager believes the practitioner is in breach of such an undertaking, the case manager must contact the professional regulatory body and the Strategic Health Authority to consider the issue of an alert letter.

ANNEX 14
THE NEW GENERAL MEDICAL SERVICES CONTRACT

1   Background[1]

On Friday 20 June 2003 the BMA announced that general practitioners had voted to accept the new general medical services contract negotiated between them and the NHS Confederation. The deal offers major strategic advantages to PCT's through:

- Better management of chronic disease leading to fewer admissions to hospital
- The ability to shape primary care services in an area according to local need
- Better, closer relationships with general practices
- Improved access to services for local people
- Improved recruitment and retention of doctors

Subject to the necessary legislation being passed, the new contract will come into force from 1 April 2004. Delivering the new contract on time will be a major and critical operational challenge for PCTs.

2   Main Points of the New GMS Contract[2]

More flexible provision of services

Practices will have greater flexibility to determine their own workload by opting out of some services, e.g. out-of hours or an additional service such as contraceptive services, and/or choosing in agreement with the PCT to provide others to higher levels than normally required e.g. specialist services for patients with MS. Patients will however be guaranteed continuing access to the range of services they currently receive in the event of their practice choosing not to provide them. PCTs will ensure that this guarantee is delivered and will be able, for the first time, to provide services themselves.

Rewards for quality

Practices will be able to achieve substantial pay increases by achieving higher levels of quality in an evidence-based system which covers clinical standards Clinical areas covered include coronary heart disease, diabetes, asthma and cancer.

Investment will be made in IT systems to support the quality and outcomes framework so that the practice can record its performance using a simple scorecard system.

Modernising the system

As part of the new contract good human resource management will be encouraged and supported for both doctors and all practice staff.

---

1   Extract from the letter dated 26 June 2003 from Andrew Foster, Director of Human Resources, Department of Health to PCT Chief Executives.

2   Extract from a Department of Health Briefing Paper on the New GMS Contract

Practices in rural and remote areas will be helped by the new allocation formula which recognises their specific problems. New powers for PCTs to employ medical staff and new options for doctors to take salaried posts may also help in rural and remote areas.

There will be substantial investment in IT and premises funding to make sure that family health services are delivered from premises which are fit for purpose and that communications within the NHS are speedy and integrated.

Investment in primary care
It is intended that the new contract will deliver the modernisation of the service, making the distribution of funding more accurate and in line with patient need, providing a guaranteed level of resources to practices in return for a better service for patients.

The investment totals £6.8 billion in England

Benefits for patients
It is intended that there will be a wider range of higher quality services for patients and funding will be allocated to practices on the basis of the needs of their local populations. Through inclusion in the quality and outcomes framework, patients will be involved in providing systematic feedback to their doctors about the services they receive and how they receive them. There will be a programme of work looking at take-up of services and how best to ensure that patients and doctors are engaged in the management of take-up.

3   Practice-based contract[3]
The new GMS contract will be a practice-based contract, in which the money flows with the patient. Practices will have the flexibility to use their resources in a way that suits local circumstances and meets patient needs.

It also means that, unlike now where the Secretary of State holds a contract with individual GPs, the new GMS contract will be between the PCO (Primary Care Organisation) and the practice. Primary legislation (under the Health and Social Care Bill) will be required to allow this to happen.

Quality and Outcomes framework
Practices will have the opportunity to receive additional funding through the achievement of a range of quality standards. The quality framework will have 3 main components focussing on clinical standards, organisational standards and the views of patients.

Out-of-Hours
The new contract allows GPs a choice as to whether they provide out of hours care. There will not be a statutory responsibility on GPs to provide care to their patients from 6.30pm to 8.00am, Monday to Friday, at weekends and on Bank Holidays. This does not prevent, however, practices continuing to provide routine surgeries in the evening or at weekends where they choose to do so in response to patient need.

---

3   Extracts from the NHS Confederation GMS Contract Negotiations, Questions and Answers and Executive Summary – available at www.nhsconfed.org/gmscontract

PCOs will be responsible for planning the delivery of out of hours care to their population. This provides the PCO with the flexibility to develop innovative models of working using a combination of service providers including the GPs themselves but also NHS Direct/NHS24, NHS walk-in centres, GP co-operatives, practice partnerships, paramedics, GPs/primary care nurses in A&E departments and deputising services.

Infrastructure
A number of new premises flexibilities are being introduced through the new contract to ensure that, where necessary, the quality of practice premises is adequate to provide a quality service to patients and funds are targeted at those areas where premises are most in need of improvement.

Career development
The new contract will recognise the different stages of a GP career and GPs will be able to adapt their career to suit their aspirations. A three-module approach is reflected in the new contract and provides for a salaried option as an alternative to independent contractor status. The three modules are: skills development; special interest development; and clinical leadership.

4   Summary of Main Points
Each contract will be between the PCT and the practice, rather than the individual general practitioner.

The 'global' sum (funding) will give practices new flexibility to appoint salaried staff, including doctors.

All practices will be required to provide essential services. Practices will have a preferential right to provide additional services (e.g. cervical screening, contraceptive advice, maternity services) and will normally do so. Both will be funded through the global sum.

PCTs may commission enhanced services, as considered appropriate. These would include essential or additional services delivered to a higher standard or services such as those provided by nurses or GPs with special interests. There will be no obligation on any GP practice to provide enhanced services.

From April 2004, PCTs will become responsible for commissioning out-of-hours care; they may contract with existing practices to supply the service.

A quality framework will reward practices' achievements in delivering a quality service. There will be four 'domains' or areas within this framework as follows:

- The clinical domain (management of CHD, strokes, mental health and other specified medical conditions);
- The organisational domain (management of records, patient information, education and training, practice management and medicines management);
- The additional services domain;
- The patient experience domain.

The inclusion of the patient experience in the key service indicators provides an opportunity for practices to obtain systematic feedback from patients about the services which they provide, to include these within their service development plans and to engage patients in these plans.

The contract will incorporate the systems to ensure the appraisal of doctors recently established and will ensure proper funding of appraisal within each PCT.

The fixed retirement age of 70 will be abolished, as each GP will instead be subject to appraisal and revalidation.

There will be a new obligation to give a warning to a patient before removal from a practice list, and to give reasons for any removal.

5   Additional Information

Comprehensive coverage of the new GMS Contract is available from the NHS Confederation website at www.nhsconfed.org/gmscontract or from the BMA website at www.bma.org.uk

APPENDICES

APPENDIX 1
THE CHAIRMAN AND PANEL OF THE AYLING INQUIRY

Dame Anna Pauffley

Dame Anna Pauffley was appointed as Chairman of the Ayling Inquiry. She was called to the bar in 1979 and is a family law specialist. In 1992, she was Counsel to the Leicestershire Children's Homes Inquiry. In 1995 she was appointed Queens Counsel. Between 1997 and 1998, she represented more than 100 witnesses before the North Wales Tribunal of Inquiry into the abuse of children in care. Dame Anna began sitting as an Assistant Recorder in 1993 and as a Deputy High Court Judge in the Family Division in 1998. On 1 October 2003 she was appointed to the High Court Bench.

Peter Berman

Peter Berman, a solicitor by profession, was the Chief Executive of Taunton Deane Borough Council in Somerset for fifteen years. He was actively involved in the founding of the National Association of Lay People in Primary Care. He has also served as the Lay member on the Taunton and Area Primary Care Group and is now Vice Chairman of the Taunton Deane Primary Care Trust and is a co-opted member of the Executive of the NHS Alliance. Peter Berman has also acted on two occasions as an official United Kingdom observer at Romanian national and local elections.

Mary Whitty

Mary Whitty joined the National Health Service in 1973 under the management training scheme and has had senior management experience as a Chief Executive of primary and community health service organisations. Prior to her retirement from the NHS in March 2002 she was the Chief Executive of Brent & Harrow Health Authority. Mary Whitty's career in the National Health Service has given her extensive experience in the planning, commissioning and monitoring of health service provision.

APPENDIX 2
THE SECRETARIAT AND THE LEGAL TEAM

Secretariat

Inquiry Secretary:	Colin Phillips
Previous Inquiry Secretary:	Pauline Fox
Assistant Inquiry Secretary:	John Miller
Inquiry Solicitor:	Michael Fitzgerald
Deputy Inquiry Solicitor:	Duncan Henderson
Commissioning Manager (Experts):	Dr Ruth Chadwick
Inquiry Co-ordinator:	Jerome O'Brien
Assistant Co-ordinator:	Anne Atkins

Counsel to the Inquiry

Counsel:	Eleanor Grey
Junior Counsel:	Peter Skelton

Legal Support Team

Kathleen Price

Lucy Cheetham

James Malam

Karoon Akoon

Natalie Davey

Adam Holliman

Nick Holman

Kevin Walsh

Administrative and Secretarial Support

Philip Otton

Emily Frost

Gurjeev Johal

Richard Partridge

Anisha Patel

Lorna Wilkinson

Virginia Berkholz

Aaron Counter

Erica Johnson

Pauline Stannard

Part 2 – Seminars

Facilitator: Ann James CBE

Co-ordinator: Kypros Menicou

Senior Administrator: Emily Frost

APPENDIX 3
LAY WITNESSES

Witnesses who gave oral evidence are designated "O"; witnesses who gave written evidence are designated "W".

In addition to the witnesses identified below, 77 former patients of Clifford Ayling gave written evidence to the Inquiry, of whom 14 also gave oral evidence.

Allison, Ms Elizabeth Anne	State Enrolled Nurse, Thanet District Hospital (1974–1999)	W
Addison, Mr Mark	Unit General Manager, South East Kent Health Authority (1991–1999) Chief Executive, South Kent Hospitals NHS Trust (1994–1999)	W/O
Alexander, Ms Ann Elizabeth	Community Midwife, Ashford Hospital (1992), Buckland Hospital (1992)	W/O
Anderson, Dr Norman Wilson	Principal in General Practice, The White House Surgery (From 1993)	W/O
Andrews, Mr Andrew Paul	Regional Legal Advisor, South East Thames Regional Health Authority (1987)	W
Andrews, Ms Elizabeth McIllroy	Deputy Unit Administrator/Operational Manager Canterbury & Thanet District Health Authority (1983–1987)	W
Appleyard, Dr James	Consultant Paediatrician, Canterbury & Thanet District Health Authority (1971–1998)	W
Ardouin, Mr Alan Peter	Consultant Ear Nose and Throat Surgeon, Kent & Canterbury Hospital (1964–1992)	W
Ashton, Dr John Bradley	General Practitioner, West Malling (1966–2000) *See Entry for Mr D Barr. Medical Secretary to the Kent Local Medical Committee	W
Astley, Mr David John	Chief Executive, East Kent Hospitals NHS Trust (From 1999)	W/O
Atley, Ms Jennifer	Nursing Officer, Margate Hospital (1979–1990), Quality, Quality Department of Queen Elizabeth Queen Mother Hospital (1990–1995), Training Coordinator Queen Elizabeth Queen Mother Hospital, (1995–2000)	W
Austin, Ms Mary	Staff Midwife, Thanet District Hospital (1974–1977), Sister, Thanet District Hospital (1977–1986)	W
Ayers, Ms Eunice Mary	Staff Nurse, Outpatients Department, Thanet District Hospital (1978–1989), Sister, Thanet District Hospital (1989–1996)	W

Ayling, Ms Jeannette Evelyn	Practice Manager, Cheriton High Street, (1977–2000)	W
Badkoubei, Dr Sharokh	Senior House Officer/Registrar in Obstetrics & Gynaecology, Thanet District Hospital (1976–1978) & (1979–1981) Locum Senior House Officer and Registrar (1987–1991), Staff Grade Doctor, Thanet District Hospital (From 1991)	W
Barr, Mr David	Clerk to Kent Local Medical Committee (gave oral evidence in place of Dr Ashton) *See Entry for Dr JB Ashton	O
Basu, Dr Mitali	Retired Medical Practitioner	W
Bateman, Dr Frederick John Afford	Medical Officer, family Planning Clinics, Folkestone, Hythe, Dover, New Romney and Ashford	W
Bayles, Dr Ian	General Practitioner, The Old School Surgery	W/O
Beautridge, DC Sean Charles	Detective Sergeant, Kent Police (1993–2003), Police Officer, Kent Police (1987–1993)	W
Bell, Ms Lynn	Secretary, (1996–1997), Post Payment Verification Manager/Patient Services Manager (From 1997) Kent Health Authorities Support Agency	W
Bentley, Mrs Delphine	Midwife, Thanet District Hospital (1983–1989)	W/O
Biffen, Ms Janice	Nurse (1984–1999), Nursing Sister (From 1999) William Harvey Hospital	W/O
Bolton, Ms Cathy	Domestic Services Manager, South East Kent District Health Authority (1986–1993) Administration Manager (1993–1994) Legal and Administration Manager (1994–1996), Legal Administration Manager, (1996–1997), Secretary (1997–1999) East Kent Health Authority	W/O
Boyd, Ms Sally Gordon	Member of Staff Committee, South East Kent District Health Authority (1979–1987), Member of Kent Family Practitioner Committee (1987–1991) Member of East Kent Health Authority (1991–1997) Lay Chair for Independent Review Procedure, South East Thames Regional Health Authority/ NHS Executive, South East Region (1997–2002)	W
Brace, Mr John Charles	Consultant Obstetrician and Gynaecologist, North Middlesex Hospital (1971)	W
Bradford, Mrs Christine Joy	Office Manager, SEADOC (1993–2001)	W
Brewster, Ms Pamela Ann	Staff Nurse, Thanet District Hospital (1973–1974), Day Sister, Thanet District Hospital (1976–1978)	W
Bridges, Ms Janet Ann	Night Sister, Margate Hospital (1971–1982)	W

Broad, Ms Hazel	State Registered Nurse/Sister Thanet District Hospital (1978–1984)	W
Broughton, Ms Gillian Mary	Midwife, Kent & Canterbury Hospital (1986–1993)	W
Brown, Ms Lucille May	Theatre Sister, Thanet District Hospital (1967–1980)	W
Burnett, Dr Andrew Cameron	Deputy Medical Director (1991–1993), Director for Primary Care Development for East Kent (1993–1995) Medical Director (1994–1996) Kent Family Health Services Authority	W/O
Bussey, Dr Alan Laurence	Area Medical Officer, Kent Area Health Authority (1978–1982), District Medical Officer/District General Manager, Maidstone Health Authority (1985–1988)	W
Butler, Mr Michael John Stewart	Member (1980–1982), Vice Chair (1982–1988), Chair (1988–1990) Canterbury and Thanet Community Health Council, Non Executive Director (1990–1992) Vice Chair (1992–1996) Kent Family Health Services Authority, Non Executive Director/Vice Chair, East Kent Health Authority (1996–2000)	W
Calver, Dr Dennis	General Practitioner, The Sandgate Road Practice (From 1987)	W/O
Chalkley, Mr Richard	Lay Member (1985), Chairman, Dental Service Committee and Deputy Chairman, Medical Service Committee, (Until 1990) Kent Family Practitioner Committee/Kent Family Health Services Authority (1990–1995)	W
Clark, Dr Jane Erskine	Community Medical Officer, Family Planning and Child Health Surveillance (1986–1990) Community Medical Officer, Ashford Family Planning Clinic	W
Clements, Mr Roger Varley	Consultant Obstetrician and Gynaecologist, North Middlesex Hospital (1973–1984), Clinical director (1988–1991), Medical Director (1991–1994) North Middlesex Hospital NHS Trust	W
Coates, Ms Jacqui	Complaints Officer, (1992–1993) Service Committee Manager (1993–1994), Deputy Complaints Manager (1994–1996) Kent Family Health Services Authority, Customer Services Manager, West Kent Health Authority (1996–2002)	W
Coleman, Ms Elizabeth	Non Executive Director, East Kent Health Authority (1996–2000)	W/O
Colledge, Dr Julian	General Practitioner, Hamstreet Surgery (1981–2001)	W
Cook, Dr David Markham	Consultant Paediatrician, Margate Hospital (1974–2000)	W/O
Cook, Mrs Elaine Mary	Director of Nursing and Midwifery Services, Canterbury & Thanet District Health Authority (1982–1990)	W
Cook, Ms Jennifer Shane	Staff Midwife/Sister, Thanet District Hospital (1975–1979)	W/O

Cooper, Ms Fay	Complaints Manager, South East London and Kent Executive Council, Kent Family Practitioner Committee Kent Family Health Services Authority (1967–1990)	W
Cresswell, Ms Mary	Chief Officer, Maidstone Community Health Council (1987–1990), District Manager (1990–1991) Complaints Manager (1991–1996) Kent Family Health Services Authority	W
Czlapka, Ms Wanda Maria Ellzbieta	Midwife/Sister, Kent & Canterbury Hospital (From 1979)	W
Darling, Mrs Merle	Assistant Director of Nursing Services, South East Kent Health Authority (1984–1989), Director of Nursing and Quality Assurance (1989–1993)	W/O
Davies, Dr John Orrell	Consultant Obstetrician, William Harvey Hospital (From 1988) Clinical Director (1990–1991) and (1999–2002)	W/O
de Caestecker, Dr James Peter	Principal in General Practice, The New Surgery (From 1989)	W/O
Dodds, Ms Valerie	Family Planning Nurse, Medway Health Authority 1969–1976) South East Kent District, Kent Area Health Authority (1976) Health Visitor Assistant (1977), Staff Nurse (1978), School Nurse I and Family Planning Nurse (1981), Locality Coordinator, Folkestone Health Centre (1998)	W/O
Dutchburn, Ms Barbara Mary	Midwifery Sister, Queen Elizabeth, The Queen Mother Hospital (1971–1991)	W
Duthoit, Ms Mary	Nursing Sister, William Harvey Hospital (1979–1999)	W
Earl, Ms Pat	Family Planning Administrator (1963–1995)	W
Ellis, Mrs Joan Margaret	Midwife, Queen Elizabeth, Queen Elizabeth, The Queen Mother Hospital (1971–1979) and (1982–1984)	W
Elworthy, Mrs Mildred Patricia	Midwife, Thanet District Hospital (1957–1958), Superintendent Midwife, Thanet District Hospital (1964–1984) and Senior Nursing Officer (Midwifery), Kent & Canterbury Hospital (1976–1984)	W/O
Embry, Mrs Elizabeth	Staff Midwife, Kent & Canterbury Hospital (1985–2000)	W
Evans, Ms Rosemary Barbara Denise	Midwife (1982–1984) Staff Nurse (From 1985) Thanet District Hospital	W
Fage, Ms Catherine Mary	Auxiliary Nurse, William Harvey Hospital (From 1987)	W
Fairman, Ms Jennifer	Complaints Officer, Kent Family Health Services Authority/Kent Health Authorities Support Agency (1993–1996)	W
Farebrother, Dr Ann	Medical Officer, Medway Health Authority (1977–1983) Senior House Officer, Community Medicine, Medway Health	W/O

	Authority, Registrar, Community Medicine (1983–1985), Senior Registrar (1985–1989), South East Thames Regional Health Authority, Consultant in Public Health, Medway District Health Authority (1989–1990), Director of Public Health, South East Kent Health Authority (1990–1994), Consultant in Public Health Medicine, East Kent Health Authority (From 1994)	
Feeney, Dr Marc	Principal in General Practice, Cedars Surgery (From 1993)	W
Fernandes, Dr Manuel Andrew Agnelo Mario	Principal in General Practice, The Manor Clinic (From 1988)	W
Flory, Ms Susan	Clerical Officer, Complaints Department (1993–1995) Complaints Officer, Kent Family Health Services Authority (1995–1996) Complaints Officer, West Kent Health Authority (1996–1999)	W
Forsythe, Professor John Malcolm	Area Medical Officer, Kent Area Health Authority (1974–1978), Regional Medical Officer, South East Thames Regional Health Authority (1978–1992)	W/O
Fullman, Mr Peter	Consultant Obstetric & Gynaecological Surgeon, Kent & Canterbury Hospital and Margate Hospital (1973–1994)	W/O
Gilday, Mrs Collette	Midwifery Sister, Queen Elizabeth, The Queen Mother (1975–1983) Senior Midwife, Queen Elizabeth, The Queen Mother (1983–1993)	W
Goodburn, Ms Hilary	Practice Manager, Guildhall Surgery, (1994–2002)	W/O
Goodwin, Dr Daryl Patrick	General Practitioner, Sandgate Road Surgery (1984–2002)	W
Grant, Ms Vadney Viola Grant	Staff Midwife/Sister, Queen Elizabeth, The Queen Mother (1973–2002)	W
Guy, Ms Susan	Finance Assistant, (1994–1995), Complaints Officer (1995–1998) Kent Family Health Services Authority, Finance Department, Kent Health Authorities Support Agency (From 1998)	W
Hall, Dr Frederick Marcus W	Consultant Radiotherapist, Kent & Canterbury Hospital (1965–1984)	
Hamilton, Ms Julie Claire	Staff Midwife/Sister, Thanet District Hospital (From 1981)	W
Hanna, Ms Susan John	Nurse, Family Planning Clinics (From 1990)	W
Hatfield, Ms Margaret Ann	Staff Midwife, Thanet District Hospital (1974–1976) and Sister and Midwifery Coordinator (1981–1999)	W/O
Heatherington, Ms Kay	Practice Manager, (1970/1–1980/1) Secretary, Community Health Council, Dartford and Gravesham (1984), District Manager, South East Kent District office, Kent Family Practitioner Committee/Kent Family Health Services Authority (1988/9–1996)	W

Heffernan, Dr John	Retired General Practitioner, The Whitehouse Surgery (1958–1992)	W/O
Heseltine, Ms Anne Elaine	Staff Midwife, Margate Hospital (1977–1979) Midwife, William Harvey Hospital (1979–1989) and (1995–1999), Senior Midwife, Buckland Hospital (1989–1995) Supervisor of Midwives, William Harvey Hospital (From 1990)	W/O
Higgins, Professor Peter Matthew	Chairman, Kent Family Health Services Authority (1990–1992)	W
Hind, Mr John	Unit Administrator, William Harvey Hospital (1983–1986), Unit General Manager, Community and Priority Health Services (1986–1993), Chief Executive, South Kent Community Healthcare NHS Trust (1993–1997)	W
Hollman, Mr Kenneth William	Deputy Administrator/Administrator, Kent Family Practitioner Committee (1956–1985)	W
Homeshaw, Mr David Francis Robert	Chief Officer, Kent Family Practitioner Committee/Family Health Services Authority (1985–1992)	W/O
Hossain, Dr Mohammed Altaf	General Practitioner, Guildhall Surgery (From 1984)	W/O
Humphreys, Ms Kathryn Janette	Midwife, Thanet District Hospital (1981–1990)	W
James, Ms Stella Ann	South East Kent Occupational Health Department, Ashford Hospital and William Harvey Hospital (1976–1978), Senior Nursing Officer for Midwifery and Paediatrics, William Harvey Hospital (1978–1981), District Nursing Officer (1981–19820 Director of Nursing, William Harvey Hospital (1982–1990)	W
Jedrzejewski, Dr John Anthony	General Practitioner, The Whitehouse Surgery (From 1984)	W/O
Jedrzejewski, Mrs Penelope Jill	Staff Midwife, Maidstone Area Health Authority (1981–1985), Flexi Bank Midwife, William Harvey Hospital (1985–1990), Community Midwife, Shepway (1990–1994), Quality Assurance Core Group (1994), Group Practice Leader Midwife, Shepway (1998), Unit Coordinator, Dover Family Birthing Centre (1999)	W/O
Jenkinson, Mrs Valerie Robertson	Director of Nursing Services, Canterbury & Thanet District Health Authority (1983–1989)	W
Jones, Ms Pamela	Foster Carer (1997)	W
Khine-Smith, Dr Trudy Kin Mae Chit	General Practitioner Guildhall Surgery (1986–2001)	W/O
Kilpper, Mrs Irmgard	Midwifery Sister, Queen Elizabeth, The Queen Mother Hospital (1972–1973) Nursing Officer, Queen Elizabeth, The Queen Mother Hospital (1973–1982)	W

Kinnis, Ms Jennifer	Midwifery Sister, Thanet District Hospital (1968–1996)	W
Kitney, Mr David Leonard	District Personnel Officer, Canterbury & Thanet District Health Authority (1987–NK)	W
Lethbridge, Ms Helen	Community Nurse (1997–1998) based in Clifford Ayling's Surgery	W
Lewis, Ms Christina Lewis	Complaints Officer, Kent Family Health Services Authority (1991–1994), Service Committee Coordinator, Kent Family Health Services Authority/West Kent Health Authority (1994–1997), Deputy Complaints Manager (1997–1998), Complaints Coordinator (1998–1999), Primary Care Development Manager, Kent Weald Primary Care Group (From 1999)	W
Lewis, Ms Gillian Mary	Ward Sister, William Harvey Hospital (1979–1982), District Nurse (1982–1986), Liaison and Night Nursing Services, South Kent (196–1987), Community Nurse Manager (1987–1992), Locality Manager (1992–1998), Strategy and Service Coordinator, East Kent Community Trust (1998–2002)	W
Lock, Ms Jacqueline Francis Noelette	Midwife, Thanet District Hospital (From 1974)	W
Lowe, Ms Vanessa Mary	Ward Sister, William Harvey Hospital (1979–1982), family Planning Service, Vicarage Lane Ashford (1985), Osteopathic Ward, Kent and Canterbury Hospital (1996–2000)	W
Lucas, Mr Michael John	Acting Sector Administrator (1982–1983) Canterbury & Thanet District Health Authority and Kent Area Health Authority Unit Administrator (1983–1986) Deputy Unit General Manager (1986–1999)	W
Luckett, Ms Gaynor Ann	State Registered Nurse William Harvey Hospital (1979–1985), Midwife, Buckland hospital (1985–1989), Health Visitor, Cheriton High Street Surgery (1990–1992), Whitehouse Surgery (1992–1997), Thames Gateway NHS Trust (1998–2001)	W
Mackie, Ms Anne	Director of Public Health, West Kent Health Authority (2001–2002)	W
Maitra, Dr Dilip Kumar	General Practitioner, Park Farm Surgery (from 1994)	W/O
Martin, Mrs Sylvia	Sister, Outpatients Department, Outpatients Departmental Nurse Manager, William Harvey Hospital (1979–1997)	W/O
McDonald, Ms Ann-Marie Theresa	Staff Nurse, William Harvey Hospital (1979–1981) Registered General Nurse (From 1998)	W
McDougall, Ms Clare	Project Officer, South East Kent District Health Authority (1992–1994), Contracts Officer, East Kent District Health Authority (1994–1996), Service Development Assistant, Healthcare Development Directorate, East Kent Health Authority (1996–1999), Thanet Primary Care Group (1999)	W

Medhurst, Ms Christine Glynis	Staff Midwife (1981–1983) Sister (1983–1998) Thanet District Hospital	W
Medlock, Ms Helen	Pharmaceutical Advisor (1989–1992), Quality Assurance Manager/Business Director (1992), Kent Family Health Services Authority, General Manager, Kent Health Authority's Support Agency (1995–1996), Principal Commissioning Manager (1996–1999), West Kent Health Authority	W
Miller, Mrs Julie Francis	Midwife, Canterbury & Thanet Area (1979–1995) Queen Elizabeth, The Queen Mother Hospital (From 1999)	W/O
Milligan, Dr Michael Peter	Consultant Obstetrician & Gynaecologist Kent & Canterbury Hospital (From 1983)	W
Millington, Ms Janet	Midwife/Sister, Queen Elizabeth, The Queen Mother Hospital (1972–1987)	W
Mills, Ms Heather Frances	Trainee Nurse, Margate Hospital (1978)	W
Mitchell, Mr Derek	Practice Manager (1986–1994), Locality Commissioner, East Kent District Health Authority (1994–1995), Service Development Manager, Ashford and Shepway, East Kent Health Authority (1995–1999), Clinical Governance Manager, East Kent Health Authority (1999–2002)	W
Moffatt, Dr William James	General Practitioner, Kingsnorth Medical Practice (From 1988)	W/O
Mohammed, Mr Ali	Human Resources, in the NHS, various areas in Kent (From 1988)	W/O
Montgomery, Dr Donald	Retired General Practitioner, The Manor Clinic (1961–1995)	W/O
Moore, Mrs Penelope Christine Elizabeth	Midwife (1978–1981), Sister (1981–1995) Queen Elizabeth, The Queen Mother Hospital	W/O
Morgan, Ms Nichola Jane	Midwife, Thanet District Hospital (1984–1985) Kent & Canterbury Hospital (1985–1993) Clinical Midwifery Manager, Kent & Canterbury Hospital (1993–2000)	W/O
Morris, Dr Peter	Consultant Obstetrician & Gynaecologist, Canterbury & Thanet District Health Authority (1983–1989)	W
Morris, Ms Candida Frances	Chief Executive, Kent and Medway Strategic Health Authority (from 2002)	W
Mulley, Ms Katherine Mary	Policy Manager, Victim Support	W

Murrells, Mr Richard	Hospital Administration, Medway Hospital (1971–1978), Canterbury & Thanet District (1978–1983) Administrator, Headquarter Services (1983–1982), Assistant General Manager (1993) South East Kent District Health Authority, Assistant Chief Executive/Head of Corporate Services, East Kent Commissioning Agency (1993–1996), Director of Corporate Affairs, East Kent Health Authority (1996–2002)	W
Musgrave, Ms Linda	Nurse, Thanet District Hospital (1972–1975) and (from 1989)	W
Nightingale, Ms Heather	Area Nurse (Personnel), Kent Area Health Authority (1979–1982), Chief Nursing Officer, Canterbury & Thanet District Health Authority (1982–1992)	W/O
Osborne, Mrs Sylvia	Auxiliary Nurse, Margate Hospital (1979–2000)	W
Outhwaite, Mr Mark Robert Canning	Chief Executive, East Kent Commissioning Agency (1993–1994), East Kent District Health Authority (1994–1996), East Kent Health Authority (1996–2002), Acting Chief Executive, West Kent Health Authority (2001–2002)	W/O
Padley, Dr Noel Richard	Consultant Pathologist, William Harvey Hospital (1979–1994) Medical Director, South East Kent Health Authority (1994–1999) and East Kent Health Trust (1999–2003)	W/O
Parsons, Mr Stephen	General Manager/Chief Executive, Kent Health Authorities Suipport Agency (From 1996)	W
Patterson, Mr William Michael	Retired Obstetrician & Gynaecologist, (1973–1995)	W/O
Pemberton, Ms Alison	Communications Manager (1997–1999), Senior Communications Manager (1999) East Kent Health Authority, Head of Communications, East Kent Hospitals Trust (2000)	W
Pickering, Dr Edward Neville	Retired General Practitioner, The Whitehouse Surgery, (1961–1995)	W/O
Piper, Ms Andrea June	Midwife, Thanet District Hospital (1980–1999)	W
Plaskett, Mr Jose	Healthcare Assistant, Thanet District Hospital and Queen Elizabeth, The Queen Mother Hospital (From 1975)	W
Pompeus, Mr Steven	Consumer Affairs Assistant (1997–1998) Assistant Consumer Affairs Manager (1998–1999) Acting Legal Services Manager (1999–2001) East Kent Health Authority	W
Premnath, Dr Pankaj	General Practitioner, The White Cliffs Medical Centre (From 1987)	W
Price, Dr Carol Ann	General Practitioner, Kingsnorth Medical Centre (From 1999)	W

Pringle, Dr Alexander	General Physician (1967) Clinical Director (1974–1995) North Middlesex Hospital	W
Reed, Mrs Clare Sussanne	Midwife, Queen Elizabeth, The Queen Mother Hospital (1978–1980's)	W
Richards, Ms Gwynneth	Divisional Nursing Officer (1983) Unit General Manager, William Harvey Hospital, South East Kent Hospitals Unit (1989–1991)	W
Richman, Ms Gillian	Midwife/Community Midwife, Thanet District Hospital (1980–1987)	W
Roberts Dr Charles Ian	Consultant General Physician, Kent & Canterbury Hospital (1974–2000)	W
Robertson-Ritchie, Dr Hugh	General Practitioner, The New Surgery (From 1983)	W
Rodway, Ms Janet Mary	Trainee Nurse (1972–1975), Midwife, Kent & Canterbury Hospital (1977), Midwife, Buckland Hospital (1986–1990)	W
Russell, Ms Jennifer	State Enrolled Nurse, Queen Elizabeth, The Queen Mother Hospital (1977–1989)	W
Sarkhel, Dr Ramaprosad	Registrar, Obstetrics and Gynaecology, William Harvey Hospital and Buckland Hospital (1967–1976), Consultant in Genito-Urinary Medicine and Venereal Diseases, South East Thames Regional Health Authority (1976), Titular Head of Family Planning (1984–1992)	W/O
Savege, Dr Peter Beverley	Medical Director (1990–1994), Acting Chief Executive (1992–1993) Kent Family Health Services Authority	W/O
Scott, Dr Paul James	Senior House Officer, Kent & Canterbury Hospital (1985–1987) and (1988)	W
Scott, Mr Finlay Macmillan	Chief Executive and Registrar, General Medical Council (From 1994)	W/O
Scott, Ms Sylvia Rae	Health Visitor, Folkestone (1972–1974), Senior Nurse (Health Visiting) (1989–1990), Director of Nursing (1990), Director of Nursing and Primary Care (1992–1994) South East Kent Health Authority, Director of Primary Care and Nurse Executive, South Kent Community NHS Trust (1998)	W
Sidwell, Mrs Christine	Director of Nursing, South Kent Hospitals NHS Trust (1994–1999) Director of Nursing and Quality East Kent Hospitals NHS Trust (From 1999)	W/O
Smailes, Ms Carolyn Margaret	Auxiliary Nurse, William Harvey Hospital (1980/1981–1997)	W

Snell, Dr Anthony David	Medical Advisor, East Kent Health Authority (1996–2002)	W/O
Stewart, Dr Robert	Principal in General Practice, Kent (From 1983)	
Stewart, Mr Charles Malcolm	Consultant Gynaecologist, William Harvey Hospital, East Kent Hospital NHS Trust (From 1987)	W
Stewart, Ms Jacqueline	Director of Primary Care of West Kent, Kent Family Health Services Authority (1993–1996), Director of Healthcare Development, East Kent Health Authority (1996–2002)	W/O
Stokes, Ms Kitty Lillian	Nursing Officer, Senior Nursing Officer, Nursing (Personnel) Officer, Kent Area Health Authority and Canterbury & Thanet District Health Authority (1968–1991)	W
Sullivan, Ms Susan Elizabeth	Health Visitor, South East Kent District Health Authority (1984–1990) Senior Nurse Health Visiting Dover/Deal (1990), Locality Manager Folkestone East (1991), Community Services Nursing Services Manager (1992–1998)	W
Sutton, Ms Ann	Chief Executive, Shepway Primary Care Trust (From 2002)	W/O
Tonge, Dr Jennifer	Medical Student, Kent & Canterbury Hospital (1963)	W
Topping, Ms Christine Salms	Nurse/Ward Manager, Queen Elizabeth, The Queen Mother Hospital (1980–1999)	W
Town, Ms Linda	Supervisor, (1983–1990) Deputy Manager (1990–1995) Health Records Department, William Harvey Hospital, Appointments Manager (From 1995)	W
Tyas, Ms Diane	Practice Manager (1989), Service Development Manager, (1998–1999), Performance Manager and Strategic Lead for Dentistry, East Kent Health Authority (1999)	W
Veenhuizen, Dr Philippa Anne	General Practitioner, The Manor Clinic (From 1997)	W
Voysey, Dr Margaret Mary	Consultant Anaesthetist (1962–1986), Unit General Manager, Canterbury & Thanet District Health Authority (From 1986)	W/O
Watkins, Ms Doreen	Nursing Officer (Midwifery), William Harvey Hospital (1984–1995), Head of Midwifery, South East Kent Hospitals Trust (1995–2001)	W
Watts, Ms Patricia Ann	Health Records Department (1979–1984) Assistant Patient Services Manager (1984–1991) Business Manager for Obstetrics & Gynaecology, South Kent (1991–2000) William Harvey Hospital	W
Weedon, Ms Dorothy	Administrative Officer, Kent Family Practitioner Committee (1974–1990)	W

Williams, Ms Pamela Ann	Radiology Services Manager, Kent & Canterbury Hospital (1996–2000)	W/O
Williamson, Ms Wendy	Health Visitor, South East Community (1988)	W
Winkler, Ms Fedelma	Chief Executive, Kent Family Health Services Authority (1993–1995)	W/O
Woolley, Ms Margaret Marion	Health Visitor, Folkestone Area (From 1981)	W

APPENDIX 4
LEGAL REPRESENTATIVES

WITNESSES AND THEIR REPRESENTATIVES

Witnesses	Representatives
Certain former patients of Clifford Ayling	Sarah Harman of Harman & Harman, Solicitors
The NHS bodies in East Kent	David Mason, James Reynolds and Lorna Hardman, all of Capsticks, Solicitors
Various General Practitioners in East Kent	Giles Colin, instructed by RadcliffesLeBrasseur, Solicitors
Mr P Fullman and Mr W M Patterson	Giles Colin, instructed by RadcliffesLeBrasseur, Solicitors
Kent Local Medical Committee	Andrew Lockhart-Mirams of Lockharts, Solicitors
Dr M M Voysey	Julia Law of Brachers, Solicitors
Andrew Andrews *	Alan Hannah of Brachers, Solicitors
Dr J B Ashton *	Robert Sumerling of RadcliffesLeBrasseur, Solicitors
Jeannette Ayling *	A P Isaacson of Rootes & Alliott, Solicitors

* These witnesses each provided a witness statement but were not called to give oral evidence.

APPENDIX 5
EXPERT ADVISERS

Mr Peter Bowen-Simpkins MA FRCOG MFFP, Consultant Obstetrician and Gynaecologist, Swansea NHS Trust

Dr Michael G Jeffries BSc MB ChB DCCH FRCGP, General Practitioner, Betws-y-Coed Practice

Mr Jonathan Lane MB BS FRCOG, Consultant Obstetrician and Gynaecologist, Royal Shrewsbury Hospital NHS Trust

Professor Linda Mulcahy, Anniversary Professor of Law and Society, Birkbeck College, University of London

Professor Ian Smith, Clifford Chance Professor of Employment Law, University of East Anglia

APPENDIX 6
THE MODIFIED FORM OF PRIVATE INQUIRY

In Chapter 1 of this Report we deal with the evolution of the Inquiry following its announcement by the Secretary of State on 13th July 2001. We explain how the private Inquiry originally established by the Secretary of State evolved into a modified form of private Inquiry. When settling upon the Inquiry Procedures document, which is at Appendix 9, we attempted to adopt procedures which recognised and reflected the somewhat changed nature of the Inquiry following the concessions made by the Secretary of State, and the decision of the court in the judicial review proceedings.

But what were the practical consequences of operating within the confines of this hybrid Inquiry? If we had been established as a Public Inquiry it is likely that all documents and statements received by the Inquiry would have been released to the public, perhaps on a website; and hearings would have been accessible to all. Our proceedings by contrast, required us to impose restrictions on the circulation of documents, statements and the record of the hearings held, essentially in private. Preserving patient confidentiality was paramount when considering distribution to participants in the Inquiry of material provided to us by other participants. We decided that, generally speaking, we would make available to a participant only that material which was considered necessary for that participant to contribute to the work of the Inquiry. Thus, contrary to what might have happened in the case of a Public Inquiry, the complete Inquiry bundle of relevant documents and witness statements was not given to each and every participant. We endeavoured to send out to their legal representatives only documentation relevant to that participant. Where necessary, documents were sent in redacted form.

There was a particular focus of attention upon the permitted use of witness statements and other documents supplied by the Inquiry to the legal representatives of the participants. Such material was supplied to the legal representatives to facilitate their informed involvement in the Inquiry process, so as to further our work. The Inquiry was content for such legal representatives to show to their clients material which was relevant to the client's particular case or their own personal history, this for the purposes of obtaining instructions, written comment and/or rebuttal. When indicating that such wider use of material supplied to legal representatives was permitted, the Inquiry emphasised that it would be necessary for the legal representatives to take steps to protect patient confidentiality. Thus, for example, it would be necessary to ensure that material relating to former patients who did not wish to involve themselves in the Inquiry processes was not made available to other witnesses.

Material supplied to the legal representatives by the Inquiry was expressly subject to their confidentiality undertaking and agreement not to use this material for purposes other than the Inquiry. Similarly, the Inquiry required the same undertaking from those who were shown such written material by their legal representatives.

There were also potentially difficult questions concerning the status of written material which was referred to in the hearing chamber. It may have been said that, to the extent that it had been discussed in the chamber, it was no longer to be considered private. Alternatively it could be argued that such material remained private, given the essentially private nature of the hearings. In the event we were not required to make any adjudication on the matter.

A further area of debate concerned the legitimate use of the transcript of the oral hearings. The transcript was made available to the legal representatives of the participants, as soon as possible after each day's hearing and at no cost, solely for the purposes of representing their clients on the Inquiry. It was supplied to them subject to the terms of the confidentiality undertaking. Thus, for example, the placing of the transcript, or any part of it, on a website was prohibited. There was some suggestion that circulation of the transcript without restriction might be permitted since, following the judicial review, patients were given the right to attend the oral hearings, and to speak about what they had heard. Thus, it was said that what was recorded in the transcript could not be confidential. An alternative view was that the written record is a permanent record of that which otherwise would be fleeting and transitory. Furthermore, the terms of the Data Protection Act, to which the Inquiry was subject, imposed conditions which further complicated the position. In the event we were not called upon to adjudicate upon these arguments.

During the course of the hearings a difficulty arose concerning the receipt by one of the legal representatives of documents, witness statements and the transcript, this in circumstances where that representative was also involved in civil litigation about matters arising out of Ayling's conduct. It was resolved by the representative deciding not to receive such material for the future, and to return to the Inquiry that which had already been supplied.

Through their legal representative, we did receive a request from some former patients for a copy of the transcript of the evidence of certain healthcare professionals in circumstances where the former patient was unable to attend the oral hearings. We thought this a reasonable request, which was granted, but subject to the former patient first signing an undertaking, both as to confidentiality and return of the transcript with no copies having been taken.

We also received a request that a supporter of a former patient should be permitted to attend the oral hearings on days other than that upon which that witness was giving oral evidence to the Inquiry. Again, this request was thought to be reasonable and was granted, subject to there being available seating in the hearing chamber. In practice this did not present any difficulties. Attendance of those wishing to be present at the oral hearings was arranged on the basis of a pre-arranged security pass.

For the former patients and other witnesses attending the oral hearings, we wished to assist them in understanding the content of the hearings. We attempted to achieve this by showing on a large plasma screen those witness statements and documents (suitably redacted where necessary) which were being discussed in the course of a witness's evidence.

APPENDIX 7
ATTEMPTS TO ENGAGE WITH CLIFFORD AYLING

In paragraph 1.24 of this Report we referred to our attempts to engage Ayling in the work of the Inquiry. In this Appendix we deal more fully with them.

On 27 September 2002 the Solicitor to the Inquiry wrote to Ayling who was then serving his sentence in HMP Lewes. Ayling was thereby informed of the appointment of the Chairman and Panel members and sent a copy of the Terms of Reference. It was emphasised in that initial letter that the purpose of the Inquiry was to investigate how concerns or complaints were handled in relation to his practice and conduct during the period 1971–2000. It was explained that this was an Inquiry into complaints handling, processes and systems, their strengths and weaknesses and how they can be improved for the future.

It was recognised by the Inquiry that, in order to participate in the Inquiry processes, Ayling would wish to consider documents coming into the possession of the Inquiry. The Solicitor to the Inquiry made arrangements with HMP Lewes for him to do that in HMP Lewes in conditions which would ensure that confidentiality was maintained. Ayling concluded that the arrangements were not suitable. As with any other prospective participant, Ayling was first asked to sign a confidentiality undertaking. This he refused to do. As a consequence of his decisions, Ayling did not engage in the Inquiry process.

On 10 June 2003, Ayling wrote to the Solicitor to the Inquiry to say that he had commenced proceedings for judicial review. He claimed that in its dealings with him the Inquiry had been biased and was in breach of the rules of natural justice and of the European Convention of Human Rights. The Treasury Solicitor was instructed to defend the proceedings and detailed summary grounds for opposing the claim were lodged with the High Court on 1 July 2003. On 9 July 2003 Mr Justice Silber refused Clifford Ayling permission to apply for judicial review, observing when doing so as follows:-

> *"This claim is based on a basic misconception of the purpose and scope of the Inquiry, which does not determine or effect any rights covered by Article 6 or Article 17. There is no arguable point of public law available to the claimant."*

Thereafter Ayling applied for an oral hearing of his application for permission to bring judicial review proceedings. That hearing took place in the High Court in London on 30 July 2003, when Ayling was brought to the court from HMP Lewes to represent himself before the Honourable Mr Justice Jackson. The Inquiry was represented by Martin Chamberlain of Counsel, instructed by the Treasury Solicitor. After hearing from Ayling and Counsel for the Inquiry, Mr Justice Jackson delivered a judgment refusing Ayling permission to apply for judicial review. In the course of his judgment Mr Justice Jackson identified the several opportunities given by the Inquiry to Ayling to engage in the Inquiry process but which he had not taken up. Notwithstanding that Ayling had told the Judge that he was now prepared to sign the confidentiality undertaking, Mr Justice Jackson said it was now too late, closing submissions being heard by the panel 24 hours later, on 31 July 2003. The Judge concluded by saying that none of the complaints made by Ayling gave rise to any public law remedy or which were arguable; he said that the claim had no prospect of success.

Ayling sought permission to appeal against the decision of Mr Justice Jackson in August 2003 but it was not until 24 February 2004 that his application was heard by Lord Justice Brooke in the Court of Appeal. After hearing Ayling (who by this time had been released from prison) in person, Lord Justice Brooke refused Ayling's application to appeal the decision of Mr Justice Jackson.

COMMITTEE OF INQUIRY
INDEPENDENT INVESTIGATION INTO HOW THE NHS HANDLED
ALLEGATIONS ABOUT THE CONDUCT OF CLIFFORD AYLING

INQUIRY CHAIRMAN: ANNA PAUFFLEY QC

TERMS OF REFERENCE

The investigation will be chaired by Anna Pauffley QC. The Panel members are Peter Berman and Mary Whitty. The Inquiry Panel will draw on other expert advice as required.

The overall purpose of the Inquiry is :

1   To assess the appropriateness and effectiveness of the procedures operated in the local health services

    (a) for enabling health service users to raise issues of legitimate concern relating to the conduct of health service employees and professionals;

    (b) for ensuring that such complaints are effectively considered; and

    (c) for ensuring that appropriate remedial action is taken in the particular case and generally; and

2   To make such recommendations as are appropriate for the revision and improvement of the procedures referred to above.

The Inquiry is asked ….

- To identify the procedures in place during the period 1971-2000 within the local health services to enable members of the public and other health service users to raise concerns or complaints concerning the actions and conduct of health service professionals in their professional capacity.

- To document and establish the nature of and the chronology of the concerns or complaints raised concerning the appointment, practice and conduct of Dr Clifford Ayling, a former GP from Kent during this period.

- To investigate the actions which were taken for the purpose of (a) considering the concerns and complaints which were raised; (b) providing remedial action in relation to them; and (c) ensuring that the opportunities for any similar future misconduct were removed.

- To investigate cultural or organisational factors within the local health services which impeded or prevented appropriate investigation and action.

- To assess and draw conclusions as to the effectiveness of the policies and procedures in place.

- To make recommendations, informed by this case, as to improvements which should be made to the policies and procedures which are now in place within the health service, (taking into account the changes in procedures since the events in question).

- To provide a full report on these matters to the Secretary of State for Health for publication by him.

APPENDIX 9

**COMMITTEE OF INQUIRY
TO INVESTIGATE INTO HOW THE NHS HANDLED ALLEGATIONS
ABOUT THE CONDUCT OF CLIFFORD AYLING**

INQUIRY CHAIRMAN: ANNA PAUFFLEY QC

INQUIRY PROCEDURES

Introduction

This Procedures Paper sets out the procedures that the Inquiry intends to adopt following a process of consultation.

The Inquiry was set up under section 2 National Health Service Act 1977. Accordingly, its remit is to inquire into the NHS and the Department of Health in accordance with its Terms of Reference which are attached (Annex A). The Inquiry does not have jurisdiction to inquire into non-NHS bodies such as the General Medical Council or private hospitals, although it is concerned with interfaces between the NHS and the GMC or other such bodies.

The participants in the Inquiry include the former patients of Clifford Ayling who provide evidence to the Inquiry (that is, provide a witness statement to the Inquiry) and the National Health Service ("NHS") health care staff, professionals and managers who worked with Clifford Ayling or were otherwise responsible for patients' care from 1971 – 2000, within the various hospitals and clinics at which he was employed and his surgery premises.

Document Gathering

1. The Inquiry is asking that anyone who holds documents that are relevant to its work to supply these documents to the Inquiry. Originals will be copied, and the originals returned to their owners.

2. The Inquiry team is analysing the documents it holds in order to build up a preliminary picture of events, and also to discover whether there are further documents that it should see. It may therefore contact people to ask for further assistance.

List of Issues

3. The Inquiry is sending a List of Issues to all participants, with this Procedure Paper. That document sets out the issues that the Inquiry wishes to explore in its work. The List of Issues is a guide for the preparation of witness statements, and more generally in the Inquiry's work.

Witness Statements

4. The Inquiry intends to gather much of its evidence in written form. It will therefore be asking anyone who wishes to participate and who has relevant evidence to give, who has not already sent a written statement to the Inquiry, to supply a written statement or to make arrangements to have one prepared. Where a written statement has already been provided, the Inquiry may ask for a further statement seeking clarification or focussing on areas of particular concern.

5. The Inquiry Solicitor, Michael Fitzgerald, will send out requests for new, or further, written statements. Each request will indicate the topics and events upon which the Inquiry seeks assistance; participants may also wish to look at the List of Issues for further guidance.

6. When it is able to do so, the Inquiry will also supply copies of the documents that may assist a witness in preparing their evidence. However, before any such material is sent to a witness, he or she will be asked to sign a 'Confidentiality Undertaking' (see further below).

7. There are a number of ways in which a person may arrange for a statement to be provided to the Inquiry. The Inquiry Solicitor or one of his colleagues can take statements, if any witness would like the Inquiry's help in making his or her statement. If so, witnesses will have the opportunity to alter, add to or amend their draft statements before signing. Or the witness may wish to prepare his or her own statement. They can seek the help of a legal representative, or other representative (such as a Trade Union official) to do so. When she thinks it appropriate, the Inquiry Chairman, Anna Pauffley QC, will make representations to the Secretary of State for Health about meeting the costs of legal representation.

Use of Statements or other Documents: seeking Comments

8. The Inquiry is concerned with complaints that touch upon private matters. These include issues of health and of sexual conduct. So a great number of the documents and written statements sent to the Inquiry are bound to be confidential in nature. It will generally be necessary for the Inquiry to obtain and consider evidence in private, so as to respect that confidence.

9. But to allow the Inquiry to explore the evidence it receives, it must, first, be able to circulate such material amongst the members of the Inquiry team, and the Inquiry Panel, for the purpose of analysis.

10. It must also be able to question other people about the witness statements and documents it has received where this is required for the purpose of seeking confirmation, clarification or rebuttal. For example, if a former patient tells the Inquiry that she made a complaint, the Inquiry needs to be able to ask those to whom she spoke, or those who had a broader responsibility for complaints-handling, about her evidence, and to discover to whom the complaint was passed. The health service personnel asked about the complaint may need reasonable access to the former patient's medical notes, to remind themselves of the patient and their contact with her at the time when the matter was raised.

11. This may mean that a statement, or a document or records, needs to be referred to or disclosed to other participants or persons when this evidence forms the basis for questioning those other persons or for seeking further information from them. The Inquiry will be concerned to ensure that the information disclosed is limited to that which the person who is being asked to comment reasonably requires to see, in order to respond and to assist the Inquiry.

12. Requests for such further information or comments may take place in writing, after the Inquiry has been sent a statement or document whose contents it needs to draw to the attention of other persons. The Inquiry might also ask a witness giving oral evidence to comment on other documents or witness statements during the oral hearings.

13. The Inquiry may also, subject to the 'confidentiality undertaking' referred to below, send copies of statements or other documents to participants in the Inquiry, or their representatives, if it considers that their submissions on the issues raised by such material would assist it in fulfilling its terms of reference. The material sent by the Inquiry may be redacted in order to preserve confidentiality.

14. The Inquiry would therefore wish all those who submit documents and statement to it to waive confidentiality to the extent of allowing such analysis, questioning and limited further disclosure to other

interested parties to be carried out. As set out below, when a statement or document is disclosed for the purpose of seeking comment, the person to whom it is sent will be bound by a confidentiality undertaking in respect of the material circulated.

15. When the Inquiry asks for a statement, it will also ask the witness whether he or she agrees to their evidence being circulated in the way outlined above. If former patients or other participants have already sent statements or other documents, in confidence, to the Inquiry, the Inquiry will also write to them to ask for their permission to use their evidence in the way outlined above.

Confidentiality Undertakings

16. However, all those who are contacted by the Inquiry with a request for information will be asked to sign a written 'Confidentiality Undertaking'. They will be asked not to disclose further any information or documents sent to them by the Inquiry. At the end of the Inquiry, they will be asked to hand back any such documents.

> It should be recognised that there is no restriction on what those present at any oral hearings held by the Inquiry can say publicly about what occurred at those hearings. Thus, to the extent that oral evidence is given at those hearings, there will be no restriction on the content of that evidence entering the public domain should those who attend the hearing choose to talk about it. However, restrictions on revealing documents or the content of documents supplied to participants and subject to the confidentiality undertaking would still remain effective.

Attending the Oral Hearings

17. As stated above, the Inquiry is gathering much of its evidence in written form. But as well as asking for written evidence, the Inquiry may also ask a witness who has given a witness statement to give oral evidence at its hearings. It is for the Inquiry Panel to decide whom it wishes to hear from in oral hearings. The choice of witnesses may be linked to a selection of "exemplars" – that is, an illustrative range of cases, relating both to patients who raised concerns at or near the time of the incident which they say took place, and to those who did not feel able to make a complaint or raise any concerns until a later date. The purpose of oral evidence will be the clarification of evidence that is insufficiently clear, the testing of evidence where this is required and the exploration of disputes of fact or controversial issues, or matters of opinion.

18. As presently established under section 2 of the National Health Service Act 1977, the Inquiry cannot compel any person to give evidence. The Panel can only hear from those who voluntarily agree to provide a statement or to attend to give oral evidence. However, if the Inquiry considers that a reasonable request to assist the Inquiry, or to attend was made, and the request was unreasonably refused, it would be open to the Inquiry to comment upon that refusal in its report. Further, should it appear necessary or appropriate to do so in light of non-cooperation by key potential witnesses, the Chairman may recommend that the Secretary of State give her powers to compel witnesses to give evidence under s.84 National Health Service Act 1977.

19. Evidence will not be taken on oath. However, the Inquiry will ask each witness to confirm that they understand the importance of their evidence to the Inquiry, and the importance of telling the truth.

20. The hearings will take place privately. Although they will be open to former patients, to the participants, and their legal representatives, the hearings will not be open to the general public or the media. The Panel will be concerned to maintain an environment in the hearings that enables open and frank discussion, that minimises distress to witnesses, and which helps to preserve patient confidentiality. The Inquiry will consider whether to exclude any attendee whose presence could materially damage these objectives, or

whose exclusion is required to further the objectives of the Inquiry. It may also consider requests to admit those whose presence would further these objectives; it has in mind, for instance, that patients giving evidence may wish a member of their family to be present as a support. Arrangements will be made for carers of patients who are ill or infirm to be able to attend with the patient concerned. Further, the Inquiry may need to restrict the number of those who may attend the oral hearings of the Inquiry on any given day, for practical reasons relating to the size of its hearing chamber, etc.

In order to verify individual entitlement to attend the oral hearings, **all** who wish to attend the oral hearings will be asked to apply to the Inquiry in advance for a pass (which will be issued on the first day they attend). Applications for a pass, in advance of the oral hearings should be made, by the participant's legal representative or directly, to John Miller, Assistant Inquiry Secretary, The Inquiry Office, 6th Floor, Hannibal House, Elephant & Castle, London SE1 6TE, explaining the reason why the applicant is eligible to attend. During the course of the oral hearings, applications for a pass may be made to John Miller, The Ayling Inquiry, c/o The Holiday Inn, A20 Maidstone Road, Hothfield, Ashford, Kent, TN26 1AR or to Lorna Wilkinson, The Inquiry Office, London as above. However, applications made at this stage may lead to a delay before admittance to the Inquiry hearings can be secured.

21. A list of intended oral witnesses will be circulated in advance, again on a confidential basis, to the participants. No patient would be mentioned by name in the hearings. When a healthcare professional is asked in oral evidence about a patient's case, they will be informed of the name of the patient whose case is being discussed; but the patient's name will not be mentioned openly. This will help to keep sensitive matters private.

Notice of Matters Requiring Explanation

22. Before any witness gives oral evidence, the Inquiry will indicate, in writing, what issues or topics it wishes to hear further about.

23. Further, if there are any matters that require explanation, because the Inquiry is concerned about the way in which events unfolded or matters were handled, the letter will indicate those areas of concern.

24. The purpose of these letters is to assist witnesses to know what topics will be addressed in questioning. It is also to enable those who face possible criticism to understand the areas of concern that may be raised at the hearing. They will not be designed to pre-judge matters, but merely to give all witnesses a full opportunity to consider all matters to be dealt with in oral evidence.

25. If new matters requiring an explanation from a participant are raised during the course of oral hearings (in particular, after that participant has already given evidence), the Inquiry will ensure that he or she is given an opportunity to respond to the new matters. Such an opportunity may be afforded by inviting the participant to comment in writing or (at the Panel's discretion) by asking them to give further oral evidence.

Opening Submissions

26. At the start of the oral hearings, the Panel will hear opening submissions by Counsel to the Inquiry that introduce the issues before the Inquiry. With the permission of the Panel, participants or their representatives may then also make an opening submission. These submissions should be designed to help the Panel in their task, by informing it of matters that the participants wish to see addressed. They are not an opportunity to give evidence, which will be heard later. Submissions will be time-limited, so as to enable all participants to have an equal voice in the time available.

Questions at the Hearings

27. As stated above, in general all former patients, and participants and their legal representatives may attend the hearings.

28. Counsel to the Inquiry will ask the witnesses questions. The interested parties or their representatives may submit written questions to the Counsel or Solicitor to the Inquiry not later than 48 hours in advance of the relevant witness giving evidence. Counsel will seek to ensure that questions or issues suggested by the parties will, if relevant, be put to the witness (subject to any time constraints for hearing evidence).

29. The witness's legal representative may ask questions at the close of the questions from Counsel to the Inquiry and from the Panel, if he or she wishes to do so, in order to clarify any evidence given during the course of the hearing. It is not envisaged that this process should take more than 15 minutes, and the Chairman may intervene to prevent further, lengthier questioning.

30. The Inquiry is inquiring into what happened in accordance with its terms of reference. Its procedures will remain investigative throughout. All questioning of witnesses will be designed to assist its investigations, and take place in order to fulfil its terms of reference only.

Closing Submissions

31. Shortly after the Panel has finished hearing oral evidence from witnesses, participants or their representatives may submit written submissions about the evidence that has been heard, and the inferences that may be drawn from it, to the Panel. The Inquiry is also likely to schedule a further one-day hearing after receipt of these submissions, at which each participant will have the opportunity of making oral concluding submissions comments to the Panel. Again, submissions will be time-limited, so as to enable all participants to have an equal voice in the time available.

Publication

32. The Inquiry will write a report for publication by the Secretary of State for Health. Patient names and case histories will remain anonymous in that report, although health and social care professionals, including managers and other staff, may be named. Sometimes, in order to explain its findings, evidence will need to be referred to or extracts quoted: but the Inquiry will make every effort to ensure that this is done in such a way as not to identify any individual patient.

33. At present, the Inquiry does not anticipate a need to publish the statements submitted to the Inquiry. If, for some reason, it takes the view that it would be helpful for a particular statement to be made public, it will approach the maker of the statement and any patient who might be identified in it, for permission.

APPENDIX 10

**COMMITTEE OF INQUIRY
TO INVESTIGATE INTO HOW THE NHS HANDLED ALLEGATIONS
ABOUT THE CONDUCT OF CLIFFORD AYLING**

INQUIRY CHAIRMAN: ANNA PAUFFLEY QC

LIST OF ISSUES

National Policy Background

1. What were the relevant national policies and guidance relating to complaints handling within the NHS from 1971 to 2000, when Dr Clifford Ayling was working either as a GP or as a healthcare professional employed by the NHS?

2. What changes have been made to those policies since 2000?

Local Policy Background

3. What were the relevant local policies, guidance or protocols relating to complaints handling from 1971-2000 within:

   a   DrAyling's general practice, at 19 Cheriton High Street, Folkestone;

   b.   The local health authority responsible for commissioning general practitioners' services; and

   c.   Each of the NHS organisations by which Dr Ayling was employed to provide clinical services?

4. What amendments have been made to those policies, guidance or protocols since 2000?

Linkages

5. What were, and are, the linkages between the national and local complaints handling systems, and other relevant processes, including: (a) disciplinary procedures relating to healthcare professionals; (b) systems for monitoring performance or the quality of clinical care; (c) user information or patient advocacy services?

6. What impact does each of these linkages have upon the effectiveness of the complaints handling process and procedures?

Employment by the National Health Service

7   To what positions within the NHS was Dr Ayling appointed from 1971–2000?

8.   Were appropriate and adequate employment procedures followed upon appointment and for the period of his employment thereafter?

General Practice

9. From what premises did Dr Ayling practice as a general practitioner from 1971–2000?

10. What were the organisational structures within each of the general practices in which he was a partner or sole practitioner, during this period?

11. Did the relevant contracting authorities follow appropriate and adequate procedures when they contracted with Dr Ayling for the provision of general practitioner services?

Complaints or concerns voiced between 1971 and 2000

12. What allegations about the professional practice and conduct of Dr Ayling were made to, or passed to:

    a. health or social care professionals, or other staff, working for local National Health services; or

    b. general practitioners or their staff; or

    c. other health or social care professionals?

13. In respect of each allegation:

    a. When was it made;

    b. Who made it;

    c. What was the nature of the allegation;

    d. To whom was the allegation made;

    e. What were the expectations of the person making the allegation: did he or she wish the matter to be treated as a complaint, and if not, what action did he or she wish to be taken;

    f. What was the immediate response of the recipient of the allegation to the person who had made it?

14. In respect of each allegation, what action was taken:

    a. to acknowledge the allegation;

    b. to record the allegation;

    c. to pass it to the appropriate authorities;

    d. to investigate it and to establish its credibility;

    e. to provide any appropriate support or assistance to the person making it;

    f. to inform the person raising the concern or complaint of the action that would be taken, and to see whether this met their expectations?

15. What action was taken to deal with the substance of the allegation?

16. Were any lessons learnt from the allegation, or from the experience of investigating it?

17. What action was taken to ensure that the likelihood of similar complaints being made in the future was reduced?

18. If it was agreed that changes to practice or procedure would be introduced, what steps were taken to implement such changes, and to monitor their implementation and effect?

Concerns and Subsequent Complaints

19. Were there patients who had concerns about the professional practice and conduct of Dr Ayling but who did not voice their concerns to any health or social care professionals or other responsible individuals, until the fact of other complaints became public knowledge in 1998?

   If so:

20. Why did they not raise their concerns at or near the time when they began to be held?

21. What were the barriers to raising concerns or complaints about healthcare services received, during the period when Dr Ayling was in professional practice?

22. Were there health or social care professionals, or other NHS staff, who formed the view that the conduct or practices of Dr Ayling raised issues of concern, but who did not voice their concerns?

23. If so, why did they not raise these concerns?

Effectiveness of procedures

24. How effective were the policies and procedures described under paragraphs 1 – 6, at capturing any of the concerns identified under paragraphs 19 – 23?

25. How effective were the policies and practices described under paragraphs 1 – 6, at investigating the allegations, and/or resolving the complaints, described under paragraphs 12–18?

26. How effective were the policies and practices described under paragraphs 1 – 6 in enabling lessons to be learned from the information received and action to be taken to reduce the likelihood of similar future complaints?

27. What were the barriers to effective complaints-handling?

Current Practice

28. To what extent would the policies and procedures presently in force address or remedy any inadequacies found under paragraphs 24 – 27?

29. If similar concerns or complaints were raised today, is it likely that they would be handled in a more or less effective manner?

30. How can current systems of clinical and corporate governance best learn from the experience of users of healthcare services of the NHS, and/or avoid the need for formal complaints to be made?

31. What examples of good practice have been identified in the course of the Inquiry, not already incorporated into present policies or practice, from which useful lessons may be learned?

Recommendations

32. What recommendations can the Panel make that would strengthen or improve the complaints-handling policies and procedures now in force within the NHS, in the light of its findings in these cases?

33. What recommendations can the Panel make that would strengthen or improve the ability of the NHS to learn effectively from the experience of users of its healthcare services?

APPENDIX 11
GLOSSARY OF ACRONYMS

AC   Audit Commission – The Audit Commission is an independent body responsible for ensuring that public money is used economically, efficiently and effectively.

ACHCEW   Association of Community Health Councils for England and Wales – The Association of Community Health Councils was the national voice of Community Health Councils to provide a focus for them and to assist in the performance of their functions including representing the interest of the public in the NHS at a national level.

AHA   Area Health Authority – An Area Health Authority is a government statutory body concerned with health scheme planning and the funding of health services in a particular geographical area.

AHT   Acute Hospital Trust – An Acute Hospital Trust is a National Health Service provision of goods and services, namely hospital accommodation and services, and community health services for the purposes of the health service at a specific hospital location.

BMA   British Medical Association – The British Medical Association represents doctors from all branches of medicine all over the United Kingdom. It is a voluntary association with about 80 per cent of practicing doctors in membership.

BoG/BdG   Board of Governors – Each NHS Trust has a Board of Governors who are responsible for representing the interests of the local community, staff and local partner organisations.

CHCs   Community Health Councils – Community Health Councils, which were established in 1992 and abolished in 2003, were non-profit community based health promotion, advocacy and policy organisations.

CHI/CHAI   The Commission for Health Improvement (which was abolished and replaced by the Commission for Health Care Audit and Inspection from 1 April 2004) is the independent inspection body for the NHS. It publishes reports on NHS organisations in England and Wales and highlights where the NHS is working well and the areas that need improvement. Now referred to as the Health Care Commission.

DoH   Department of Health – The Department of Health is a Government Department with the aim of improving the health and well being of people in England.

DHA   District Health Authority – The Health Service Act 1980 established 192 District Health Authorities to replace Area Health Authorities. On 1 April 1982 DHAs became the main operational authorities of the NHS. They were abolished with effect from 1 April 1996 under the Health Authorities Act 1995.

DHSC   Directorate of Health and Social Care – Four Directorates for Health and Social Care were set up in 2002 within the Department of Health to oversee the development of local health services. They were abolished in 2003.

DHSS   Department of Health and Social Security – The Department of Health and Social Security was the Government Department with responsibility for health issues. In July 1988 it was split into the two separate departments of Health and Social Security.

EC   Executive Councils – Between 1948-74, primary care services were run by 117 Executive Councils who were responsible for contracting these services from self-employed doctors, dentists, opticians and pharmacists.

FHSA   Family Health Services Authority – Family Health Services Authorities replaced Family Practitioner Committees s in 1991 and became accountable to the Regional Health Authorities with additional powers to strengthen their strategic management role in relation to the services for which they were responsible. They were abolished in 1996 under the Health Authorities Act 1995.

FPC   Family Practitioner Committee – Family Practitioner Committees were responsible for administering the Terms of Service for GPs, monitoring and enforcing standards (including investigating complaints against GPs) and ensuring access to GP services for the local population. They were renamed Family Health Services Authorities in 1991.

GMC   General Medical Council – The General Medical Council, under the legal authority of the Medical Act, is the regulator of the medical profession. It has legal powers which are designed to maintain the standards the public have a right to expect of doctors. Any doctor failing to meet those standards can be struck off the register and have their right to practice removed by the GMC.

HMC   Hospital Management Committee – Hospital Management Committees reported to the Regional Hospital Boards between 1948-74 and were responsible for supervising hospitals.

ICAS   Independent Complaints Advocacy Service – Independent Complaints Advocacy Services were introduced on 1 September 2003. Section 12 of the Health and Social Care Act places a legal duty on the Secretary of State to make arrangements to provide Independent Advocacy Services to assist individuals making complaints against the NHS and its services.

IPR   Independent Professional Review – An Independent Professional Review is an arrangement for assuring, controlling or promoting an activity that involves scrutiny by appropriate people independent of those carrying out or with responsibility for the activity. It can include, but is not limited to, peer review arrangements.

IRP   Independent Review Panel – An Independent Review Panel will deal with, on request, complaints that arise from people who are not happy with the local NHS resolution. The panel consists of three people:- a lay chair (nominated from a list of people held by the Department of Health); a convenor (who will be specially trained and will be a non-executive director of the NHS organisation concerned with the complaint) and; a third person (either from the local Primary Care Trust or from the Department of Health list).

266

JCC	Joint Consultants' Committee of British Medical Association – The Joint Consultants Committee was set up in 1948, by the Medical Royal Colleges and the British Medical Association (BMA), to represent the medical profession in discussions with the Department of Health. The Committee focuses on matters relating to the standard of professional knowledge and skill in the hospital service and the encouragement of education and research. Members include the presidents of the Medical Royal Colleges and their faculties and representatives from the BMA.
LMC	Local Medical Committee – A Local Medical Committee is a statutory body which represents NHS General Practitioner principals whose rights and responsibilities are governed by NHS Acts and Regulations.
MDU	Medical Defence Union – The Medical Defence Union, established in 1885, is a mutual non-profit organisation, owned by members of doctors, dentists and other health care professionals. The MDU defends the professional reputations of their members when their clinical performance is called into question.
MPS	Medical Protection Society – The Medical Protection Society is the largest mutual medical protection organisation operating internationally. It helps doctors with legal problems that arise from their clinical practice. In the United Kingdom it has more than 100,000 members across healthcare professionals.
MDOs	Medical Defence Organisations – Medical Defence Organisations is the generic definition for the bodies that can represent doctors in situations where representation and defence advice is necessary. It includes such bodies as the Medical Defence Union and the Medical Protection Society.
NAO	National Audit Office – The National Audit Office scrutinises public spending on behalf of Parliament. The office is entirely independent of Government and it audits the accounts of all government departments and agencies as well as a wide range of other public bodies. It reports to Parliament on the economy, efficiency and effectiveness with which government bodies have used public money.
NICE	National Institute for Clinical Excellence – The National Institute for Clinical Excellence is part of the NHS and is an independent organisation responsible for providing national treatments and care for those using the NHS in England and Wales. Its guidance is for healthcare professionals and patients and their carers to help them make decisions about their treatment and healthcare.
NCAA	National Clinical Assessment Authority – The National Clinical Assessment Authority is a special health authority established as one of the central elements of the NHS's work on quality. It began work in April 2001 and aims to provide a support service to health authorities, Primary Care Trusts and hospital and community Trusts who are faced with concerns over the performance of an individual doctor.
NCSC	National Care Standards Commission – The National Care Standards Commission was set up under the Care Standards Act 2000 and became fully operational on 1 April 2002. From April 2004, (as set out in the Health and Social Care (Community Health and Standards) Act 2003), the Commission for Social Care Inspection (CSCI) will take on the NCSC's role of regulating independent social care providers and the regulation of private and voluntary healthcare providers will move from the NCSC to the Commission for Healthcare Audit and Inspection (CHAI).

NHSE	National Health Service Executive – The NHS Executive was an integral part of the Department of Health reporting to the Chief Executive of the NHS [before the post was brought together with that of the DH Permanent Secretary under Sir Nigel Crisp]. It provided leadership and a range of central management services to the NHS, supported Ministers in developing policy on health and health services and was responsible for the effective management of the NHS and stewardship of NHS resources.
NMC	Nursing & Midwifery Council (formerly UKCC) – The Nursing and Midwifery Council is an organisation set up by Parliament to ensure nurses, midwives and health visitors provide high standards of care to their patients and clients.
NPSA	National Patient Safety Agency – The National Patient Safety Agency is a Special Health Authority which was created in July 2001. It was established to improve the quality of care through reporting, analysing and learning from mistakes and problems that affect patient safety in the NHS.
P&HSO	The Parliamentary and Health Service Ombudsman – The Parliamentary Ombudsman and Health Service Ombudsman undertake independent investigations into complaints about government departments, a range of other bodies and the National Health Service. The same person holds both posts.
PALS	Patient Advice and Liaison Services – The Patient Advice and Liaison Services provide instant, on the spot information and help to patient, their families and carers. They act independently on matters that are brought to their attention and the aims are to advise and support patients, their families and carers, provide information on NHS services, listen to concerns, suggestions or queries and help sort out problems quickly.
PCT	Primary Care Trust – A Primary Care Trust is a free-standing body with responsibility for the delivery of better health care and health improvements to its local area. A Primary Care Trust can both provide and commission health services.
PHLS	Public Health Laboratory Service – The Public Health Laboratory Service was set up under the National Health Service Act 1946. Its overall purpose was to protect the UK population from infection by maintaining national capability of the highest quality for the detection, diagnosis, surveillance, prevention and control of infections and communicable diseases. PHLS became part of the Health Protection Agency on 1 April 2003.
PLP	Public Law Project – The Public Law Project is an independent, national legal charity which aims to improve access to public law remedies for those whose access is restricted by poverty, discrimination or other similar barriers. It has adopted three key objectives of increasing the accountability of public decision makers, enhancing the quality of public decision making and improving access to justice.
RDPH	Regional Director of Public Health – The Regional Director of Public Health is responsible for the development and performance management of clinical governance to ensure sound clinical performance and patient safety across the full range of local NHS organisations.

RHA	Regional Health Authority – 14 Regional Health Authorities were set up in 1974 under the NHS Reorganisation Act 1973 to oversee hospitals, primary care services and community services. They were abolished with effect from 1 April 1996 under the Health Authorities Act 1995 and were replaced by the 8 regional offices of the NHS Executive.
RHB	Regional Hospital Board – The management structure of the NHS from 1948 until 1974 consisted of 14 Regional Hospital Boards and 35 Teaching Hospital Boards reporting direct to the Ministry of Health. Between them, these Hospital Boards supervised about 400 Hospital Management Committees.
RMO	Regional Medical Officer – Regional Medical Officers worked for the Regional Medical Service (RMS) and were mainly responsible for medically refereeing social security applications in respect, for instance, of incapacity or injury benefits. They were also responsible for visiting GPs to discuss issues such as premises, prescribing costs, the management of controlled drugs and national insurance certification. There were six regional divisions in England. In 1991, the RMS was transferred to the Department of Social Security (DSS).
RO	Regional Office (of NHS Executive) – Regional Offices of the NHS Executive were set up in 1996 within the Department of Health to replace the Regional Health Authorities and to performance manage the NHS in the 8 NHS Regions through Health Authorities and directly with NHS Trusts. They were abolished in 2002.
SHAs	Special Health Authorities – Special Health Authorities have been established to provide a national service to the NHS or the public, under Section 11 of the NHS Act 1977. They are independent, but can be subject to ministerial direction like other NHS bodies.
StHAs	Strategic Health Authorities – Strategic Health Authorities are responsible for developing strategies for local health services and ensuring high-quality performance. They manage the NHS locally and are the key link between the Department of Health and the NHS. They also ensure that national priorities (such as programmes for improving cancer services) are integrated into local plans.
UKCC	United Kingdom Central Council for Nursing & Midwifery was established in 1979 under the Nurses, Midwives and Health Visitors Act. It was a corporate body with responsibilities under the act set standards for education, practice and conduct, maintain a register of qualified nurses, midwives and health visitors, provide guidance to registrants and handle professional misconduct complaints and allegations of unfitness to practice due to ill health. The Nursing and Midwifery Council replaced it in 1999.

EXPENDITURE OF THE AYLING INQUIRY: AUGUST 2001 – JULY 2004

Type of Expenditure	2001/02 (note 2)	2002/03	2003/04	2004/05	Total
	£k	£k	£k	£k	£k
Panel (note 3)	–	24	164	8	196
Counsel	–	72	220		295
Legal Fees: (note 4)	–	26	109		135
Expert Contributors	–	6	46	1	53
Staff	24	154	378		556
Premises	53	63	142		258
Information Technology & Telecommunications	17	42	234		293
Other administrative costs	23	40	43		106
TOTAL	**117**	**427**	**1,336**	**12**	**1,892**

These are the full provisional accounts up to the publication of the Inquiry Report. Final accounts will be prepared in due course.

NOTES

1. The financial year runs from 1 April to 31 March.
2. The Inquiry was announced in July 2001 and the Secretariat established shortly thereafter.
3. The Chairman and Panel Members were appointed on 6 September 2002.
4. Costs of the legal representation of former patients and another participant.

APPENDIX 13
SEMINARS PARTICIPANTS LIST

SEMINAR 1 – SUPPORTING PATIENTS IN RAISING CONCERN ABOUT THEIR CARE

Mrs Sue Benn – Patient Advice & Liaison Service Manager, University College London Hospitals NHS Trust

Leslie Forsyth – Director of Patient and Public Involvement (North) Designate, Commission for Patient and Public Involvement in Health

Liz Dimond – Complaints Lead, Transition Team, Commission for Healthcare Audit and Inspection

Frances Blunden – Principal Policy Adviser, Health, Consumers' Association

Hilary Scott – Programme Manager, Complaints & Clinical Negligence Reform, Department of Health

Professor Linda Mulcahy – School of Law, Birkbeck College, University of London

Tessa Harding MBE – Senior Policy Adviser, Help the Aged

David Gilbert – Director of Patient and Public Involvement, Commission for Health Improvement

Dr Joan Martin – Lay Member, General Medical Council

Bill McClimont – Director of Corporate Affairs, Nestor Healthcare Group

Joe Nichols – Professional Adviser, Nursing & Midwifery Council

Sarah Squire – Director of Patient Experience, NHS Modernisation Agency

Liz Thomas – Head of Policy & Research, Action for Victims of Medical Accidents

SEMINAR 2 – SUPPORTING STAFF IN RAISING CONCERNS ABOUT THEIR COLLEAGUES

John Adsett – Independent Human Resources and Management Consultant in Healthcare Sector, NHS Confederation

Don Brand – Consultant to Social Care Institute for Excellence

Dr Elizabeth Cheshire – Medico-Legal Adviser, Medical Defence Union

Melanie Every – Regional Manager Southern Office, Royal College of Midwives

Dr Janice Gosby – Professional Adviser, Education, Nursing & Midwifery Council

Hilary Scott – Programme Manager, Complaints & Clinical Negligence Reform Department of Health

Professor Linda Mulcahy – Birkbeck College, University of London

Sue Osborne – Joint Chief Executive, National Patient Safety Agency

Professor Ian Smith – Clifford Chance Professor of Employment Law, Norwich Law School, University of East Anglia

Miss Heather Mellows – Vice President, Royal College of Obstetricians and Gynaecologists

Anna Myers – Deputy Director, Public Concern at Work

Dr Linda Patterson – Medical Director, Commission for Health Improvement

Dr Joan Trowell – Medical Member, General Medical Council

Professor Linda Mulcahy, School of Law, Birkbeck College, University of London

SEMINAR 3 – THE EMPLOYMENT CONTEXT

Dr Edwin Borman – Chairman of the International Committee, British Medical Association

Stephen Collier – Independent Healthcare Association

Dr Mark Dudley – Medico-Legal Adviser, Medical Protection Society

Paul Loveland – Head of Post-Qualification Learning and CPD, Department of Health

Professor Ian Smith – Clifford Chance Professor of Employment Law, Norwich Law School, University of East Anglia

Dr George McIntyre – Chief Executive, South Leeds Primary Care Trust

Sean King – Human Resources Directorate, Department of Health

Ian Stone – CMO Advisor for Long Term Suspension/Human Resources Adviser to National Clinical Assessment Authority

Bruce Sharpe – GMC Registration & Education Directorate, General Medical Council

Pauline Young – Chair, Association of Medical Secretaries, Practice Managers, Administrators and Receptionists (AMSPAR)

SEMINAR 4 – SHARING INFORMATION ACROSS DIFFERENT BODIES ABOUT INDIVIDUAL CONDUCT AND PERFORMANCE

Lynne Berry – Chief Executive, General Social Care Council

Frances Blunden – Principal Policy Adviser, Health, Consumers' Association

Linda Charlton – Director of Investigations, Health Service Ombudsman's Office

Dr Christine Dewbury – Medical Advisor, Wessex Local Medical Committee

Hilary Scott – Programme Manager, Complaints & Clinical Negligence Reform, Department of Health

David Bawden – Commission for Healthcare Audit and Inspection, Transition Team

Dr Bill Holmes – Medical Director, Nestor Healthcare Group

Dr Christine Hopton – Adviser, National Clinical Assessment Authority

Richard Jefferies – Acting Finance Director, Council for the Regulation of Healthcare Professionals

Anne Jones – Assistant Information Commissioner, Office of the Information Commissioner for Wales

Liz McAnulty – Director of Professional Conduct, Nursing & Midwifery Council

Finaly Scott – Chief Executive, General Medical Council

Sally Taber – Head of Operational Policy, Independent Healthcare Association

Simon Ward – Compliance Officer, Health Team, Office of the Information Commissioner

SEMINAR 5 – THE ROLE OF CHAPERONES

Dr Maureen Baker – Director of Primary Care, National Patient Safety Agency and Honorary Secretary, Royal College of General Practitioners

Tessa Harding MBE – Senior Policy Adviser, Help the Aged

Dr Susan Bewley – Clinical Director Women's Services, Guys & St Thomas' Hospitals NHS Trust

Dr Patricia Crowley – Senior Lecturer in Obstetrics and Gynaecology, Trinity College, Dublin and Consultant Obstetrician & Gynaecologist, Coombe Women's Hospital, Dublin

Lee Edwards – Director of Virtual Theatre Projects, St Mary's Hospital, London

Dr Charlie McGarrity – Associate Medical Director, Eastern Leicester Primary Care Trust and Medical Adviser for NCAA

Kevin Miles – Nurse Consultant in Sexual Health, Camden Primary Care Trust

Dr Orest Mulka – GP, Measham

Dr Alan Russell – SFCOG, British Medical Association

Dr Peter Schutte – Medico-Legal Adviser and Acting Head of Advisory Services, Medical Defence Union

Dr Nicola Toynton – Medical Member, General Medical Council

Gillian Trainor – Professional Officer/Professional Advisor, Nursing & Midwifery Council

Printed in the UK by the Stationery Office limited
on behalf of the Controller of Her Majesty's Stationery Office
172946   09/04